**Urban Asymmetries.**
Studies and
Projects on
Neoliberal
Urbanization

# Urban Asym metries. Studies and Projects on Neoliberal Urbanization

itors Tahl Kaminer, Miguel Robles-Durán and Heidi Sohn

th contributions by **M. Christine Boyer, Stephanie Choi, Roberto Eibenschutz**

d Laura O. Carrillo, Beatriz García Peralta, Arie Graafland, Rodrigo Hidalgo,

ıl Kaminer, Mark Krasovic, Margit Mayer, Mexico City Study Group,

wark Study Group, Miguel Robles-Durán, Santiago Study Group, Heidi Sohn,

k Swyngedouw

0 Publishers **Rotterdam 2011**

# Santiago

# Newark

# Foreword

**M. Christine Boyer**

*Urban Asymmetries* is dissatisfied with uneven urban development produced in the wake of neo-liberal policies. These policies, adopted since the late 1960s, entail the globalization of market forces, the deregulation of financial institutions, the privatization of public services. The effects not only devastate the public provision of services, but expose an expanding gap between the extremes of poverty and wealth in cities of both the developing as well as developed world. These discrepancies plus the evisceration of Welfare State programmes offering at least a minimum of subsistence have eroded even a pretence of commonality amongst urban citizenry. As an effect of such neoliberal policies *Urban Asymmetries* examines why architects have abandoned their long-standing position that modern architecture is a response to human needs, a guarantee against insecurity and risk.

Thus *Urban Asymmetries* frames its inquiry by asking why architects suffer from amnesia over the production of uneven spatial formation, why the urban condition, long the foundational base of modern architecture, has been removed from its agenda, and why a set of neoliberal assumptions has been erected instead? Why do architects assume nothing can be done to stop what they call the 'natural' expansion and formation of cities, why have they turned to pragmatism, adopting a post-critical approach to market demands as a legitimating factor in architectural practice, and why do they adopt a post-political agenda that leaves human agency out of the decision-making process of urban development? *Urban Asymmetries* is a reflection on and inquiry into these post-critical and post-political processes and assumptions, which have produced uneven spatial forma-tions evidenced in the three case studies of Mexico City, Santiago de Chile and Newark N.J. In opposition to neoliberal assumptions, *Urban Asymmetries* calls for a series of actions in order to develop a new theory of urban politics, new social housing agendas and new forms of human agency.

The questions *Urban Asymmetries* raises are those of the bio-politics of population or the struggle for life, for its continual strengthening and for the will to power that will constitute such. It is a conflict of forces of unequal measure, those that strengthen and those that diminish. The state seeks to protect individuals in their struggle against each other, but if it goes too far on the side of preservation it enfeebles, devastates, even destroys the individual. Hence uneven development of life, of territory, of cities, occurs within a framework of prevision and prevention. Neoliberalism protects against the over-zealous prevision by the state, just as the state is a bulwark against the destructive conflicts of individualism. Conservation and development are indissolubly linked as action and reaction moving in opposite directions towards survival and security or conflict and death.[1]

---

**1** Roberto Esposito, **Bios: Biopolitics and Philosophy** (Minneapolis: University of Minnesota Press, 2008).

Modern architecture emerged as part of this bio-political machine, producing not only disciplined bodies but securing the protection of life at the city level through public hygiene, housing projects, educational services, provisions for leisure and food and at the individual level securing freedom from exemptions and privileges, freedom of mobility of people and things, security against an array of risks and disasters.[2] Security and discipline are the two poles around which the bio-politics of population unfurls and as Michel Foucault described, they treat planned spatial distributions differently.[3] Security focuses above all on the city as a home of disease, a place of revolt, a site of pestilence and death. Discipline focuses on the individual, breaking down space into grids in which the individual can be seen and modified. With the shift towards neoliberalism the apparatus of bio-politics is transformed as well. Now it is a matter of spatial distribution via vast networks of communication, working through a series of mobile elements to be monitored and modulated continuously and flexibly. Such a shift puts the spatial distributions of both discipline and security in crisis: schools, housing, factories, people at risk, people facing uncertainties and evictions, deskilling and depoliticization. It is towards an understanding of what spatial redistribution this new bio-politics requires in the twenty-first century that *Urban Asymmetries* is directed.

**2** Sven-Olov Wallerstein, **Bio-Politics and the Emergence of Modern Architecture** (New York: Princeton Architecture Press, 2009).
**3** Michel Foucault, **Security, Territory, Population: Lectures at the College de France 1977–1978** (New York: Palgrave Macmillan, 2004).

# Introduction: Urban Asymmetries

**The editors**

*The logic of uneven development derives specifically from the opposed tendencies, inherent in capital, towards the differentiation but simultaneous equalization of the levels and conditions of production.*
(Neil Smith)[1]

## Uneven urban development

Uneven development is a phenomenon which is hardly limited to capitalist conditions, yet is exacerbated by them and is a prominent and fundamental principle of capitalist growth. Capitalism can never achieve the equilibrium between production and consumption which it desires; the free market and laws of competition create dynamism and instability, with producers constantly searching for new markets and opportunities, for cheaper materials and labour, or for real estate deals. The dynamism, instability and absence of equilibrium of capitalist markets result in uneven geographical development, a phenomenon originally identified by Marx and thoroughly studied in recent decades by urban geographers such as Neil Smith and David Harvey.

Uneven geographical development begins with a disparity of natural conditions in different regions or states: different natural resources – raw materials – and different geographical locations – natural harbour, trade route etc. However, the importance of natural conditions and of the proximity to raw materials has diminished over time thanks to improved means of production and cheaper and faster means of transport. As Neil Smith points out, 'the present reality of New York City, such an impressive symbol of the productiveness of human activity, has long since outgrown any naturalistic explanation based on bedrock or physical accessibility'.[2] Smith quotes Bukharin's comment that '[i]mportant as the natural differences in the conditions of production may be, they recede more and more into the background compared with differences which are the outcome of the uneven development of productive forces'.[3] Therefore the natural conditions are surpassed by additional conditions which encourage uneven development: availability of labour, means of transportation and production, regulations and controls, and other conditions which are mostly the result of prior development; each moment of development, in effect, prepares the ground and takes part in pre-determining future development. The sweatshops in China's southern cities, in Vietnam or India, currently producing cheap commodities later sold to affluent consumers in cities such as Beijing or Hamburg, perfectly exemplify this process: the availability of cheap labour, compounded by tax free zones and lax labour regulations provide an opportunity to capitalists, and engender a situation in which different territories follow a very disparate trajectory of development, increasing socio-economic differences in the process.

Uneven geographical development is a phenomenon which is highly visible in contemporary cities. The same cities which are currently home to mass-sweatshops are often also the playground

**1** Neil Smith, **Uneven Development: Nature, Capital, and the Production of Space**
(Oxford; Cambridge, Mass.: Blackwell, 1991), p. xv.
**2** ibid., p. 103.
**3** ibid., p. 104.

of a highly affluent class, living in very different neighbourhoods and conditions than the sweatshop labourers. Uneven urban development has many facets, but arguably its most visible is the real estate market – the disparity of property values in different parts of cities, the constant attempt to devalue land in order to be able to buy it cheap, and subsequently the attempts of developers and city governments to raise the real estate value by diverse initiatives and investments.

More than a single force is at play. In the early twentieth century, for example, large industrial firms offered their employees affordable housing in order to counter real estate speculation and prevent pressures to raise salaries.[4] Capitalism thus encourages competition not only within specific sectors of economy, but also a competition between the different sectors for diverse resources which affect surplus value – labour, land, materials, transport, government and local policies.

The need to re-invest surplus profit is one of the reasons that investment in the building industry and urban development is a major practice of capitalists. Property is typically perceived by middle-class society as a 'safe investment', despite widespread speculation in real estate and property and fluctuation in value, as demonstrated recently by the collapse of the subprime mortgage sector in the United States. Consequently, urban development is an enterprise which absorbs surplus profit from other economic sectors, channelling the capital towards the construction or reconstruction of urban areas, and becoming an impetus for initiating development – in other words, the need to re-invest capital being one of the major reasons for initiating urban development in the first place.

The last thirty years of urban development have been dominated by the wide implementation of neoliberal policies aimed at furthering globalization, deregulation, privatization and free markets. These policies, which have given the market – investors and developers – a free hand in the urban arena, have further increased social disparities within cities, creating conditions which are extreme by any criterion or standard: acute poverty contrasted with excessive wealth, urban territories purged of the poor and needy, affluent gated communities, renovated loft apartments, Disneyfied shopping palaces, sprawling slums, shoddy tenements worthy of nineteenth-century cities. The evidence of the hardship and inequalities caused by neoliberal urban policies is everywhere, though conveniently hidden from view, located in urban outskirts or the global south rather than in Western city centres.

Before the onset of neoliberalism, the state was the principal organ in charge of planning, financing and constructing the dwelling modes for the lower income groups of society. In many Western cities, the retreat of government in recent decades has meant a shortage in affordable housing for the poor. In contrast, across the developing world, once the interventionist policies of the state – whether politically populist or social – were curtailed, private corporations and other non-public interest groups have adopted the now very profitable business of building for the poor, for the working classes, and for the lower middle classes of society. No longer can we speak of 'social housing', or, as was the case in Mexico until the 1970s, of subsidized 'social *interest* dwelling'. In any case, and despite severe problems with housing provided by the state in the past, the failure rate in state-driven urban developments (in terms of social adaptation, use, accessibility and provision of secondary urban infrastructure and urban servicing) was substantially lower than in the contemporary market-driven developments.

Formally and spatially, the housing developments that have become ubiquitous are nothing but appalling: located in the furthest fringes of the urban periphery, far removed from anything that resembles an urban core or centre, and at unacceptable commuting distances from sources of employment. These 'sleep-burbs' are designed as compounds, as camps, intended for furthering social integration by infusing a 'desire for ownership'. This desire fuels the generation of a new social class. In order to own one of these dwelling units, the aspirational poor are forced into the formal economic sector (which is not always a desirable condition); the buyers are often plunged into ruthless credit conditions for life. In short, such a system finances the individual rather than the object. This, needless to say, is 'good' for the larger economy and for the moneyed elites, but proves disastrous for the small, household economies of the already materially deprived.

Whereas ownership – such as Thatcher's Right to Buy policy of selling social housing to its residents – has been the last in a string of tactics used to assimilate the Western working class, in the global south the integration of the poor into bourgeois society is far from complete. Consequently, in global centres such as Mexico City, the mass housing which imitates the housing typologies of the middle class as a substitute for the self-built, unplanned housing currently dominating the urban periphery, presents the opportunity to introduce the urban poor to a way of living modelled on the bourgeoisie, though without any of the qualities and comforts available in real middle-class housing. Social integration produces a class which shares a worldview and ideals with the middle class, despite its limited economic means and lack of power, and prevents the instability and threat of an excluded mass which shares nothing with the dominant class.

However, the social well-being of the residents of the urban peripheries has hardly been in the centre of architectural and urban discourse in recent times. Instead, the world looked with awe in the last decade at the megalopolises rising in China and at urban apparitions such as Dubai, captivated by the scale and radicalism of such mass developments. The standard opening sentence of

**4** Peter Marcuse, 'Do Cities Have a Future?', in Robert Chery [ed.], **The Imperiled Economy: Through the Safety Net** (New York: Union of Radical Political Economists, 1988), pp. 189-200.

numerous articles and books on architecture or urbanism in recent times typically thundered a list of facts and numbers regarding the unprecedented growth of Chinese cities and of the world's urban population, marginalizing, consequently, other urban phenomena. Such uncritical work, characterized by a romanticization – if not outright idolization – of the mass urbanization in the Third World, typically ignores the inequalities and injustices caused by these developments – developments which are driven by neoliberal forces and are measured by a single yardstick: the production of surplus profit. *Urban Asymmetries* confronts such apologia to neo-liberalism and joins a growing chorus of critical thought which is directed at overturning urban policies driven by market interests, and dares to suggest inter-ventionist practices which are not subjugated to a neoliberal agenda.

## Critique of current urban and architectural strategies

It is thus the intention of *Urban Asymmetries* to challenge some of the assumptions and conventions as well as strategies and methodologies which are currently prevalent within the disciplines of architecture and urbanism. This necessitates questioning and overturning some of the aspects of thought and action which have dominated the two disciplines for the last decades, beginning with the schism of theory and practice. Architectural practice has opted either to embrace abstract theories which do not intervene in praxis and function primarily as a means of legitimating architectural design,[5] or, alternatively, to refute theory altogether, boasting of a pragmatism which suggests practice is directly derived from and completely determined by existing reality, with no need for theoretical mediation, that current conditions pre-define architectural practice – and hence demand a subordination to the status-quo. Theory has not fared much better, opting for an academism which enables critical distance but shies away from con-crete proposals of action and intervention. Consequently, theory has produced insightful analysis and damning critique, but in the absence of engagement with practice lacks the necessary leverage to implement the critique; in effect, the result is a toothless 'critique for critique's sake'.[6]

In this context, one of the most problematic approaches to cities that have sur-faced in recent times is the understanding of the city as 'a given' or as an organic, natural phenomenon. Propagated by diverse practitioners and theorists, including Rem Koolhaas and Winy Maas,[7] such an understanding veils the actual forces at work in the development and transformation of cities; it locates urban change in a natural force beyond the reach of man. The city as 'a given' or as an organic phenomenon can be seen at best as a Foucaultian understanding and at worst as merely an affirmation of market forces and a total surrender to their agenda – the accumulation of capital. The forces which are portrayed as the makers of the city are characterized as self-generative, self-propelling and immune from human agency. Absent is the manner in which human subjects take part in creating the city, in which human agency affects the urban environment and shapes its outcome. The absence of the human agency, whether the result of pessimism regarding the human subject's prowess or of an acceptance of market dictates, is arguably one of the most troubling outcomes of such an approach.

Often, in studies which adhere to such approaches history is itself circumvented, preventing the ability to understand or explain urban change and transformation. Similarly, the understanding of the city as a finite object – typical of many architects, though by no means a recent development – avoids history and process and focuses on issues such as form and context – but stripped of the understanding of the historical specificity of urban environments. Things appear 'just as they are'; the process which *is* the city disappears in a static conception of reality; fatalism replaces critical cognition. It is little wonder that such an approach leads to the eclipsing of critique and to a subjugation to the status quo.

In the absence of history and the human subject, the urban environment is naturalized, and the specific struggles, social movements, economic changes or political decisions which construct the city become invisible. Moreover, knowledge of the ability to steer urban transformation via political, social or economic endeavours disappears. All this is related to the emergence of post-politics, of economy 'freeing' itself from the dictates of politics and society, allowing its most basic goal, the accumulation of capital, to be the sole determinant of its development and the only measure of its success or failure. The post-political condition marries truth with fiction: the – very real – weakening of political agency by transferring power to markets and to international organizations such as the IMF or WTO, on the one hand, and, on the other, the popularity of anti-political sentiments which vilify politics rather than the corporations which, at the end of the day, directly shape today the human subject's daily life. The current condition both undermines the population's desire to act politically and limits the efficacy of political action.

In his recent musings about the architectural profession and his own practice, Alejandro Zaera-Polo of FoA follows in the footsteps of Koolhaas and Maas, accepting the basic conditions of architectural practice – in this case, the limitation of the territory of architectural influence to the

**5** In this sense, the work of architects such as Peter Eisenman, who freely alluded to the writings of the philosophers Jacques Derrida and Gilles Deleuze and claimed his own architectural projects implemented the philosophical ideas, does not express a theory and praxis relationship, for it lacks the dialectical relation necessary: the transposition of theory to practice, to the extent that it took place in Eisenman's work, is one-directional. See more in T. Kaminer, **Architecture, Crisis and Resuscitation: The Reproduction of Post-Fordism in Late-Twentieth-Century Architecture** (London: Routledge, 2011).
**6** This was not limited to architecture and urbanism. The work of Jean Baudrillard, for example, was rebuked by his ex-professor Henri Lefebvre as 'hypercritical' – a critique which leads to a dead end, not to transformational practice. Lefebvre wrote that '[t]he abuse of critical thinking, which has lapsed into hypercriticism, must also be acknowledged'; Henri Lefebvre, **The Critique of Everyday Life, Vol. III: From Modernity to Modernism (Towards a Metaphilosophy of Daily Life)** (London: New York: 2005), p. 6.
**7** See, for example, Rem Koolhaas, 'What Ever Happened to Urbanism?', Rem Koolhaas, OMA & Bruce Mau, **S, M, L, XL** (New York: Monacelli Press, 1996), pp. 959-71.

building's facades, surrendering the programme, the layout and organization to developers and consultants.[8] The situation on the urban scale is significantly worse, for the pressures on urban development from economic powerhouses are enormous and the stakes higher. The urbanist and architect have been stripped of much of their means of affecting any aspect of life which has social meaning; their role has shrunk to a form of city-branding, addressing the packaging of buildings and cities rather than their (social) content.

The grievances listed above are but a concise demonstration of the aporia in which architecture, urbanism, cities and society find themselves today. This book, and particularly the work of the Urban Asymmetries study group – excerpts from its work are included in the project sections of this volume – wishes to address the issues which prevent the emergence of a meaningful urbanity – ranging from the absence of history to the limited role of architects and urbanists – and to identify alternative options, strategies and methodologies which offer social and political commitment and a route to the betterment of city and society. The methodologies employed by the Urban Asymmetries study group were developed as a means of overturning many of the ideas and assumptions which have animated architects and urbanists in recent decades – ideas which were widely implemented to satisfy the demands of neoliberalism and are deeply flawed from the perspective of society's good.

## Devising alternative urban strategies

*The new aesthetic paradigm has ethico-political implications because to speak of creation is to speak of the responsibility of the creative instance with regard to the thing created.* (Felix Guattari)[9]

The Urban Asymmetries projects depart from the premise that in order to advance any inquiry or investigation regardless of the 'nature' of the subject or object in question, it is necessary to frame it within an appropriate theoretical perspective and body. It considers the 'problem of theorizing' as foundational to its rationale and scope and centres on an understanding of *problématique* as more than an analytical or positivistic research tool.[10] As *Problemstellung*, this would include elements of definition and contextualization, and necessarily rely on rigorous analysis to untangle and comprehend its mechanisms and operations beyond mere common sense.

Conceptually, however, Urban Asymmetries understands a *problématique* to be a more complex construction comparable perhaps to a horizontal structure composed of interconnected political, economic and ideological/aesthetic instances that ignite and sustain a broad array of processes; as a set of interrelated forces that when analysed properly, will clearly evidence the connection between issues and developments, and in a more strict sense, expose and expound the productive forces, specific power-relations and interest agendas located at the core of the problem, thus generating relational readings across many levels. Examples of this theoretical model abound and deviate only slightly in their treatment of 'overdetermination': Althusser's semi-autonomous model, Harvey's conception of the 'web of life', Foucault's *dispositif*, or Deleuze's assemblage theory via the theorization of Manuel De Landa. In this sense, notions of how power-relations operate within contemporary 'democratic', neoliberal domains, as well as how decision-making practices and other social organizations influence a given process are of crucial importance to comprehend complex ensembles.

An important aspect of the work of the study group was to re-introduce theory-based practice and practice-based theory, in a sense mending the schism of theory and practice of the last decades. The understanding of theory and practice as inter-related activities was central to Marxist thought until the 1960s; Jürgen Habermas and Henri Lefebvre are, arguably, the last heavyweight scholars to emphasize this aspect of knowledge and action in a period in which many practitioners in diverse fields expressed a freedom from the dictates of theory and theorists kept practice at arm's length for fear of contamination by commodified and compromised practices.

The Greek term 'praxis' suggests actions aimed at the activities themselves, as opposed to instru-mental actions aimed at achieving a clearly defined goal which is external to the activities (*poiesis*). The plan, in praxis, is within the activities, is intimately involved with the actions. In Marxism, praxis is understood 'to designate a kind of self-creating action, which differed from the externally motivated behaviour produced by forces outside man's control. [...] *praxis* in Marxist usage was seen in dialectical relation to theory. In fact, one of the earmarks of *praxis* as opposed to mere action was its being informed by theoretical considerations. The goal of revolutionary activity was understood as the unifying of theory and *praxis*, which would be in direct contrast to the situation prevailing under capitalism.'[11]

The dialectical relation between theory and praxis means an ongoing development of each, with theory adapting to conclusions reached via practice and practice implementing the proposals of theory, a relation which constantly develops, enriching both theory and praxis in the process; practice depends on theory, and theory depends on practice – they cease to be autonomous, exclusive activities pursued in total separation.

One of the major hurdles to creating a tight relationship between theory and practice is the difficulty of transition from one to the other: theory, being text-based and formed via discourse,

**8** Alejandro Zaera-Polo, 'The Politics of the Fold' (part I), **Log** 13/14, Fall 2008, pp. 193-207.

**9** Felix Guattari, **Chaosmosis: An Ethico-Aesthetic Paradigm** (Indianapolis: Indiana University Press, 1995), p. 107.

**10** David Harvey, **Justice, Nature and the Geography of Difference** (Oxford: Blackwell, 1996), p. 9.

**11** Martin Jay, **The Dialectical Imagination: A History of the Frankfurt School and the Institute of Social Research, 1923-1950** (Berkeley & Los Angeles; London: University of California Press, 1996), p. 4.

does not easily lend itself to application in the world of action. The philosopher and literature critic Georg Lukács commented that '[i]f the theory is juxtaposed to an action without mediation, without it becoming clear how its effect on the latter is intended, thus, without making clear the organizational links between them, then the theory itself can only be criticised with respect to its immanent theoretical contradictions'.[12] Mediation therefore is a central instrument of guaranteeing a successful transition from theory to practice and its reverse.

Establishing a dialectical relationship between theory and praxis was one of the principles guiding the work of the Urban Asymmetries study group, and is present in this volume as well – in the juxtapositioning of theoretical essays and projects which feed into each other, albeit in a relatively loose manner. In the work of the Urban Asymmetries study group the mediating instruments included diagrams of the conclusions of the analysis, which enabled the development of a strategy, and proposals which articulated the agencies which would be able to undertake the project – identifying the means of organization needed to implement the theory.

In order to understand urban transformation, the forces which determine such transformation, and to comprehend the city as a process rather than as a static object, the projects of Urban Asymmetries begin with an historical analysis. Harvey has commented that 'I stand, in short, to learn far more about urban process under capitalism by detailed reconstruction of how a particular city has evolved than I would from collection of empirical data sets from a sample of one hundred cities'.[13] Rather than a reciting of facts, the historical analysis is a means of identifying the major forces at work in a specific urban context, delineating the diverse agencies in operation as well as the power structures which determine the environment and its social composition. As the projects aim to intervene in an existing environment and transform it, the in-depth understanding of the manner in which transformation takes place and is shaped in the specific context is vital.

Beyond the capitulation of local politicians and urban planners to the demands of investors and developers who press for more business-friendly conditions such as tax breaks or the removal of regulations, the last decades have seen the growing power of local urban movements, typically comprised of diverse groups united around a single cause in an ad-hoc organization. While such movements have been particularly common in middle-class areas, leveraging the access of the local population to media and lawyers, they have not been limited to the affluent or to NIMBI protests. The many successes of such urban movements should remind professionals, including architects and urbanists, that market forces are not the only forces at play, that as professionals, they have a responsibility to society rather than to the accumulation of capital.

The re-instatement of the agency of the architect and the urbanist are thus part of the Urban Asymmetries agenda, for it is the urbanist who can prevent speculation and opportunism which leaves urban devastation, and the architect who can provide proper housing solutions or affective micro-interventions which articulate parts of a larger strategy or plan. But in order to discover architectural or urban agency, it is also necessary to expand these fields beyond the limits delineated for them – limits which were designated to guarantee that the work of urbanists and architects aids rather than undermines the accumulation of capital. Such an expansion of the field means a multi-disciplinary approach, accessing disciplines which provide a perspective of social processes, including urban geography, sociology, economics or political science. The city, after all, not only comprises the buildings and the infrastructure, but also its inhabitants, the social networks, the daily rhythms, working life, power relations and so on.

The Urban Asymmetries projects address the dissolution of social housing – one of the major issues for the study group – as a symptom of larger losses at the levels of society, politics and culture. One of the most important elements in the development of a healthy urbanity is intimately associated with the satisfactory provision of dignified housing for the weaker segments of the population, especially in regions characterized by asymmetrical development. The projects argue that the loss of social commitment and political engagement visible in many of today's (private) urban development agendas is producing a process of erosion of 'citiness'. Urban Asymmetries intends to set the theoretical groundwork for a series of strategic recommendations, counter-proposals and ultimately design interventions that may address, answer or even challenge some of these negative forces in the production of the city.

The re-instatement of the architect and urbanist suggested by Urban Asymmetries is thus in a somewhat transformed role: re-assuming agency and responsibility for the city by engaging the residents, politicians, advocacy groups, funding organizations, social movements. Only a broad coalition can initiate meaningful urban change which departs from neoliberal solutions and defies the demands of the market for the general benefit of society. Hence, not only architectural agency is resurrected, but human agency as well, envisioning the empowerment of urban dwellers to steer their life and determine their environment.

**The book**  This volume includes excerpts from three pilot projects by the Urban Asymmetries study group; the underlying aim of these three projects was to disclose the correlation between the introduction of neoliberalism during the 1970s, its spread in the 1980s and its consolidation in the 1990s in three strategically located cities in the Americas: Santiago de Chile, Mexico City and Newark. The three cities demonstrate the dire condition of contemporary cities, contrasting the

**12**  Georg Lukács, in Jürgen Habermas, **Theory and Praxis** (Boston: Beacon Press, 1974), p. 34.
**13**  David Harvey, 'Notes Towards a Theory of Uneven Geographical Development', **Spaces of Global Capitalism: Towards a Theory of Uneven Geographical Development** (London; New York: Verso, 2006), p. 86.

glossy magazine images of glittering shopping districts and affluence which have dominated the representation of urban life in mass media since the mid-1990s. The three represent very different expressions of very similar policies carried out in diverse scales – international, national and local. Each of the cities has been shaped by a different aspect of uneven urban development in the Americas. In the 1970s, Santiago under General Pinochet was the laboratory for the Chicago School of Economics, experimenting with economic policies which would later be implemented in the United States, the United Kingdom and many other countries. Thus, Santiago was chosen for an Urban Asymmetries project because it is the locus in which neoliberalism was launched, the 'cradle' of neoliberalism. Mexico City represents the condition of uneven urban development prompted by international agreements which formed the large trading block NAFTA. It is the locus of city sprawl, of areas of extreme affluence contrasting urban destitution, of unplanned development and mass standardization – a city of contradictions. Newark represents the special case of the ex-industrial city which has lost its role in post-industrial society, a city which stands in stark contrast to the affluence of nearby Manhattan or New Jersey's suburban sprawl.

The excerpts included here from the three Urban Asymmetries projects emphasize the analysis carried out. These projects are the backbone of three corresponding sections which provide an introduction and insight into contemporary Santiago, Mexico City and Newark. Each section offers, in addition to the project excerpts, an introductory text, as well as essays and interviews which unfold the specific condition of these cities. These three sections are complemented by more general articles and interviews which address issues of uneven urban development under neoliberalism. David Harvey discusses urban development and its crisis; Erik Swyngedouw outlines new modes of urban governance in the post-political world which necessitate the withering of the state; Margit Mayer correlates contemporary urban oppositional movements to neoliberal ideas; and Arie Graafland provides a critical evaluation of the Urban Asymmetries projects and of everyday urbanism.

The current economic crisis, which is far from over, has only underlined the urgent need for an alternative to contemporary urban policies and practices. *Urban Asymmetries* offers a critique of neoliberal urban policies and current urban conditions, as well as a – somewhat hesitant – step towards devising interventionist strategies which could delineate a very different trajectory for society and the city, a trajectory which is driven by the general wellbeing of society rather than the narrow interests of economic elites.

# The Zero-Ground of Politics: Musings on the Post-Political City

**Erik Swyngedouw**[1]

*There is a shift from the model of the* polis *founded on a centre, that is, a public centre or* agora, *to a new metropolitan spatialisation that is certainly invested in a process of de-politicisation, which results in a strange zone where it is impossible to decide what is private and what is public.* (Agamben, 2006)[2]

The city offers a privileged scale for dissecting the social body, for rummaging through the innards of our most intimate fantasies, desires, and fears; for excavating the symptoms of the city's political condition. As the ancient Greek polis was for Aristotle and Plato the experimental site for the performance of civic and political life, the contemporary city also holds for us the key to unlocking the contours of the present political constellation.

It is indeed unmistakably so that the city has undergone radical change over the past two decades or so, most dramatically in its modes of urban governing and polic(y)ing.[3] We shall argue that, while the city is alive and thriving at least in some of its spaces, the polis, conceived in the idealized Greek sense as the site for public political encounter and democratic negotiation, the spacing of (often radical) dissent, and disagreement, and the place where political subjectivation emerges and literally takes place, seems moribund. In other words, the 'political' is retreating while social space is increasingly colonized by policies (or policing). The latter refers to a constellation of technocratic managerial practices of good governance within a generic neoliberal frame that remains uncontested. The suturing of social space by consensual managerial policies and the evacuation of the properly political (democratic) dimension from the urban – what will be described below as the post-political condition – constitutes what I would define as the ZERO-ground of politics. The leitmotiv of this chapter will indeed be the figure of a de-politicized Post-Political and Post-Democratic city.

I shall argue that urban governance at the beginning of the twenty-first century has shifted profoundly, giving rise to a new form of governmentality in the Foucaultian sense of the word, one that is predicated upon new formal and informal institutional configurations – forms of governance that are characterized by a broadening of the sphere of governing, while narrowing, if not suspending, the space of the properly political. Urban governing today is carried by a wide variety of institutions and organizations. It operates through a range of geographical scales, and mobilizes a wide assortment of social actors, including private agents, designers, architects, and planners, non-governmental organizations, civil society groups, corporations, and the more traditional forms of local, regional, or national government. I shall characterize these new regimes of policing the city as Governance-beyond-the-State.[4] It is a governance regime concerned with policing, controlling and accentuating the imperatives of a globally connected neoliberalized market economy, a condition further re-

1 An earlier version of this paper was published in **NewGeographies** – After Zero Theme Issue (Harvard University Design School), issue 1, pp. 52-61.
2 G. Agamben, Metropolis. **Metropoli/Moltitudine Seminario nomade in tre atti** (Venice, 2006).
3 J. Rancière, **La Mésente**. (Editions Galilée, 1995); M. Dikeç, **Badlands of the Republic. Space, Politics and French Urban Policy** (Oxford: Blackwell, 2007).
4 E. Swyngedouw, 'Governance Innovation and the Citizen: The Janus Face of Governance-beyond-the-state', **Urban Studies** 42, 2005, pp. 1-16; E. Swyngedouw, 'Civil Society,

enforced by the elite-led restructuring in the aftermath of the global financial crisis that erupted in 2008.

This new 'polic(y)ing' order reflects what Slavoj Žižek and Jacques Rancière define as a post-political and post-democratic constitution. In other words, contrary to the popular belief that these new forms of neoliberal urban governance widen participation and deepen 'democracy', I shall insist that this post-political condition in fact annuls democracy, evacuates the proper political dimension – i.e. the nurturing of disagreement through properly constructed material and symbolic spaces for dissentient public encounter and exchange – and ultimately perverts and undermines the very foundation of a democratic polis. This regime exposes what Rancière calls the scandal of democracy: while promising equality, it produces an oligarchically instituted form of governing in which political power seamlessly fuses with economic might and a governance arrangement that consensually shapes the city according to the dreams, tastes and needs of the transnational economic, political, and cultural elites.[5] Proper urban politics fosters dissent, creates disagreement and triggers the debating of and experimentation with more egalitarian and inclusive urban futures, a process that is fraught with all kinds of tensions and contradictions but also opens up spaces of possibilities. Exploring these will constitute the final part of this contribution. But first I shall highlight the contours of present-day urbanity.

## Urban post-political governance-beyond-the-State: the zero-ground of politics

My entry into excavating the constellation of present-day urbanity is through the large scale redevelopment projects that are dotting the urban landscape worldwide. I take my cue from the emblematic urban interventions that are staged and erected as attempts to reconfigure the urban socio-cultural, economic, and physical fabric in line with the aspirations and dreams of urban elites that prefigure a particular form of urbanity, one that simultaneously redraws the wider and globalizing spatio-temporal co-ordinates in which the city is enmeshed. Whether one considers the Amsterdam-Zuid project, Bilbao's Guggenheim Museum and the Abandobarra re-development, Abu Dhabi's urban dreamscape, Berlin's feeble attempt to reposition itself as a global city through signature urban reconstruction on Potzdamer Platz, or London's and Barcelona's mission to take spectacular large scale architectural and development cathedrals as the lynchpin to reposition the city as competitive, creative, cosmopolitan and globally connected, they all exhibit, despite their differences, an extraordinary degree of similarity.[6] While the reader can come up with his or her own favourite list of cities and their emblematic buildings or projects, the key point is their ubiquitous presence in contemporary urban strategies to plug their city as a vibrant, cosmopolitan, entrepreneurial, dynamic environment that sits comfortably within a neo-liberal market-driven global competitive urban order.

Of course, these newly built environments express a series of wider transformations and signal, if not actively manufacture, new political, socio-cultural, and economic realities. Contrary to the mainstream argument that urban leaders and elites mobilize such competitive tactics as a response to the assumed inevitability of a neoliberal global economic order, I insist that these strategies in fact construct and consciously produce the very conditions that are symbolically defined as global urbanism. Equally important, of course, is the question of the institutional and political orderings that permit such emblematic and dramatic interventions to take place. Put differently, the very possibility of a new competitive globalized city requires the reconfiguration of the polic(y)ing order, of the regime of governmentality as Foucault would have it, and is predicated upon a profound transformations of the 'traditional' horizons of urban governance, most notably through the formation of new institutional and civic arrangements that centre around the inclusion of private and other non-state actors in the act of governing. Moreover, these emerging new regimes of urban governance fuse together actors, elites, and institutions not only from the local social milieu, but also from the national or international level. In sum, large scale urban interventions embody in their crystalline structure the very dynamics through which new forms of governmentality, reconfigured elite networks, and new parameters of competitiveness, economic dynamics and spatial linkages are constructed.

Elsewhere, I have defined the newly emerging forms of urban governing as arrangements of Governing-beyond-the-State (but often with the explicit inclusion of parts of the state apparatus).[7] These are institutional or quasi-institutional constellations that are organized as horizontal associational networks of private (market), civil society (usually NGO), and state actors.[8] These forms of apparently horizontally organized, networked, and polycentric *ensembles* in which power is dispersed are increasingly prevalent in rule making, setting and implementation at a variety of geographical scales.[9] These modes of governance frame an emerging new form of governmentality or 'the conduct of conduct'.[10] Such network-governance implies a common purpose, joint action, a framework of shared values, continuous interaction and the wish to achieve collective benefits that cannot be gained by acting independently,[11] and is predicated upon a consensual agreement

Governmentality and the Contradictions of Governance-Beyond-the-State', in J. Hillier, F. Moulaert, and S. Vicari (eds) **Social Innovation and Territorial Development** (Aldershot: Ashgate, 2009), pp. 63-78.

5  J. Rancière, **La Haine de la Démocratie** (Paris: La Fabrique éditions, 2005).

6  E. Swyngedouw, F. Moulaert, and A. Rodriguez, 'Neoliberal Urbanization in Europe: Large-Scale Urban Development Projects and the New Urban Policy', **Antipode** 34, 2002, pp. 542-77.

7  E. Swyngedouw, 'Governance Innovation and the Citizen: The Janus Face of Governance-beyond-the-state', 2005.

8  K. Dingwerth, 'Democratic Governance beyond the State: Operationalising an Idea', 2004, http://www.glogov.org (accessed 16 May 2005).

9  M. Hajer, 'Policy without Polity? Policy Analysis and the Institutional Void', **Policy Sciences** 36, 2003, pp. 175-95; N. Brenner, **New State Spaces** (Oxford: University Press, 2004).

10  M. Foucault, 'On Governmentality', **Ideology and Consciousness** 6, 1979, pp. 5-21; T. Lemke, 'Foucault, Governmentality, and Critique', **Rethinking Marxism** 14, 2002, pp. 49-64.

11  G. Stoker, 'Public–Private Partnerships in Urban Governance', in J. Pierre (ed.) **Partnerships in Urban Governance: European and American Experience** (Basingstoke: Macmillan, 1998), pp. 34-51.

on the existing conditions ('The state of the situation')[12] and the main objectives to be achieved ('The partition of the sensible'). This model is related to a view of 'governmentality' that considers the mobilization of resources (ideological, economic, cultural) from actors operating outside the state system as a vital part of democratic, efficient, and effective government.[13] In sum, Governance-beyond-the-State is constituted by presumably horizontally networked associations, and based on interactive relations between independent and interdependent actors that share a high degree of consensus and trust, despite internal conflict and oppositional agendas, within selectively inclusive participatory institutional or organizational settings.

Whilst in pluralist democracy, the political entitlement of the citizen is articulated via the twin condition of 'national' citizenship on the one hand, and the entitlement to egalitarian political participation in a variety of ways (but, primarily via a form of (constitutionally or otherwise) codified representational democracy) on the other, network-based forms of urban governance do not have codified rules and regulations that shape or define participation and identify the exact domains or arenas of power.[14] As Beck argues,[15] these practices are full of 'unauthorized actors'. The status, inclusion or exclusion, legitimacy, system of representation, scale of operation, and internal or external accountability of such actors often take place in non-transparent, ad-hoc, and context-dependent ways and differ greatly from those associated with egalitarian pluralist democratic rules and codes. Moreover, the internal power choreography of systems of Governance-beyond-the-State is customarily led by coalitions of economic, socio-cultural, or political elites.[16] Therefore, existing social and political power geometries are changed, resulting in a new constellation of governance articulated via a proliferating maze of opaque networks, fuzzy institutional arrangements, with ill-defined responsibilities and ambiguous political objectives and priorities. The state still plays a pivotal and often autocratic role in transferring competencies (and consequently for instantiating the resulting changing power geometries) and in arranging these new networked forms of governance.

For Žižek, Mouffe, and Rancière, among others, such arrangements signal the emergence of a post-political and post-democratic condition. They define the post-political as a political formation that actually forecloses the political, that prevents the politicization of particulars:[17] 'post-politics mobilizes the vast apparatus of experts, social workers, and so on, to reduce the overall demand (complaint) of a particular group to just this demand, with its particular content – no wonder that this suffocating closure gives birth to "irrational" outbursts of violence as the only way to give expression to the dimension beyond particularity.'[18] Post-politics rejects ideological divisions and the explicit universalization of particular political demands. Instead, the post-political condition is one in which a consensus has been built around the inevitability of neoliberal capitalism as an economic system, parliamentary democracy as the political ideal, humanitarianism and inclusive cosmopolitanism as a moral foundation. As Žižek puts it: '[p]ost-politics is thus about the administration (policing) of social, economic or other issues, and they remain of course fully within the realm of the possible, of existing social relations',[19] they organize 'the partition of the sensible',[20] the distribution of functions and places. 'The ultimate sign of post-politics in all Western countries', Žižek continues, 'is the growth of a managerial approach to government: government is reconceived as a managerial function, deprived of its proper political dimension.'[21] Post-politics refuses politicization in the classical Greek sense, that is, as the metaphorical universalization of particular demands, which aims at 'more' than negotiation of interests. Politics becomes something one can do without making decisions that divide and separate.[22] A consensual post-politics thus arises, one that either eliminates fundamental conflict or elevates it to antithetical ultra-politics. The consensual times we are currently living in have thus eliminated a genuine political space of disagreement. However, consensus does not equal peace or absence of fundamental conflict.[23]

Difficulties and problems, such as re-ordering the urban, that are generally staged and accepted as problematic, need to be dealt with through compromise, managerial and technical arrangement, and the production of consensus. 'Consensus means that whatever your personal commitments, interests and values may be, you perceive the same things, you give them the same name. But there is no contest on what appears, on what is given in a situation and as a situation'.[24] The key feature of consensus is 'the annulment of dissensus ..... the "end of politics"'.[25] Of course, this post-political world eludes choice and freedom (other than those tolerated by the consensus). The only position of real dissent is that of either the traditionalist (stuck in the past and refusing to accept the inevitability of the new global neoliberal order) or the fundamentalist. The only way to deal with them is by sheer violence, by suspending their 'humanitarian' and 'democratic' rights. The post-political

**12**  A. Badiou, **Being and Event** (London: Continuum, 2005).

**13**  J. Pierre, **Debating Governance: Authority, Steering and Democracy** (Oxford: University Press, 2000).

**14**  M. Hajer (ed.) **Deliberative Policy Analysis: Understanding Governance in the Network Society** (Cambridge: University Press, 2003).

**15**  U. Beck, **World Risk Society** (Cambridge: Polity Press, 1999).

**16**  E. Swyngedouw, F. Moulaert, and A. Rodriguez, 'Neoliberal Urbanization in Europe: Large-Scale Urban Development Projects and the New Urban Policy', 2002.

**17**  S. Žižek, 'Carl Schmitt in the Age of Post-Politics', in C. Mouffe (ed.) **The Challenge of Carl Schmitt** (London: Verso, 1999), p. 35; S. Žižek, **The Parallax View** (Cambridge, Mass.: MIT Press, 2006); C. Mouffe, **On The Political** (London: Routledge, 2005).

**18**  S. Žižek, **The Ticklish Subject – The Absent Centre of Political Ontology** (London: Verso, 1999), p. 204.

**19**  S. Žižek, **The Ticklish Subject**, p. 198.

**20**  J. Rancière, **Le Partage du Sensible: Esthétique et Politique** (Paris: La Fabrique, 2000).

**21**  S. Žižek, **Revolution at the Gates – Žižek on Lenin – The 1917 Writings** (London: Verso. 2002), p. 303.

**22**  A.J.P. Thomson, 'Re-Placing the Opposition: Rancière and Derrida', **Fidelity to the Disagreement** (London: Goldsmith's College, University of London, 2003), p. 19.

**23**  J. Rancière, **Chroniques des Temps Consensuels** (Paris: Seuil, 2005), p. 8.

**24**  J. Rancière, 'Comment and Responses', **Theory & Event** 6, 2003, p. §4.

**25**  J. Rancière, 'Ten Theses on Politics', **Theory & Event** 5, 2001, p. §32.

relies on including all in a consensual pluralist order and/or on excluding radically those who posit themselves outside the consensus. For them, as Agamben argues,[26] the law is suspended – the 'police' order annuls their rights; they are literally put outside the law and treated as extremists and terrorists. That is why for Agamben the 'Camp' is the seminal space of late modernity. This form of ultra-politics pits those who 'participate' in the consensual order radically against those who are placed outside. The riots in Paris in the fall of 2005 and the 'police' responses (by both the forces of repression and the political elites) were classic violent expressions of such urban ultra-politics.[27]

Late capitalist urban governance and debates over the arrangement of the city are not only perfect expressions of such a post-political order, but in fact, the making of new creative and entrepreneurial cities is one of the key arenas through which this post-political consensus becomes constructed, when 'politics proper is progressively replaced by expert social administration'.[28] The post-political consensus, therefore, is one that is radically reactionary, one that forestalls the articulation of divergent, conflicting, and alternative trajectories of future urban possibilities and assemblages. This retreat of the political into the cocoon of consensual policy-making within a singular distribution of the givens of the situation constitutes, I maintain, the zero ground of politics.

## Urban populism as symptom of post-democracy[29]

This Post-Political condition articulates with a consensual populist tactic as the conduit to instigate 'desirable' change. Urban polic(y)ing is a prime expression of the populist ploy of the post-political post-democratic condition.[30] Put differently, a depoliticized urban populism has become a key symptom of the post-democratic institutional consensus. We shall briefly chart the characteristics of populism and how this is reflected in mainstream urban concerns.[31]

Populism invokes 'THE' city and 'THE' (undivided) 'people' as a whole in a material and discursive manner. All people are affected by urban problems and the whole of urban life as we know it is under threat from potential catastrophes (globalization, non-competitiveness, global warming, uncontrolled immigration). As such, populism cuts across the idiosyncrasies of different forms and expressions of urban life, silences ideological and other constitutive social differences and papers over fundamental conflicts of interest by distilling a common threat or challenge. Urban populism is also based on a politics of 'the people know best' (although the latter category remains often empty, unnamed), supported by an assumedly neutral scientific technocracy, and advocates a direct relationship between people and political participation. Populism customarily invokes the spectre of annihilating apocalyptic futures if no direct and immediate action is taken. If we refrain from acting (in a technocratic-managerial manner) now, our urban future is in grave danger. It instils a sense of millennialist angst and existentialist urgency. Populist tactics do not identify a privileged subject of change (like the proletariat for Marx, women for feminists, or the 'creative class' for neoliberal capitalism), but instead invoke a common condition or predicament, the need for common action, mutual collaboration and co-operation. There are no internal social tensions or generative internal conflicts. Instead the enemy is always externalized and objectified. Populism's fundamental fantasy is that of a threatening *Intruder*, or more usually a group of intruders, who have *corrupted* the system.[32] The 'immigrant', 'terrorist', and 'globalization' stand here as classic examples of fetishized and externalized foes – empty signifiers – that require dealing with if a new urbanity is to be attained. Problems therefore are not the result of the 'system', of unevenly distributed power relations, of implicit or explicit silences and marginalizations, of the networks of control and influence, of rampant injustices, or of a fatal flaw inscribed in the system, but are blamed on an outsider, a 'pathological' syndrome that can be cut out without affecting the functioning of the system. Populist demands are always addressed to the elites. Urban populism is not about changing the elites, but calling on the elites to undertake action. A non-populist politics is exactly about obliterating the elite, imagining the impossible. Furthermore, no proper names are assigned to a post-political populist politics.[33] Post-political populism is associated with a politics of not naming in the sense of giving a definite or proper name to its domain or field of action. Only vague concepts – floating signifiers – like the creative city, the competitive city, the inclusive city, the global city, the sustainable city replace the proper names of politics. These proper names are what constitute a genuine democracy, that is a space where the unnamed, the uncounted, and, consequently, un-symbolized claim name and (ac)count. Finally, populism is expressed in particular demands (get rid of immigrants, lower taxes, increase 'participation', improve sustainability) that remain particular and foreclose universalization as a positive urban project. In other words, the urban problem does not posit a positive and named socio-environmental situation, an embodied vision, a desire that awaits its realization, a fiction to be realized.

**26** G. Agamben, **State of Exception** (Chicago: The University of Chicago Press, 2005).

**27** For details, see Dikeç, **Badlands of the Republic. Space, Politics and French Urban Policy**, 2007.

**28** S. Žižek, 'Against Human Rights', **New Left Review**, 2005, p. 117.

**29** For further discussion, see, among others, E. Swyngedouw, 'The Post-Political City' in BAVO (ed.) **Urban Politics Now. Re-imagining Democracy in the Neo-liberal City** (Rotterdam: Netherlands Architecture Institute NAI Publishers, 2007); E. Swyngedouw, 'Wal-Marting the Urban: Reflections on the Post-Political and Post-Democratic City', in B. Hofmeyr (ed.) **Wal-marting the City** (Maastricht: Jan Van Eyck Academy, 2008), pp. 107-140; and F. Moulaert, A. Rodriguez, and E. Swyngedouw (eds) **The Globalized City – Economic Restructuring and Social Polarization in European Cities** (Oxford: University Press, 2002).

**30** C. Crouch, **Post-Democracy** (Cambridge: Polity Press, 2004); see also R. Rorty, 'Post-Democracy', **London Review of Books**, 2004.

**31** See, among others, M. Canovan, 'Trust the People! Populism and the Two Faces of Democracy', **Political Studies** 47, 1999, pp. 2-16; E. Laclau, **On Populist Reason** (London: Verso, 2005); Mouffe, **On The Political**, 2005; S. Žižek, 'Against the Populist Temptation', **Is The Politics of Truth still Thinkable? A conference organized by Slavoj Žižek and Costas Douzinas** (Birkbeck College, University of London: The Birkbeck Institute for the Humanities, 2005); E. Swyngedouw, 'Impossible/Undesirable Sustainability and the Post-Political Condition' in J.R. Krueger, and D. Gibbs (eds) **The Sustainable Development Paradox** (New York: Guilford, 2007), pp. 13-40.

**32** S. Žižek, **In Defense of Lost Causes** (London: Verso, 2008).

**33** A. Badiou, 'Politics: A Non-Expressive Dialectics', **Is The Politics of Truth still Thinkable?, A conference organized by Slavoj Žižek and Costas Douzinas** (London: Birkbeck Institute for the Humanities, Birkbeck College, 2005).

### Reclaiming the political city: beyond the 'zero' ground of urban polic(y)ing

'[T]he political act (intervention) proper is not simply something that works well within the framework of existing relations, but something that *changes the very framework that determines how things work* .... [A]uthentic politics ... is the art of the *impossible* – it changes the very parameters of what is considered "possible" in the existing constellation.' (Žižek, 1999; emphasis in original) [34]

A genuine politics, therefore, is 'the moment in which a particular demand is not simply part of the negotiation of interests but aims at something more, and starts to function as the metaphoric condensation of the global restructuring of the entire social space'.[35] It implies the recognition of conflict as constitutive of the social condition, and the naming of the urban spaces that can become. The political is defined by Žižek and Rancière as the space of litigation,[36] the space for those who are not-All, who are uncounted and unnamed, not part of the 'police' (symbolic, social and state) order; where they claim their right to the polis. A true political space is always a space of contestation, in the name of equality, for those who have no name or no place. As Diken and Laustsen put it: '[p]olitics in this sense is the ability to debate, question and renew the fundament on which political struggle unfolds, the ability to criticize radically a given order and to fight for a new and better one. In a nutshell, then, politics necessitates accepting conflict.'[37] A radical-progressive position 'should insist on the unconditional primacy of the inherent antagonism as constitutive of the political'[38] and 'always works against the pacification of social disruption, against the management of consensus and "stability" .... The concern of democracy is not with the formulation of agreement or the preservation of order but with the invention of new and hitherto unauthorised modes of disaggregation, disagreement and disorder';[39] it is about demanding the realization of the impossible. In sum, as Badiou argues,[40] 'a new radical politics must revolve around the construction of great new fictions' that create real possibilities for constructing different urban futures. To the extent that the current post-political condition that combines consensual 'Third Way' politics with a hegemonic neoliberal view of social ordering constitutes one particular fiction (one that in fact forecloses dissent, conflict, and the possibility of a different future) and reveals its perverse underbelly each time it becomes geographically concrete in the world, there is an urgent need for different stories and fictions that can be mobilized for realization. A genuine democratic political sequence starts from an axiomatic egalitarian position, recognizes conflicting socio-spatial processes and radically different possible urban futures, and struggles over the naming and trajectories of these futures.[41] It is about re-centring the political as space of dispute/litigation/disagreement.

The courage of the intellectual imagination of progressive urbanities is one of the ingredients in this process of reclaiming political space and of excavating the archaeology of future possibilities. There is a clear agenda here, one that revolves around the ruthless critique of the impossibility (in egalitarian democratic terms) of the neoliberal utopia. The promises of a free-floating, globally interconnected, inclusive and phantasmagorical liberal paradise are clearly endearing and captivating for some, promising that the ultimate realization of our desires is just lurking around the corner, provided we stick it out until the neoliberal prescriptions have done their healing work. While this may indeed be true for some, it invariably brings with it all manner of distortions, inequalities, and new barriers. Consider, for example, how the promise of mobility and the freedom of place are highly and unevenly truncated. While the spatial freedom and mobility of capital in the form of money is virtually frictionless, the freedom to roam the world for capital as commodities is already highly unevenly regulated and organized. For capital in the form of labour force, of course, the most unspeakable mental and physical violence is inflicted upon roaming labouring bodies. We call them immigrants or refugees (once upon a time we called them (guest-) workers, identifying them by their class position and assigned socio-spatial function); yet they are one of the crucial forms of capital, a capital that neoliberals desperately wish to keep in their place and out of the elite spaces. While there is indeed a global world for capital, there are many worlds for others, whose borders are strictly demarcated, walled, patrolled, policed, and contained.[42] The market utopia of a free mobility is one that is only accessible to some, while others are kept in place and/or outside. All manner of polarizing and fragmenting forces divide and separate in a globalizing neoliberal order. My urban Nikes at $ 140.00 a pair are stitched together in Chinese sweatshops by teenage girls at 13 dollar cents. The spread of capitalism worldwide has propelled the proletarianization process to unparalleled heights. Freeing peasants from their land, of course, permits freedom to move, to the city, to the global North. The spread of global capitalism and the generalization of market forces brings therefore unprecedented migration. Many of those de-territorialized bodies are now becoming an integral part of the global north's urban citizenry, yet remain conspicuously absent from the new orders of governing.

The post-political 'glocal' city is fragmented and kaleidoscopic. Worldwide integration unfolds hand in glove with increasing spatial differentiations, inequalities and combined but uneven development. Within the tensions, inconsistencies and exclusions forged through these kaleido-

**34** S. Žižek, **The Ticklish Subject**, p. 199.
**35** S. Žižek, **The Ticklish Subject**, p. 208.
**36** S. Žižek, 'For a Leftist Appropriation of the European Legacy', **Journal of Political Ideologies** 3, 1998, pp. 63-78.
**37** B. Diken and C. Laustsen, '7/11, 9/11, and Post-Politics', 2004, p. 9, see http://www.comp.lancs.ac.uk/sociology/papers/diken-laustsen-7-11-9-11-post-politics.pdf (accessed 15 September 2005).
**38** S. Žižek, 'Carl Schmitt in the Age of Post-Politics', p. 9.
**39** P. Hallward, 'Jacques Rancière and the Subversion of Mastery', **Paragraph** 28, 2005, pp. 34-35.
**40** A. Badiou, 'Politics: A Non-Expressive Dialectics', 2005.
**41** E. Swyngedouw, 'The Communist Hypothesis and Revolutionary Capitalisms: Exploring the Idea of Communist Geographies for the 21st Century', **Antipode** 41, 2010, pp. 1439-60.
**42** A. Badiou, **De Quoi Sarkozy est-il le Nom?** (Paris: Nouvelles Éditions Lignes, 2007).

scopic yet incoherent transformations, all manner of frictions, cracks, fissures, gaps, and 'vacant' spaces arise;[43] spaces that, although an integral part of the 'police' order, of the existing state of the situation, are simultaneously outside of it. These fissures, cracks, and 'free' spaces form 'quilting' points, nodes for experimentation with new urban possibilities. It is indeed precisely in these 'marginal' spaces – the fragments left unoccupied and non-sutured by the urban police order that regulates, assigns, and distributes – that all manner of new urban social and cultural energies and practices emerge; where new forms of urbanity come to life. While transnational capital flows impose their totalizing logic on the city and on urban polic(y)ing, the contours of and possibilities for a new and more humane urban form and life germinate in these urban 'free' spaces. These are the sort of spaces where alternative forms of living, working, and expressing are experimented with, where new forms of social and political action are staged, where affective economies are reworked, and creative living is not measured by the rise of the stock market and pension fund indices.

Reclaiming the democratic polis revolves around re-centring/re-designing the urban as a democratic political field of dispute/disagreement: it is about enunciating dissent and rupture, literally opening up spaces that permit speech acts that claim a place in the order of things. This centres on re-thinking equality politically, i.e. thinking equality not as a sociologically verifiable concept or procedure that permits opening a policy arena which will remedy the observed inequalities (utopian/normative/moral) some time in a utopian future (i.e. the standard recipe of left-liberal urban policy prescriptions), but as the axiomatically given and presupposed, albeit contingent, condition of democracy. Political space emerges thereby as the space for the institutionalization of the social (society) and equality as the foundational gesture of political democracy (presumed, axiomatic, yet contingent, foundation). This requires extraordinary designs (both theoretically and materially) that cut through the master signifiers of consensual urban governance (creativity, sustainability, growth, cosmopolitanism, participation, etc...) and their radical metonymic re-imagination. Elements of such transgressive metonymic re-designs include:

- Thinking the creativity of opposition/dissensus and reworking the 'creative' city as agonistic urban space rather than limiting creativity to musings of the urban 'creative class'.
- Thinking through the city as a space for accommodating difference and disorder. This hinges critically on creating ega-libertarian public spaces.
- Visionary thinking and urban practices: imagining concrete spatio-temporal utopias as immediately necessary and realizable.
- Re-thinking and re-practicing the 'Right to the City' as the 'Right to the production of urbanization'. Henri Lefebvre's clarion call about the 'Right to the

City' is indeed really one that urges us to think the city as a process of collective co-design and co-production.

Most important, however, is to traverse the fantasy of the elites, a fantasy that is sustained and nurtured by the imaginary of an autopoietic world, the hidden-hand of market exchange that self-regulates and self-organizes, serving simultaneously the interests of the Ones and the All, the private and the common. The socialism for the elites that structures the contemporary city is really one that mobilizes the commons in the interests of the elite through the mobilizing and disciplinary registers of post-democratic politics. It is a fantasy that is further sustained by a double fantasmagoria: on the one hand the promise of eventual enjoyment – 'believe us and our designs will guarantee your enjoyment'. It is an enjoyment that is forever postponed, that becomes a true utopia. On the other hand, there is the promise of catastrophe and disintegration if the elite's fantasy is not realized, one that is predicated upon the relentless cultivation of fear (ecological disintegration, excessive migration, terrorism, economic crisis and disintegration), a fear that can only be managed through technocratic-expert knowledge and elite governance arrangements. This fantasy of catastrophe has a castrating effect – it sustains the impotence for naming and designing truly alternative cities, truly different emancipatory spatialities and urbanities.

Traversing elite fantasies requires the intellectual and political courage to imagine egalitarian democracies, the production of common values and the collective production of the greatest collective *oeuvre*, the city, the inauguration of new political trajectories of living life in common, and, more importantly, the courage to choose, to take sides. Traversing the fantasy of the elites means recognizing that the social and ecological catastrophe that is announced everyday as tomorrow's threat is not a promise, not something to come, but is already the REAL of the present. As the Invisible Committee put it in *The Coming Insurrection*,

> It's useless to *wait* – for a breakthrough, for the revolution, the nuclear apocalypse or a social movement. To go on waiting is madness. The catastrophe is not coming, it is here. We are already situated *within* the collapse of a civilization. It is within this reality that we must choose sides.[44]

**43** E. Swyngedouw, 'The Mont des Arts as a Ruin in the Revanchist City', in B. De Meulder and K. Van Herck (eds) **Vacant City – Brussels' Mont des Arts Reconsidered** (Rotterdam: NAI Publishers, 2000), pp. 267-81.
**44** The-Invisible-Committee, **The Coming Insurrection** (Cambridge, Mass.: MIT Press, 2009).

# The Neoliberal City: Investment, Development and Crisis

**David Harvey in Conversation with Miguel Robles-Durán**[1]

**Miguel Robles-Durán**  I want to begin with your understanding of the emergence of neoliberal agendas – what were or what are from your point of view the major manifestations in the city of the immediate economic transformations that started to happen, not only in the UK under Thatcher, but also in Latin America, the United States, etc.?

**David Harvey**  I think the fundamental underlying problem from the 1970s onwards is what I call the capital surplus disposal problem. Capitalists are always producing surpluses and they always have to absorb them, and you've got to get your 3% growth or 5% growth, or whatever you are aiming for, which means the system has to expand and there is a big problem of how to expand it; and neoliberalism, if you look at its class trajectory, it was about concentrating assets in the upper classes, and the certain system legitimating that was that the upper classes invest – but what do they invest in? So, since the 1970s we have seen a whole series of asset bubbles with a vast wave of investment in the 1970s going into developing country debt, Mexico being obviously one of them; there's also Brazil, even Poland, so when the crash came all of those countries were in dire circumstances and the only way you can pay for that indebtedness is to put the screws on the people.

So you extract wealth from all of these countries; so you lure them into the debt trap, and then you squeeze it and pull it out. We've been through a whole succession of things like that. One of the things that strikes me is that wave after wave of investment ends up going into urban development. I was stunned when I saw in Mexico City the amount of high-rise buildings and condominiums and office spaces; same in Santiago. There is this area called Little Manhattan in Santiago. You go to São Paulo; you go to Mumbai. You see all of these condos and everything in the midst of surging poverty. And then of course there are the ridiculous ones, such as Dubai.

There was a report in the New York Times just two days ago about what's happening in China. And it's a bit like Dubai, big time, really big time. And you kind of figure it is going to crash too and you go to these places and there are all these big urban projects like in Seville [1992 Expo], and now they're planning to build some big kind of new infrastructure which actually isn't productive. And it is particularly unproductive in relation to popular requirements and popular needs.

Keynes once kind of said that you could have projects which were about digging ditches and filling them in again. A lot of urban investment has been precisely of that nature, it's what we call a white elephant, you just build something, and nobody knows what to do with it; like all of these new stadiums. In Athens you look at all of the stuff that was built for the Olympic Games, which sits there not being used at all… The subway is used and the airport is used but most of the infrastructure remains totally unused. And now of course everybody is going on about how profligate

**1** This is an edited version of the transcripts of a conversation between David Harvey and Miguel Robles-Durán which took place on 6 March 2010 in New York. Transcripts by Heidi Sohn, editing by Tahl Kaminer.

the Greeks were for getting into debt and being screwed because of the indebtedness, but a lot of this stuff is just useless from the standpoint of the population.

Here in Manhattan we have this surplus of condominiums which have been built specifically for upper income residents while we have a chronic shortage of housing which is affordable – and leaving aside the fact that 'affordable' is defined in such a way to exclude those really in need; so you got this urbanization going on which includes a lot of crazy urbanization projects which have nothing whatsoever to do with the real needs of the mass of the population; it's absorbing surpluses and then speculating on it. And everybody is getting indebted and then at some point or other the debts get called in, and then somebody has to pay. So now who pays when New York gets indebted, super-indebted? Well, it's the people who pay. So you build all these projects which don't give anything to the people, and then you make the people pay for them because when the indebtedness comes you cut their services. It goes on and on again and again and again. I really don't understand why people don't revolt against it. That's the thing that's so surprising.

**MR-D** Interurban competition is becoming very visible in the international competition between cities for World Expos, Olympic Games and so on, from Lisbon to Hanover to Athens. Basically it's cities or mayors trying to attract investment by arguing that their city is the best place, has this famous architect or other things to offer, but there comes a point when most of the cities that enter this interurban competition all start doing the same things.

**DH** A city that I like a lot but that distresses me more and more is Barcelona. There was a moment when Barcelona was great, and I increasingly date its decline from the Olympic Games. After that all the big name architects started to get involved there and Barcelona had to create new spaces and do new things, and prices went up and housing became almost impossible. This appalling thing was built, the Forum or whatever it is – I mean, just ghastly. But then why would you go to Barcelona to see the same sort of harbour development that you could see in every other city around the world? I mean I get to visit all these places, and people go 'oh you've got to see…', and I reply 'I don't want to see another one of those' – I mean why would I want to see another one of those?

**MR-D** What is really telling is that this type of development has lasted for the past twenty years, some cities being more successful than others. And such practices and policies continue to unfold. I mean Barcelona, a few months ago, was giving away public property at the harbour to build the W Hotel, and there was a huge protest at the inauguration of this hotel which is on what used to be public property.

**DH** Public space disappears, you know, it all gets semi-privatized, or fully privatized, and it just goes on and on and on. And you know you mentioned this interurban competition and building all this stuff, I suppose you would say that Barcelona is a city which did alright; it probably didn't lose too much by the Olympic Games, but you could also say there are two ways to measure this. The city maybe did well but the people did not necessarily do well at all. And it's so interesting right now. I'm thinking of Berlin for example. I find Berlin a liveable city. And low-income people can find accommodations which are half-way decent to live in. The result of that is that Berlin, by all the indexes which are typically used to describe success, is considered a very unsuccessful city, that developers can't get much going, that there is not much of a market for what they do, and therefore it is not considered a very dynamic city. So the authorities call in Richard Florida to see how they can create a creative city. They wanted to take over this one area where all the anarchists were located, and the anarchists did a great thing – they put up all these banners that said: 'we are the creative class,' which they are! They are very creative. They find creative ways to live in these spaces; they do all kinds of interesting things, their graffiti is just an absolutely incredible form of art, but it is not the kind of creative class that is the entrepreneurial. So you know actually I think to be unsuccessful in this is not a bad thing at all.

About four, five years ago there was a conference here in New York with a lot of French urbanists who were complaining that Paris had not captured as much of the wealth that's connected with globalization as everywhere else, and that Paris was being bypassed and that it couldn't compete with London and New York and so on. I said to them 'well, can you live reasonably close to the centre of the city?' and they said 'oh yes, oh yes', so I said 'well, consider yourselves lucky because you can't do that in London and in Manhattan it's out of the question for almost everyone, unless you happen to be lucky like me', but I kind of said that not being successful means that many people who would not have an adequate lifestyle can have an adequate lifestyle as they do in Berlin, and then I think that Berlin has an adequate lifestyle for almost all social classes. But the result of that is that Berlin is looked down upon by the rest of Germany, and it is depicted as a backward kind of city.

**MR-D** There are now many policies right now, also in Berlin, which enable you to buy very cheap housing that you have to fix up. I have seen that process in the Netherlands, it is called *Klushuizen* and it's an instrument that the government uses precisely to gentrify spaces. They condition the process. You buy very cheap, € 60,000 for 100m², but you sign a contract and in two years you have to transform this house or this apartment into one which follows all the codes and regulations that are needed, and to make that possible you need to invest possibly even more than if you buy a new house that already meets these codes. And not everyone is attracted to do that, so it is very young people normally, people who want to make changes to their house, and this programme absolutely does not address the lower classes, and the lower classes are in this urgency to enter the housing. And you see that starting to happen in Berlin and of course in other places.

**DH** Yes, certainly. I had the impression last summer when I was there that property prices were shooting up and things were beginning to change. Now that's maybe stopped a bit by the current crisis.

**MR-D** Another thing that has happened in such areas is the red lining of neighbourhoods, which is becoming an important instrument of urban transformation and gentrification. For example, in certain areas which are considered of high criminality or very problematic, the banks decide not to give mortgages, or not to give any loans in order to buy properties, so they deteriorate and in the future allow speculation, or are acquired by people and companies with enormous amounts of assets who can do without bank loans.

**DH** In some places they've got greenlining going on, where banks concentrate all their lending in some area to bring it up. So it's redlining and there's greenlining.

**MR-D** This is one of the big transformations that Europe has seen, especially the northern parts of Europe, from the Netherlands all the way to Scandinavia, where the social property used to be twenty, thirty years ago the majority, you had percentages of 80% social property, and 20% only the very rich or the very few actually owned, until the sort of massive transformation where every single person has to go to a bank in order to acquire some form of property. But have you seen any sort of shifts into the logical line of neoliberal intervention in the city or transformation since the experimentation in Chile, let's say, or early tryouts in the United States or in Britain in the 1970s?

**DH** Well, two things have happened. One was that there was not much urban development in the early 1980s for example. And the development that there was in commercial real estate ended up in a mess at the end of the 1980s with the savings and loan crisis for example. So the property development of the urbanization was not the centre of neoliberal activism. Then the other thing that was going on during the 1980s was a massive deindustrialization of many of the older cities. A city like Sheffield for example lost 60,000 jobs in steel in about four years. Bethlehem Steel here in the town of Bethlehem, and also Baltimore, began to see the deindustrialization of Detroit during those years so that neoliberalism generated a tremendous relocation of manufacturing activity, so that Silicon Valley replaced Detroit as the centre of economic activism. These shifts were facilitated by all of the movements that eventually ended up with the WTO, the lower transport costs,

China and all the rest of it. So neoliberalism was about deindustrialization in which the financial services played a very crucial role. In other words the financial bourgeoisie within the United States was perfectly happy to destroy the industrial bourgeoisie. If you look at the 500 richest people in the United States right now compared to the list in the 1970s – now they are much more in media, telecommunications, finance, those kinds of areas, whereas those engaging in manufacturing are less and less represented in such lists. Of course, some of the capitalists engaging in manufacturing were actually speculating with the currency swaps and all that kind of thing so that you had some of those ostensibly in manufacturing, such as Enron, which turned out to be just a derivatives company with no manufacturing going at all, and which of course eventually went bust. So I think the initial period of neoliberalism in the 1980s was about deindustrialization and about financialization.

**MR-D** So not so much involving urban transformation because there was not enough surplus?

**DH** No, there was urbanization because you were abandoning factories all over the place and then there was the question of how to reuse them. Places like Sheffield decide that they are going to have the Commonwealth Games and start to have cultural stuff and blah-blah-blah, and you do start to see this shift beginning towards the end of the 1980s, and that is when the entrepreneurial thing became much, much stronger, basically because central governments said to cities 'we're not going to have a set of policies to help you', so there was this shift in the positionality of urban decision-making, but it only took off in a big boom during the 1990s, and in an even bigger boom after 2001 when the stock market crashed, and other asset bubbles came to an end, like when the dot com bubble came to an end, and that's when you see a huge shift into urban transformation.

I think the 1980s was a difficult period. In general, I think that most cities were treading water in the 1980s; they did not know quite what to do with deindustrialization, they were looking for things to do, they had to switch to a much more entrepreneurial mode and that meant quite a lot of adjustment in their policies and in their politics. For instance British cities, many of which were run by the Labour Party, and it took ten years for the Labour Party to move from dealing with its traditional constituents and fighting Thatcher to becoming entrepreneurial. In other words, the fights that went on during the 1980s over, say, the militant tendency in Liverpool, over the Greater London Council – which was in the hands of the left and Thatcher had to abolish it in order to disempower the left. The politics of the 1980s were generally pretty confused, and there was a rearguard action fought by leftist forces in many of the cities.

By the time you get to the end of the 1980s even the Labour councils are becoming very entrepreneurial, and here in the United States traditional democratic unionized labour strongholds are also becoming much more entrepreneurial in what they are doing. You then start to get this literature emerging towards the middle to the end of the 1980s and 'we have to completely readjust our sights and get them to think about finding new investment', 'attracting new investment', 'how can we do it', 'we all would like to be like Silicon Valley' – so everybody starts saying we have to have these start-ups where blah-blah-blah, and they kind of go, 'well, we've got to become a cultural centre, so we've got to have museums and we've got to have a Gehry design'.

Thatcher introduced free enterprise zones in Britain, for example, urban development corporations and things like that. That was the 1980s and I think that by the time you get to the end of the 1980s the left has lost the battle for the cities and has become as entrepreneurial as everybody else. So New Labour becomes entrepreneurial in Britain, the Democratic Party in the United States becomes much more pro-business, pro-corporate, pro-investment. So you know, I think the real big-time in Anglo-American and European perspectives was really the 1990s when a new form of urbanization began to crystallize out of this tumultuous period of the 1980s. Things were different in Asia. The 1980s was a period of a huge kind of boom in Tokyo in terms of construction, and I think also in Taipei and Singapore. So the Asian story is somewhat different. But of course the Japanese boom in real estate came to an end in the 1990s; you know, and hasn't really recovered yet.

**MR-D** You have explained that in the 1980s the actual investment, the investment within interurban competition and free enterprise zones was central; currently the centre of transformation seems to be not the modality of thought of the government, or governance, but more in how things are being financed.

**DH** When you read the IMF report it is always saying the world is awash with surplus liquidity that nobody knows what to do with. The banks are always saying 'what are we going to do with this?' They lend to the housing construction industry and of course they build like crazy; they generally prefer to build for an upper income bracket, so then the question rises: who is going to buy? That's when the financial institutions go to the consumer and say: 'we'll lend you under favourable terms, you can get this big house with this small down payment,' and you get teaser interests rates. The first three years you pay 5% or nothing on the capital and then after that you reset it to commercial rates. The financial institutions are playing on both ends: they are lending to the developer and they are lending to the consumer, so they are both lending to the producer and the consumer, and of course, this means that everybody is indebted on both ends. This is a beautiful system for a little while until loans are reset and reset, and then we get the foreclosure crisis. So I think that one of the big issues is this issue of surplus liquidity and what you would do with it, and how can you dispose of it, and a lot is being disposed through urbanization projects, I mean, it's as simple as that.

**MR-D** We were talking before of the derelict warehouses of the 1980s – and investment possibly waiting, speculating for times to get better and markets to rise. Do you actually foresee any sort of continuation of these strategies?

**DH** I think that the hope is that the situation is going to revive. I mean in some places it has obviously not. There is a big difference between, say, Baltimore and Cleveland, on the one hand, and Manhattan and San Francisco on the other. Here in New York the hope is that it's going to revive: unemployment has stabilized in the city, and the fallout of the financial sector has stopped, the bonuses have revived – and the bonuses are a very important driving force in terms of the upper income market, and so things are moving here; they have recovered somewhat and I guess everybody is beginning to say 'oh well, we've gone through this rough patch; lets hope it'll go away'. I don't see it going away. I really don't.

**MR-D** And what happens to the immense surplus generated during these times? Are we talking about an addition on top of this addition, bubbles on top of bubbles, that is trying to sustain the whole situation?

**DH** Well the surplus has been absorbed. The Federal Reserve in the United States has absorbed vast amounts of surplus. The European Union just absorbed the surplus and they are just holding it; they're not doing anything with it. But they can't hold it indefinitely, and at some point or other they are going to have to release this surplus back into the system. There's a lot of nervousness about how fast they do it, and what they will do, where will it go when it comes back into the system. And what are the banks going to do with it once they get it back? They can just hold it – that's the principle of hoarding, which means that you will have a very non-dynamic capitalist economy, you are going to have very low growth, and of course with very low growth you can have unemployment, you can have all those things. I think it's a very awkward situation right now.

**MR-D** You mentioned the China phenomenon. I remember when I was in Shanghai in 2004 and you already started to see that 80% of the buildings were absolutely empty. You continued to go, and buildings continued to be built with the same vacancy rates.

**DH** Yes, but people are buying them, you know, but not holding them, warehousing them. That is a weird thing…

**MR-D** It's a very strange phenomenon – the accumulation on top of this accumulation and the warehousing. One of the things that we have seen in the current crisis is that for some reason it is sustained between countries and continents.

**DH** It's moving around. It's interesting, it started in California, Arizona, Nevada, Florida real estate markets, and to some degree older cities like Cleveland; it moved into the financial system, it's been taken out of the financial system and you have now got fiscal crisis of state expenditures, so you have got Greece and you have got all the problems with Ireland and Spain and Portugal and Italy and so on, and at some point or other people are actually looking at Britain, and saying the sovereign debt in Britain is unsustainable. China has gone its own way for certain reasons. The Chinese have a problem: they have mass unemployment, they have about 20 million people unemployed with the collapse of the export markets, and they had to reabsorb that for fear of social unrest. So they have been using their surpluses and generating surpluses in this huge kind of Keynesian project of 'developmentalism', and it seems to have been relatively successful in the short run. But there are a lot of people around who are prepared to say that this is unstable and that we could see a collapse of, for instance, the Chinese real estate market. Everything I hear about it, is that it is unsustainable.

I don't know what's going to happen to China but this is where the uneven geographical development works: there is a crisis located here, it moves to there, it goes somewhere else, and somewhere else it leaps up and holds the system together. And if it weren't for the Chinese right now, other countries would be in dire trouble, places like Chile and to some degree much of Latin America has been stabilized a bit because of the huge growth in the China trade. And Australia has not been hit too hard because it is a primary source of raw materials for the China market and there is a huge demand for raw materials.

**MR-D** And nevertheless, in talks immediately after the crisis, in big economic forums, you always sensed that China expressed a sort of opposition to the type of economic development proposed by most Western countries, such as the idea of de-dollarizing many conditions. So on one hand you have this massive trade that is being handled or that is being sustained by them, which is playing the very same sort of game, but on the other hand you have the people or the governments from the West trying to shift precisely trade and economic relations with China.

**DH** They have difficulties because many of the countries in Western Europe, particularly Germany, are selling a lot to the Chinese in terms of technology. So I think it's very difficult to curve the textiles and all the rest of it because their primary exporter is becoming China. My guess is that the Chinese are incredibly preoccupied by internal affairs right now; yes, they have a lot of things going on outside right now, but their biggest threat is unrest inside of China, which the Communist Party is very aware of and is probably constantly trying to find ways to cope with it.

**MR-D** One thing that for me was incredibly puzzling and still is, is that with this crisis what happens in the case where most of the major governments, and I think this was the thing that China was very much against, are to continue to agree on the monetary value of the currency. Are we talking here of the ultimate form of capitalist economy, where as long as the agreement continues, different forms of trade surplus can be accumulated indefinitely?

**DH** It can, but a lot of it is fictitious, it's like the Marxist category of fictitious capital, and it can remain fictitious as long as people believe in it. But once somebody stops believing in it, then all hell breaks loose.

**MR-D** This idea of unsustainable growth being abolished by the confidence between each of the countries – China has voiced some opposition, but it cannot afford to actually kill the whole system.

**DH** No, no, I don't think the Chinese are interested in destroying the system at all. They would pay a very heavy price and I think they know that. I don't think they are interested in contesting the United States militarily, or anything like that.

**MR-D** But of course, the United States is producing money like hell, massive amounts, trillions of trillions, it sounds like this process could go on for ever.

**DH** Yes, it can, but the big fear they have is that it will be inflated away. At the end of the 1970s the inflation rate in this country was up to around 15%, 16%, and you had stagflation, which was more or less when the Volcker Rule came in; but look at the inflation rates in Zimbabwe or in Argentina. And they start to produce official statistics to hide it. Occasionally the government has an inflation rate, which everybody realizes … even as a casual visitor I know that the data they are using is crazy.

**MR-D** When the crisis first burst, Erik Swyngedouw and many others suggested it was the end of neoliberalism.

**DH** No, no, I think it is not over. I think certain aspects of it are deepening rather than cracking. I think the legitimacy of the ideological mask is seriously being questioned, but its practices are not changing. The fundamental practice which I argue is crucial to neoliberalism is the defence of the integrity of financial institutions at all costs, including if necessary at the cost of the people. What have we been doing? We've been doing exactly that. That is the foundational principle that the neoliberalist order was all about, from the New York fiscal crisis to the Mexican debt crisis. What did they do in the Mexican financial crisis in 1982? They defended the financial institutions and sacrificed the Mexican people.

**MR-D** But what is there when, for example, governments take over financial institutions as in the case of the United States or Britain? One of the most discussed principles of a socialist economy was that the people, or the public, would have ownership of the banking, or the financial institutions. And it seems as though this is the situation at this point, even if we're not saying that.

**DH** The government takes a stake but then doesn't exercise any power over it. The government becomes a major stakeholder in many of these institutions but then says 'I don't go to the border and I do not vote'. And there is certainly this ideological thing about socialism or communism… it's crazy.

**MR-D** It is very difficult for me to imagine what's next. I just try to see in cities I visit how things are being developed, and I always like to look at the housing of the poor, and there's no question that this is becoming worse and worse. Capital investment is focused on the sort of middle class who are able to get some loans or get into the financial system. I mean it is deteriorating at a very fast rate, but at the same time it is very difficult for me to imagine a shift or change in the situation. You go to these places and you see the tents of families living and gathering, in displacement, foreclosures.

**DH** But one of the problems is we have been so indoctrinated into neoliberal thinking that a lot of people who go through that actually blame themselves. They don't see it as a systemic failure of capitalism at all. They see it as something to do with accidents. They will say things like: 'well, I did take out this loan, I knew I couldn't afford it, but I hoped I could get away with it, and then my husband got sick and my aunt died… and I couldn't pay…'. So they will tell you a story of that kind. And it is not only a story of systemic failure; they personally made a bunch of wrong decisions. A lot of people who have been foreclosed upon take that view. If everybody who had been foreclosed upon would start to form a big social movement attacking capitalism – but of course you cannot attack capitalism because if you do you're a socialist or a communist.

**MR-D** They blame you as irresponsible. There is something very telling about, let's say, Paris in the transformation process, and this massive displacement and the deterioration of the housing of the poor – people actually living in these pauper circles around the city.

**DH** There is a lot of loss of any sense of solidarity and of course one of the ways that loss of solidarity is exasperated is through the anti-immigration rhetoric. That is the rhetoric of the right. I was very impressed. Have you seen the German newspapers telling the Greeks that they are lazy? And they went and said, 'you should start selling off some of your islands and to sell off the Acropolis'. What on earth has happened to political solidarities?

**MR-D** Should we get a coffee?

**DH** Uhm, yes, let's go.

# Neoliberal Urbanization and the Politics of Contestation

**Margit Mayer**

**Editors** Many of the late 1960s protest movements emphasized spontaneity and freedom in their critique of society. Spontaneity and freedom are also features of neoliberalism's self-perception. To what extent did the protest movements of the 1960s share the agenda of neoliberalism? Did the critique of Fordist, Keynesian society by the leftists of the 1960s pave the way for the roll-back neoliberalism of the 1980s?

**Margit Mayer** There have been several affinities between neoliberal ideas and the claims of 1960s movements besides the emphasis on freedom and spontaneity. They also share an explicit anti-statism: instead of the state, individuals, communities, or 'voluntarism' should be playing stronger roles for vibrant societies. Both view 'too much state intervention' as hindering not only personal development and self-realization, but also societal self-regulation (which the neoliberals prefer to see happening via the market and economic rationality, whereas progressive movements would like to see it happening through alternative networks). Hence, there are strong overlaps in the appreciation for autonomy, self-determination and self-management.

On the side of the 1960s movements, these attitudes emerged out of the experience with and therefore critique of an often overbearing, paternalist, and bureaucratic (welfare) state. The Left rejected that its social programmes usually came in the form of authoritarian and intrusive paternalism, which sought to coercively integrate its 'clients' into mainstream society. Against these constraints, activists called for more autonomy, personal freedom, independence, self-realization, as well as individual responsibility and initiative. But their critique was not only directed against the bureaucratic and authoritarian rationality of the state, but also against the economic rationality of the market, and they called not only for individual but also collective agency and mobilization, with an emphasis on solidarity.

Neoconservatives and neoliberals on the other hand have sought to dismantle the welfare state both as a means to shrink public expenditures and expand market rationality and entrepreneurial logics into further realms of society, including into social service provision. While self-activation and self-discipline here are conceived as social technologies with which to increase surplus value production, the emphasis on individual freedom, autonomy, independence from overbearing and anonymous bureaucracies, and instead the promise of more choice and enhanced effectiveness proved very persuasive in this context for gaining support beyond the affluent and upwardly mobile middle classes.

Among many of the alternative projects of the 1960s and 70s and especially among their successors, who increasingly found themselves within harsher climates of leaner municipalities and tighter welfare states (as I will discuss below), these attitudes of anti-statism would lead to self-exploitation and precarious work conditions. This experience in turn led many activists to rationalize their efforts as 'social entrepreneurship' and give a positive connotation to their status as 'precariat' – when in fact such forms of micro-enterprise, no matter how 'innovative' or 'rebellious',[1] tend to reduce 'freedom' to the freedom of participating in a race to the bottom. Still, this insistence on individual freedom from the state (while downplaying other systems of control and domination, such as the market) enjoys popularity within certain left-alternative milieus, especially among the Greens who propose solving social and environmental problems with business means.[2] This liberal current within the alternative milieu, which presents its creative while precarious existence as rebellious and innovative, dovetails nicely with the neoliberal activation of all human creativity into pervasive competition and contributes, if inadvertently, to the deterioration of labour conditions and social security more broadly.

But the relationship between and mutual influence of neoliberalism and new social movements is far more complex. In the course of the neoliberalization of urban governance, a series of political demands as well as organizational forms of the new social movements have become incorporated into the neoliberal project. With new public management and the shift from public to private and semi-public institutions via outcontracting, not only established third-sector but also oppositional organizations were integrated into this regime; and with the shift from centralized to local and more differentiated modes of decision-making, also more consensus-oriented and participatory modes found their way into local governance.

On the other hand, as the movements became increasingly institutionalized and professionalized, they partially adapted to neoliberal modes of governance and reproduction, whether in community revitalization (where tenants' and citizens' initiatives as well as [ex-]squatter groups became part of 'careful urban renewal' regimes or community management landscapes) or in anti-poverty work and social service provision (where self-organized survival strategies became instrumentalized as coping mechanisms in local workfare states).

Thus we can see the impacts of the 1960s and following movements as ambivalent: while themselves a symptom of the crisis of Fordism, they were also agents of social transformation towards post-Fordism and neoliberalism in that they contributed to the cultural pluralization of Western societies, introduced new issues on to the political agenda (ecology, gender), and brought about participatory openings in local politics. What in many cities started out as radical squatters' movements, frequently ended up 'saving' neighbourhoods near the CBD and making them attractive for corporate investors and high-income residents, thus contributing to gentrification. On the one hand, these movements succeeded in generating public pressure and contested Fordist hegemony on the local scale by building autonomous infrastructures of tenants' councils, by squatting buildings, and by creating alliances between their own radical organizations and supportive intellectuals and other local initiatives, and by intervening into and collaborating with institutional politics, thereby realizing their core goals of enhanced citizen participation as well as establishing forms of self-organization. On the other hand, some of these successes facilitated the integration and cooptation of some movement actors (based on the overlap of goals between neoliberal restructuring and radical self-realization), which led to the fragmentation of local movement scenes, and, on the part of those who routinized their cooperation with local governments, to an abandonment of some of their original goals, especially those pertaining to the role of private property.

**E** The idea of civic or public service, framed in the United States by figures such as president Obama, Hilary Clinton or Oprah Winfrey, is often presented as a contrast to the self-centred individualism and greed of neoliberal society. However, you have argued that the community organizations, many of which were born in the 1970s, by taking upon themselves governmental responsibilities, have enabled governmental retreat from civic responsibilities. Were these organizations, therefore, facilitators of neoliberalism, despite their best intentions?

**MM** Not only the Clintons and Obama, but already Bush Sr. as well as G. W. Bush have been calling for volunteerism and civic engagement as an antidote to the devastating social effects of neoliberalism. Starting with Bush Sr.'s *1000 Points of Light* campaign, leaders of both political parties have sought to mobilize the voluntary sector, with presidential summits and national initiatives for community service,[3] to compensate for the growing gaps in the social safety net. While these campaigns have mostly occurred on the level of symbolic politics, they have been playing an important role in depoliticizing the engagement of civil society organizations that has always been vibrant, especially in the US context.

Civic engagement did not need much official encouragement during the 1960s and 70s, when struggles around housing, rent strikes, campaigns against urban renewal (which was dramatically

---

**1** German adherents of this position celebrate themselves as 'digital bohème'.

**2** See Ralf Fücks, lecture in 'Labor für Entrepreneurship: Grüne Marktwirtschaft – Öko-Entrepreneurship', 2007 ('Laboratory for Entrepreneurship: Green Market Economy – Eco-Entrepreneurship'), available at: <http://labor.entrepreneurship.de/blog/?s=Heinrich+Boell+Stiftung> (accessed 22 March 2010).

**3** President Clinton's 'Third Way' communitarianism leaned left, while G. W. Bush's compassionate conservatism leaned right. Both presidents instituted national initiatives for volunteerism (AmeriCorps, Freedom Corps), while funding programmes for community development and social services were cut back and/or tightly subordinated to the goals of national urban policy (in Clinton's National Urban Policy Report defined as '(to) promote solutions that are locally crafted and implemented by entrepreneurial public entities, private actors, and the growing network of community-based corporations and organizations'). This emphasis on entrepreneurialism and on inclusion of local actors and community-based groups and public-private partnerships continues to characterize neoliberal urban and anti-poverty policy, it merely shifted towards faith-based initiatives under G. W. Bush.

reorganizing cities and, in the process, displacing particularly poor residents), and struggles for youth and community centres were widespread both in North America and Western Europe. This form of civic action was often rather politicized by the wider 'threat context' which the student, anti-war, and leftist mobilizations of the 1960s had set up, and by the political openings which governments (generally in the mould of a social-democratic compromise) allowed at that time. The protests, even those around public transport, schools, child care and other public services, were contesting the cultural norms of the institutions of collective consumption, their price, their quality, and the limited options to participate in their design. The struggles around these urban services and infrastructures often brought together rebellious middle class students with marginalized and deprived groups, and were embedded in wider claims for civil rights, protest against US imperialism, and generally in a movement to build a more progressive, more democratic society.

Many of the movement organizations which were established during this first wave of broad and politicized movements entered into a more ambiguous relationship with local governments during the next phase. The background for this development was the austerity politics of the 1980s which everywhere began to grind away at Keynesian-welfarist and social-collectivist institutions. These institutions had earlier provided a material base for much of the progressive movement activity – even if this was not widely admitted by the activist beneficiaries. Now roll-back neoliberalization brought so-called 'old' social issues back on to the agenda of urban movements, next to the struggles for self-determined spaces and higher quality public infrastructures. Increasing unemployment and poverty, a 'new' housing need, riots in housing estates, and new waves of squattings changed the make-up of the urban movement milieus, while local governments – confronted with intensifying fiscal constraints as their expenditures were growing – became interested in innovative ways to solve their problems.

These pressures led to a reconfiguration in the relations between movements and local states: they transformed from opposition to cooperation. Local governments discovered the potential of community-based organizations for helping them solve their fiscal as well as legitimation problems, and the movements shifted their strategies 'from protest to programme' in order to put their alternative practice on to more stable footing. The reorientation of both was urged on by a new generation of comprehensive programmes for neighbourhood and urban revitalization. As a result, many formerly confrontational groups that used to organize rent strikes and public hearings or disrupt the authorities' business as usual with militant actions, in the course of the 1980s turned towards development and delivering (more or less alternative) services. These activities 'within and against the state' encouraged the social movement organizations to professionalize and institutionalize their activities, which, however, had the effect of distancing them from newly mobilizing groups operating outside of these forms of increasingly routinized cooperation. Those organizations who were successful in putting their reproduction on a stable footing by developing stable relations with the local state or even managed to contract with higher-level (provincial, national, EU) or private funding agencies, one might say, did contribute to allowing governmental retreat and facilitate the neoliberalization of local politics.

But while such organizations became co-opted into an emerging community management landscape and new regime of service provision, other groups, whose needs were not addressed by these arrangements, would in turn radicalize. The movement terrain overall became not only more fragmented and polarized, but also more complex due to the entry of a panoply of middle class-based movements embracing a variety of concerns, and locating themselves across the political spectrum, from NIMBY to environmental, from defensive, even reactionary, to progressive, from *Freie Fahrt für freie Bürger!* (No speed control for free citizens) to less possessively individualist forms of self-realization. Squatting activities also continued, but here, too, a bifurcation took hold: while many of the first-wave squatters were now busy nesting in their sweat equity-liberated spaces and became upwardly mobile, the new (rehab-)squatters across European cities were increasingly more needs-oriented. In sum, cities experienced during this second phase more varied and more fragmented forms of urban protest, the movement milieu split into distinct components, and there was less convergence in joint action.

**E** What are the urban protest movements which characterize our times, and to what extent are they an outgrowth of 1960s movements?

**MM** The contemporary urban protest movements are shaped by the regime of roll-out neoliberalism which has replaced the previous phase of retrenchment characteristic of the 1980s. This new regime, while still radically prioritizing market mechanisms, introduced more consensus-oriented and participatory politics and integrated some of the earlier social movements' demands, thereby responding to some of the contradictions of roll-back neoliberalism. In the urban context, the basic neoliberal imperative of mobilizing city space as an arena for growth and market discipline remained the dominant municipal project, but from the 1990s on it was accompanied by more flanking mechanisms such as local economic development policies and community-based programmes to alleviate what is no longer called 'poverty', but rather 'social exclusion'.[4] But not just social, also political and ecological criteria have become included (while also redefined) in the efforts to promote economic competitiveness; social infrastructures, political culture, and ecological foundations of the city have become transformed into economic assets wherever possible. New

4  Neil Brenner, Nik Theodore, 'Cities and the Geographies of "Actually Existing Neoliberalism"', in: Neil Brenner, Nik Theodore (eds) **Spaces of Neoliberalism** (Oxford: Blackwell, 2002), pp. 26-27.

vocabularies of reform (the activating state, community regeneration, social capital) as well as new institutions and modes of delivery have been fashioned (such as integrated area development, public-private partnerships in urban regeneration and social welfare, all with a strong emphasis on civic engagement). These discourses and policies in many ways integrated earlier movement critiques of bureaucratic Keynesianism, and have been successful in seizing formerly progressive goals and mottos such as 'self-reliance' and 'autonomy' – while redefining them in a politically regressive, individualized and competitive direction. Through this hijacking of the language of earlier movements, their critical energy was harnessed towards the development of a revitalized urban growth machine.

The consequences of these new urban development policies and of the *de facto* erosion of social rights they implied have further fragmented the movement terrain: on the one hand they triggered the emergence of new defensive movements that would seek to protect themselves and whatever privileges they enjoyed from the effects of intensified intra-urban competition; on the other hand they politicized struggles over whose city it is supposed to be. Again and again waves of anti-gentrification struggles have swept across New York, Paris, Amsterdam, Berlin, Hamburg, also Istanbul and Zagreb, and slogans such as 'Die, yuppie scum!' became literally global. *Reclaim the Streets* and similar local mobilizations of the anti-globalization movement popularized the slogan 'Another world is possible', as well as 'Another city is possible!'

As urbanization has gone increasingly global through the integration of financial markets (that have used their flexibility to debt-finance urban development around the world),[5] and as economic growth rates began to stagnate (or, where growth has still occurred, it is increasingly jobless, as has been the case in the Euro-North American core), the sharper social divides have become expressed in intensifying socio-spatial polarization, while welfare is increasingly replaced with workfare. The new urban, social, and labour market policies have not only the effect of 'activating' large parts of the urban underclass into (downgraded) labour markets, but they also impacted many (former) social movement organizations, which increasingly reproduce themselves by implementing local social and employment programmes or community development – and are seen by many as doing a better job at 'combating social exclusion' than any competing (private or state) agency could. However, their mobilizing capacity has eroded, and most have buried formerly held dreams of 'the self-determined city' or even of liberated neighbourhoods, as they limit themselves to what seems feasible under the given circumstances. And local governments which contract with these community-based service delivery and development organizations have come under enormous pressure, as more and more responsibilities and risks have been passed down to municipal administrations, while their budgets are squeezed as never before.

These developments have restricted and narrowed the space for contemporary social contestation in many ways. But mobilization has continued to form at least along three fault lines, all of which turn on one or another form of the neoliberalization of urban governance:[6]

One fault line revolves around the way neoliberal urban governance works through the dominant pattern of growth politics. This has triggered protests by movements that challenge the forms, goals, and effects of corporate urban development;[7] they fight the commercialization of public space, the intensification of surveillance and policing of urban space, the entrepreneurial ways in which cities market themselves in the global competition, as well as the concomitant neglect of neighbourhoods that fall by the wayside of these forms of growth politics. Another fault line sparks mobilizations against the neoliberalization of social and labour market policies, against the dismantling of the welfare state, and for social and environmental justice, which increasingly come together in community/labour coalitions and (immigrant) workers' rights organizations. In Germany it is the local Anti-Hartz mobilizations, in Italy the Social Centres, in the US the workers' centres, which bring worksite and community organizing together in new coalitions of social rights organizations and unions, and unite the demands of the precariously employed as well as the unemployed. A third fault line is addressed by transnational anti-globalization movements[8] that have discovered 'the local', their city, as a place where globalization 'touches down' and materializes, where global issues become localized. These movements demand not only the democratization of international institutions such as the IMF, WTO, World Bank, EU, G8 etc., but are also mobilizing in defence of public services and institutions in the cities, discovering that issues such as privatization and infringement of social rights are actually connecting them with movements across the globe. They attack global neoliberalism in the form of global corporations, investors and developers (symbolically, as in happenings and street parties at Mayday protests, which *Reclaim the Streets* organized in central business districts across Europe), but also entrepreneurial local governments that help implement the neoliberal corporate agenda and use their political leverage to shape their cities in the interest of global corporate investors and affluent residents. Organizations such as the Social Fora or Attac have taken the message of 'global justice' to the local level, where they campaign against welfare cuts and for rights for migrants as well as workfare workers and build alliances with local unions, social service organizations and churches. And a broad spectrum of local, more or less militant, anarchist, autonomous, leftist groups with various ties to

**5** See David Harvey, 'The Right to the City', **New Left Review** 53, September/October 2008, p. 30.
**6** See for a more elaborate version of the following argument Margit Mayer, 'Contesting the Neoliberalization of Urban Governance', in Helga Leitner, Jamie Peck, Eric Sheppard (eds) **Contesting Neoliberalism: The Urban Frontier** (New York: Guilford Press, 2007), pp. 90-115.
**7** Such as investments in glitzy new city centres filled with glass-and-steel architecture, offices and condominiums, mega-projects for sports and entertainment etc.
**8** The World Social Forum (WSF) emerged in 2001 out of protests against the latest form of globalization, most famously the massive protests in Seattle against the World Trade Organization. Held simultaneously with the World Economic Forum annually in Davos, Switzerland, the WSF provides an 'open space' where activists from around the planet can discuss alternatives to neoliberal, free market globalization. The Forums have been held in different parts of the world such as India, Venezuela, Mali, Pakistan, and Kenya, but primarily in the home of its founding movements, Brazil.

regional and supra-national networks have regularly been converging at counter summits not just for blockading actions and demonstrations, but also to exchange insights and experiences with their national and international comrades, and to plan and coordinate upcoming joint civil disobedience and other actions.[9]

Thus, while the neoliberalization of the city has in many ways created a more hostile environment for progressive urban movements, it has also allowed for a more global articulation of urban protest, and it has spawned a renewed convergence of some of these strands under the umbrella of the Right to the City slogan. The different movements active these days around the three fault lines just sketched have brought deprived and excluded groups on the one hand and anti-neoliberal or anti-globalization groups on the other together in ways that were not quite possible in 1968, when both 'deprivation' and 'discontent' were key moving forces, but could not yet be merged. Today, the Right to the City concept, developed by Henri Lefebvre in the context of the 1960s movements, merges and concentrates a set of highly charged issues, as more and more groups of urban residents see long-accustomed rights erode. Accumulation by dispossession has accelerated on heretofore unseen levels, which entails enormous losses of rights – civil, social, political, as well as economic rights. Cities have transformed into gated communities and privatized public spaces, where wealthy and poor districts are increasingly separated if by invisible barriers, and access of the poor to the amenities and infrastructures that cities once held for all have become more and more restricted. In this context, the slogan 'Right to the City' resonates with activists, as it makes sense as a claim and a banner under which to mobilize one side in the conflict over who should have the benefit of the city and what kind of city it should be. Whether the nation-wide Right to the City Alliance in the us,[10] or more local Right to the City alliances as, for example, in Hamburg,[11] these movements are building on the Lefebvrian conception, whereas urbanization stands for a transformation of society and everyday life through capital. Against this transformation Lefebvre sought to *create* rights through social and political action: the street, and claims to it, are establishing these rights. In this sense, the right to the city is less a juridical right, but rather an oppositional demand, which challenges the claims of the rich and powerful. It is a right to redistribution, as Peter Marcuse once called it, not for all people, but for those deprived of it and in need of it. And it is a right that exists only as people appropriate it (and the city). In this revolutionary form of appropriation, which Lefebvre discovered in the Paris of 1968, today's struggles can be seen as an outgrowth – and further development – of the 1960s movements.

**E** Considering the cooptation of so many of the grass-roots movements of the 1960s, what effective means of urban protest have you encountered in recent years? How does such activism and protest gain political leverage?

**MM** Success of protest movements is not only measured by political leverage. Certain projects may boost emancipatory efforts while failing in terms of power politics. On the other hand, there are movements that long ago failed in terms of emancipatory and transformative criteria, but have continued with powerful political leverage for some time. Thus evaluating the 'effectiveness' of urban protest is a complex endeavour.

For example, the right to the city has not only become a powerful slogan informing current struggles over shaping the city, but it has also gained significant traction with international NGOs and advocacy organizations, if with somewhat different connotations than described above. Such traction might be viewed as an exemplary case of urban protest having gained political leverage. When policies get defined, by official international gatherings and organizations, and codified in national constitutions that are to guarantee sustainable, just and democratic cities, this might be viewed as political leverage par excellence. Together with UNESCO and UN-Habitat, human rights groups as well as groups involved with the WSF process have drafted a World Charter on the Right to the City and established a Working Group on 'Urban Policies and the Right to the City', with regular annual meetings taking place either at UNESCO headquarters or various municipalities. In Latin American cities, such charters (or parts of them) were widely circulated, and in Brazil a City Statute was even inserted in 2001 into the Brazilian Constitution to recognize the collective right to the city.[12]

**9** Since the onset of the financial/economic crisis, these movements attract growing numbers of youth, whose hopes for a decent future are eroding as education systems and public infrastructures are crumbling, spawning their protest under the banner (not only in Athens) of 'money for the banks, bullets for the kids'.

**10** The RTTCA includes 36 core member organizations spanning seven states and over a dozen metropolitan areas. Organized as regional collaborative networks, the RTTCA operates in the areas of Boston/Providence, Washington D.C./Northern Virginia, Los Angeles, Miami, New Orleans, New York, Oakland/San Francisco. Network members collaborate on the basis of themes as well as regions, such as civic engagement, tenants' rights, subsidized housing, and 'a just reclamation of the Gulf Coast' (see Jacqueline Leavitt, 'Right to the City Builds Alliance, Confronts Mayors', **Progressive Planning,** Summer 2009, available at Archived Progressive Planning Magazines: < http://www.plannersnetwork.org/publications/2009_summer/leavitt. html> (accessed 22 March 2010); and Jacqueline Leavitt, Tony Roshan Samara, Marnie Brady, 'Right to the City: Social Movement and Theory', **Poverty & Race**, 19/5, September/October 2009, available at: <http://www.prrac.org/full_text.php?text_id=1238&item_ id=11801&newsletter_id=107&header=Community+Organizing&kc=1> (accessed 22 March 2010)).

**11** Initially such groups sprang up primarily in Western Europe, bringing together anti-gentrification leftists, squatters, and artists with middle class preservationists (see for Hamburg: Philipp Oehmke, 'Who Has the Right to Shape the City? Squatters Take on the Creative Class', **Spiegel Online**, January 7 2010, available at: <http://www.spiegel.de/international/germany/ 0,1518,670600,00.html> (accessed 22 March 2010); <http://esregnetkaviar.wordpress. com/>, <http://wilhelmsburg.blog.de/>; for Leipzig <http://www.sozelei.net>), but recently a 'Right to the City' group has formed also in Zagreb, which has protested an investor plan to develop a central square (Flower Square) into an upscale, exclusive, traffic-rich plaza with underground parking, to jumpstart gentrification of the surrounding area. When the group handed over 54,000 signatures protesting the development to the mayor, his response was: in four years you can elect someone else, in the meantime, leave us to do our job! (See Ognjen Caldarovic, Jana Sarinic, 'Inevitability of Gentrification', paper presented at the ISA Meeting in Barcelona, September 2008).

**12** See Edésio Fernandes, 'Constructing the "Right to the City" in Brazil', **Social and Legal Studies** 16/2 2007, pp. 201-19.

However, while these statutes and charters seek to influence public policy and legislation in a way that combines urban development with social equity and justice, they are removed from actual struggles and the interests of those whom they presumably seek to protect. In their effort to put 'our most vulnerable urban residents' rather than investors and developers at the centre of public policy, they enumerate specific rights which a progressive urban politics should particularly protect. Thus they refer to such rights as to housing, social security, work, an adequate standard of living, leisure, information, organization and free association, food and water, freedom from dispossession, participation and self-expression, health, education, culture, privacy and security, a safe and healthy environment, and more. These rights are supposed to hold for all 'urban inhabitants', both as individuals and collectively, but some groups are highlighted as deserving particular protection (poor, sick, handicapped, and migrants get mentioned).

The problem with such a legalistic definition of the right to the city and with enumerating different disenfranchised groups is that every list invariably excludes those that do not get listed. And the problem with the generic category of 'urban inhabitants' is that it reflects a view of civil society as basically homogenous and, as a whole, worthy of protection from (destructive) neoliberal forces – as if it itself did not encompass economic and political actors who participate in and profit from the production of poverty and discrimination; it thus obfuscates the fact that this entity is deeply divided by class and power. Furthermore, this institutionalized set of rights boils down to claims for inclusion in the current system as it exists, it does not aim at transforming the existing system – and in that process ourselves. The demands for rights as enumerated merely target particular aspects of neoliberal policy, e.g. in combating poverty, but not the underlying economic policies which systematically produce poverty and exclusion. Since 'collective transformative action always begins on the terrain and within the constraints set by the oppressor' (de Sousa Santos), success of the collective action is measured by the capacity to transform, in the course of the struggle, the terrain and the constraints of the conflict. Thus, remaking the city is always simultaneously a struggle about power, which cannot be left to (local) governments, not even social-democratic ones. Left to their devices and to the networks of NGOs, the political content and meaning of the contested right to the city will get diluted. It will become depoliticized as so many movement issues have, reframed into a discourse of civil society which has invaded movement milieus in the era of neoliberalism.

In this discourse, strengthening civil society networks is regarded as positive because it enhances efficiency; collaboration of urban residents and municipalities is seen as good because it furthers endogenous potentials and local growth; in this view, we can reconcile local autonomy with international competitiveness, and sustainability with economic growth, we can have neoliberalism with a human touch. This, of course, constitutes one of the most powerful mystifications of the contemporary era; exposing that and proposing the radical right to the city instead, would seem to be the best way to fight neoliberal instrumentalization of movement demands. Hence, urban protest has been most effective where it does both, build autonomous structures and, simultaneously, pursue a strategy of political intervention in institutional politics. Neglecting the former leads to political cooptation via professionalization or economic commodification, neglecting the latter leads to political marginalization. Along this vein, many struggles have been successful in recent years, whether it be the campaign against MediaSpree in Berlin[13] or saving the Gängeviertel in Hamburg;[14] the RttC Alliance has won several victories in US localities, including winning affordable housing provision, maintaining access to public space, stopping demolition of public housing, and raising the pay of abused domestic workers.[15] But spaces won or saved by progressive movements are always threatened to become (re)absorbed into the dominant praxis. Neoliberalism has been particularly successful in hijacking and integrating oppositional and rebellious claims and repertoires into its regime. We can observe this among former squatters and the newly engaged cultural activists, who frequently become more interested in projecting a city where *their* – self-determined, autonomous – liberated space is guaranteed, and less concerned with the exclusion and repression of less fortunate ones. Such activists increasingly succeed today in securing their own survival by buying into the new 'creative city' policies that exploit the vibrant local cultural scenes for branding and as a locational asset in the intensifying interurban competition. Thus, movements need to be aware of the ever present possibility that their claims and their liberated places can become co-opted into the ongoing reinvention and re-adaptation of neoliberal hegemony.

**E** In an interview in *Critical Planning* you have raised the question of whether protest is now concentrated in the global South and outside the global Western cities. Could you expand on this point?

**MM** I do think we need to realize that Western cities, or cities of the global North, are no longer the site of politically mobilized working classes nor do they harbour any longer the vibrant proletarian public sphere as was the case during the nineteenth and early twentieth centuries. They are also no longer the site of struggles around collective consumption, as was the case in the 1960s when contestations over public infrastructures and public space were still perceived by the ruling class as unrest threatening broader catalytic effects. While for Marx as well as for Lefebvre revolutions were emanating from the city, the movements visible in today's first world metropoles

**13** Albert Scharenberg, Ingo Bader, 'Berlin's Waterfront Site Struggle', **CITY** 13/2-3, June-September 2009, pp. 325-35.
**14** Philipp Oehmke, 'Who Has the Right to Shape the City? Squatters Take on the Creative Class'; Klaus Irler, Maximilian Probst, 'Gängeviertel ist vorerst gerettet', **tageszeitung**, December 17, 2009, p.7.
**15** Harmony Goldberg, 'Building Power in the City: Reflections on the Emergence of the Right to the City Alliance and the National Domestic Worker's Alliance', **In the Middle of the Whirlwind**, 2008, available at: <http://inthemiddleofthewhirlwind.wordpress.com/building-power-in-the-city/> (accessed 22 March 2010).

seem to have lost this potential of radiating transformative change into society at large. Instead of harbouring a potentially revolutionary class, first world cities now appear as global suburbs, privileged spaces for more and less gentrified 'creative classes', and breeding grounds for a mix of alternative, critical and 'bohemian' milieus. The class composition of first world cities has fundamentally transformed in the course of global urbanization and the outsourcing of manufacturing to the global South, leaving us with a new antagonism (and hence new types of conflict) between top-end users of the city versus growing advanced marginality. That is not to say that the struggles over this antagonism are not relevant (especially since [low] waged work has expanded to include more women and more immigrants, making first world cities important sites of anti-colonial struggles as well as struggles against racism and sexism), but they are hemmed in by a variety of structural factors that impede transformative change, especially the increasing societal fragmentation and the erosion of public space. Privatization, security measures, the proliferation of zones of segregation, and the retrenchment of municipal services and infrastructures have all contributed to the disappearance of spaces for collectivization, and to the disintegration of the role public space might play in the formation and politicization of (class) subjects and for building alliances.

The contemporary struggles under the banner of the right to the city and some of their victories referred to above do provide evidence that these odds are not insurmountable. But many of these struggles are merely defensive, seeking to save a piece of urbanity or protect their alternative lifestyles; for others, the risk of co-optation and partial integration into an urban model in the image of corporate and financial interests is immense, especially if we account for the fact that the benefits of the growth of the last 30 years have overwhelmingly gone to those living in the West/North under immeasurably higher living standards than the greater part of the world, even higher than for most but the very rich in the dynamic economies which have been keeping the world economy going.[16] Under these conditions, we need to ask: are first world cities still educing the social forces with an interest in transforming them into more equitable and attractive living environments for all? In whose interest would it be to form alliances that would challenge the structures of global inequality? Do the comparatively privileged urban activists in the global North have the motivation for *global* justice?

Obviously, networks and linkages with movements and actors constituting the global proletariat in those other places will be helpful. And actually, connections between struggles in first world metropoles and those in cities of the global South, where the fight against privatization, speculation, eviction and displacement is far more existential, have become quite tangible and real, as many Social Forum meetings have shown. It is often the same real estate developers and the same global corporations that are responsible for the displacement, eviction, or privatization of public goods as in the global South. The last ten years of dialogue, information sharing and collective mobilization via the Social Forum process and the get-togethers of the anti-globalization movement at counter summits have been used by activists from around the globe to explore the shared experiences and commonalities in their various struggles against privatization and dispossession, which is a good start. For first world urban struggles to have a broad and transformative impact, networking and cooperation with the dispossessed and excluded from around the globe will have to be intensified, and cities will have to be envisioned and built that reflect their hearts' desire as well as ours.

**E** Around autumn 2008 there was much talk about restructuring following the crisis, of a significant shift in the political economy, and many signs of a return to Keynesian policies. Would a return to the safety of Keynesian policies mean also a return to the lifeless urban development of the 1950s and 1960s, to assembly-line architecture and spiritless bureaucratic new towns and urban peripheries?

**MM** If local politicians intent on bringing in global investors, affluent middle classes and the type of 'creative class' that Richard Florida hypes as the path to success for every city, encouraged by Green Party support for innovative social entrepreneurs,[17] are the only ones who get to shape the city, then we need not 'worry' about a return to Keynesian policies. Instead of safety, there will be precarious living and working conditions; instead of spiritless and inhospitable homogenous new towns, there will be social polarization: glitz, creativity, and trendy urban environments in the privileged quarters; precariousness, insecurity, blight and devastation of varying degrees in the marginalized ones.

Instead of Keynesian redistribution, the financial and economic meltdown of 2008 has been met with responses that intensified and expanded the dispossession of taxpayers and the public purse, which had already been going on over the last thirty years – i.e. with a new type of state interventionism in support of investment bankers. This has aided the concentration processes and the strengthening of finance capital as well as the growth of the state debt, thereby contributing to the further polarization of society and the deepening of impoverishment of both the people and places disadvantaged by this redistribution and excluded from the upscale parts of the city. While some authors now speak of a 'post-neoliberal' phase,[18] it seems to me that in spite of the

**16**  See Eric Hobsbawm, 'Is the Intellectual Opinion of Capitalism Changing?', **Today** programme, BBC Radio 4, October 20 2008, available at: <http://news.bbc.co.uk/today/hi/today/newsid_7677000/7677683.stm>

**17**  See note 2, above.

**18**  See Neil Smith, 'Neoliberalism is Dead, Dominant, Defeatable—Then What?', **Human Geography**, 1/ 2, 2008, pp. 1-3; Ulrich Brand, Nikola Sekler (eds) 'Postneoliberalism – a Beginning Debate,' **Development Dialogue** 51, January 2009, pp. 5-13. Even the Left Party's Rosa Luxemburg Foundation in some of its analysis claims that the crisis 'has forced [the ruling hegemonic block] to modify its neoliberal strategies'. Rosa Luxemburg Foundation, 'Die Krise des Finanzmarkt-Kapitalismus – Herausforderung für die Linke', **kontrovers** 01/2009, available at: <http://www.rosalux.de/cms/index.php?id=18514> (accessed 22 March 2010); cf. also Rosa Luxemburg Foundation, 'The World Crisis – and Beyond' conference, Brussels, Oct 28-Nov 1, 2009.

obvious crisis of neoliberalism, neoliberal rule continues to be pervasive. The current regime seeks more than ever to organize all social relations 'in a way that makes markets and competition work', where 'market-like forms of governance' prevail in all sectors of society.[19] Even though neoliberalism no longer has the solutions, no longer guarantees sustained economic growth, nor enjoys legitimation any longer, it is still dominant, enjoys the support of the political elites, and provides both the context and targets for urban social movements' activities.

So rather than worry about the return of homogenizing Keynesian policies, we *should* be worrying about how urban marginality is addressed nowadays by a welfare/workfare state that is simultaneously more punitive, more activating, and more locally specific than its Keynesian predecessor. While enormous resources are being poured into upgrading city centres into magnets for tourism, consumption, and work-play environments for the affluent, poor people as well as 'weak neighbourhoods' are now urged, with new-style empowerment programmes, to mobilize what few resources and potentials they may have, and to develop 'social capital' in order to become competitive. To meet this practically impossible task, civil society and grassroots engagement are now mobilized, not only symbolically, but through funding so-called comprehensive programmes which aim at 'activating' marginalized urban groups into state-enforced low-wage labour markets and 'problematic' neighbourhoods into harnessing their own networks to stop their downward drift.[20] At the same time, disciplinary sanctions are increased and the arsenal of the penal state serves to insure the subordination of the poor to these low-wage markets and the rules of the informal economy.[21] These trends towards intensely polarized societies are truly worrisome and require the urgent attention of urban planners as well as progressive movements.

**19** Alex Demirovic, 'Postneoliberalism and Post-Fordism – Is There a New Period in the Capitalist Mode of Production?', **Development Dialogue** 51, January 2009, p. 46.
**20** See Margit Mayer, 'The Onward Sweep of Social Capital: Causes and Consequences for Understanding Cities, Communities and Urban Movements', **International Journal of Urban and Regional Research**, 27/1, 2003, pp. 110-32; Margit Mayer, 'Armutspolitik in amerikanischen Städten', **Prokla** 38/4, December 2008, pp. 569-93.
**21** See Loic Wacquant, **Punishing the Poor: The Neoliberal Government of Social Insecurity** (Durham: Duke UP, 2009).

## BIBLIOGRAPHY

Ulrich Brand, Nikola Sekler (eds) 'Postneoliberalism – a Beginning Debate', **Development Dialogue** 51, January 2009, pp. 5-13.

Neil Brenner, Nik Theodore, 'Cities and the Geographies of "Actually Existing Neoliberalism"', **Antipode** 34/3, July 2002, pp. 349-79.

Ognjen Caldarovic, Jana Sarinic, 'Inevitability of Gentrification', paper presented at the ISA Meeting in Barcelona, September 2008.

Alex Demirovic, 'Postneoliberalism and Post-Fordism – Is There a New Period in the Capitalist Mode of Production?', **Development Dialogue** 51, January 2009, pp. 45-57.

Ralf Fücks, lecture in 'Labor für Entrepreneurship: Grüne Marktwirt-schaft – Öko-Entrepreneurship', 2007 ('Laboratory for Entrepre-neurship: Green Market Economy – Eco-Entrepreneurship'), available at: <http://labor.entrepreneurship.de/blog/?s=Heinrich+Boell+Stiftung> (accessed 22 March 2010).

Harmony Goldberg, 'Building Power in the City: Reflections on the Emergence of the Right to the City Alliance and the National Domestic Worker's Alliance', **In the Middle of the Whirlwind**, 2008, available at: <http://inthemiddleofthewhirlwind.wordpress.com/building-power-in-the-city/> (accessed 22 March 2010).

David Harvey, 'The Right to the City', **New Left Review** 53, September/October 2008, pp. 23-40.

Eric Hobsbawm, 'Is the Intellectual Opinion of Capitalism Chang-ing?', **Today** programme, BBC Radio 4, October 20 2008, available at: <www.news.bbc.co.uk/today/hi/today/newsid_7677000/7677683.stm>

Klaus Irler, Maximilian Probst, 'Gängeviertel ist vorerst gerettet', **tageszeitung**, December 17, 2009, p.7.

Jacqueline Leavitt, 'Right to the City Builds Alliance, Confronts Mayors', **Progressive Planning,** Summer 2009, available at Archived Progressive Planning Magazines: < http://www.planner-snetwork.org/publications/2009_summer/leavitt.html> (accessed 22 March 2010).

Jacqueline Leavitt, Tony Roshan Samara, Marnie Brady, 'Right to the City: Social Movement and Theory', **Poverty & Race**, 19/5, Sep-tember/October 2009, available at: <http://www.prrac.org/full_text.php?text_id=1238&item_id=11801&newsletter_id=107&header=Community+Organizing&kc=1> (accessed 22 March 2010).

Margit Mayer, 'The Onward Sweep of Social Capital: Causes and Consequences for Understanding Cities, Communities and Urban Movements', **International Journal of Urban and Regional Research**, 27/1, 2003, pp. 110-32.

Margit Mayer, 'Contesting the Neoliberalization of Urban Governance', in Helga Leitner, Jamie Peck, Eric Sheppard (eds) **Contesting Neoliberalism: The Urban Frontier** (New York: Guilford Press, 2007), pp. 90-115.

Margit Mayer, 'Armutspolitik in amerikanischen Städten' ('Poverty Politics in American Cities'), **Prokla** 38/4, December 2008, pp. 569-93.

Philipp Oehmke, 'Who Has the Right to Shape the City? Squatters Take on the Creative Class', **Spiegel Online**, January 7 2010, available at: <http://www.spiegel.de/international/germany/0,1518,670600,00.html> (accessed 22 March 2010).

Rosa Luxemburg Foundation, 'Die Krise des Finanzmarkt-Kapitalis-mus – Herausforderung für die Linke', **kontrovers** 01/2009, available at: < http://www.rosalux.de/cms/index.php?id=18514> (accessed 22 March 2010).

Rosa Luxemburg Foundation, 'The World Crisis – and Beyond' conference, Brussels, Oct 28-Nov 1, 2009.

Albert Scharenberg, Ingo Bader, 'Berlin's Waterfront Site Struggle', **CITY** 13/2-3, June-September 2009, pp. 325-35.

Neil Smith, 'Neoliberalism is Dead, Dominant, Defeatable—Then What?', **Human Geography**, 1/ 2, 2008, pp. 1-3.

Loic Wacquant, **Punishing the Poor: The Neoliberal Government of Social Insecurity** (Durham: Duke UP, 2009).

# Mexico

# Denationalization: The Subjugation of Mexico and its Capital City

**Heidi Sohn**

# 1 Challenging the 'inevitability' of global capitalism

*The truth today in the so-called advanced industrial world is that our stunted imaginations have largely lost the ability to think what a society other than capitalism – with all its repressive and oppressive aspects, and spanning the gamut of social relations – might look like.*[1]

This elaboration departs from one single premise, from a conventionally accepted fact, namely that contemporary human reality is dominated by the capitalist system. In more than one sense, this is a reductionist, but deterministic and universalizing assumption that nevertheless has been able to engulf and encroach itself upon the entirety of what this system has construed as its world. Hence, capitalism today is legitimized by a strong globalizing impetus, subjecting the world to a new economic configuration of unprecedented dimensions, scales and effects. Aided and sustained by the implementation of the neoliberal doctrine, 'the central guiding principle of economic thought and management',[2] and fuelled by renewed imperialist drives, globalization under capitalism has usurped what some scholars consider a planetary status,[3] and this, not unimportantly, has assisted capitalism to legitimize its position and to establish itself as a hegemonic factuality. The kinship of contemporary capitalism, globalization and neoliberal economic policy is thus undeniable; to refer to one is to refer to all at once. Hence, to refer to contemporary human reality is to refer to a state of being in which all domains of human endeavour are defined and guided by an extremely crafty and refined economic logic geared by the rather unsophisticated and vulgar goals of profit maximization, the accumulation of wealth, and the restoration of class power.[4]

A decade into the twenty-first century and almost forty years since the first experiments in neoliberal development were implemented have proven that contrary to what this economic doctrine claims to achieve, in many respects it has been a blatant failure with dramatic social, economic, environmental and political consequences. Much of the literature that focuses on a critique of capitalism highlights its dialectic character, seeing development as a culprit of uneven development, retrogression as a necessary condition for progress, destruction as a prerequisite for creation, dispossession as the means for accumulation, and so on. Arguably, this has had two effects in discourse: on the one hand, it has contributed to the normalization and naturalization of the discourse that considers capitalist development as necessary and thus unavoidable, thus naturalizing capitalism and the legitimacy of private monopoly ownership as common sense,[5] either by neglecting its

---

**1** Neil Smith, 'Another revolution is possible: Foucault, ethics, and politics', in **Environment and Planning D: Society and Space** 2007, volume 25, pp. 191-93.
**2** David Harvey, **A Brief History of Neoliberalism** (Oxford: Oxford University Press, 2005), p. 2.
**3** See for example Wolfgang Sachs, **Planet Dialectics: Explorations in Environment and Development** (London, New York: Zed Books, 1999).
In his work, Sachs develops the notion of global management. In relation to sustainability he claims that starting in the 1960s with the space race and new technological developments environmentalists began exploiting the image of 'planet Earth' as a finite, closed system. Not long after, a 'new tribe of global ecocrats is ready to act upon the newly emerged reality of the planet, imagining that they can preside over the world'. Further, he argues that '[I]t is the implicit agenda of this endeavour to be eventually able to moderate the planetary system, supervising species diversity, fishing grounds, felling rates, energy flows and material cycles'. (Sachs, **Planet Dialectics**, pp. 43-44)
**4** See David Harvey, et al..

counter-effects, apologetically considering them as simply the 'inevitable' side of development, or worse, by capitalizing on them.

But while discourse and critique debate on the inevitability or the irreversibility of global capitalism, the material consequences become patent at all scales as political, economic and social practices are absorbed and deeply transformed by the capitalist machinery. The impact on space, on the ground, is imminent as geographical differences are increasingly evened out and pre-neoliberal forms of territoriality are declared obsolete. As regional, national, domestic or local spatial configurations are incorporated into this new geography of power other, non-capitalist forms of socio-spatiality are threatened, and this weakens the possibilities of mounting a strong case for anti- or non-capitalist alternatives.
Against the conventional reactions to this realization, which tend to either paralyse critique, overshadowing it with pessimistic resignation, or on the contrary, inflaming it and turning it into forms of reactionary, romanticized anti-capitalism, there exists the possibility of what Ernesto Laclau proposes as the construction of an alternative project, of a non-capitalist alternative, which 'is based on the ground created by those transformations [entailed by capitalism] and not on opposition to them'.[6]

This necessarily brings to the fore the urgency and importance of challenging the 'inevitability' of capitalism on the one hand, and on the other, the problematic question of just how to devise alternatives to the capitalist system from a wide array of scales, which do not resist it, but which instead work within the processes brought about by it in order to *change* it. This, putting all its many problems aside for now, will be the guiding premise in this elaboration. In other words, it departs from a position that has assimilated advanced capitalism with all its apparatuses and applications as not only its context, but essentially as an all-encompassing system, which leaves a very narrow room for formulations on a state of reality developing somehow outside or beyond its confines. However, and against the all-too easily accepted consensus that sees global capitalism as inevitable, and in fact, as a necessary requirement for human development and progress, I argue that, while by now it is commonly accepted that the inner conflicts of the capitalist system, as well as the myriad of contradictions that result from its forces, dynamics and processes are in fact inevitable, this by no means implies that these cannot – or should not – be challenged, reversed and changed. Today more than ever, the search for radical alternatives – either reformist or revolutionary – should not be abandoned.

Borrowing the concepts of 'theoretical ethics' and 'strategic politics' from Michel Foucault's essay 'Useless to Revolt?' of 1967 as interpreted by Neil Smith[7] this elaboration attempts to integrate these as the main components towards the formulation of urban alternatives that extend critical theory to encompass also the domains of practice. In other words, the ultimate aim of this chapter is to trace the outline of a sort of conceptual model based on ethics, which regards urban politics as the nexus between substantive contents and performance. Among others, the notions of government and governance are crucial to this model, as I will explain further on.

The contextual framework of this model is shaped by three interrelated trends conventionally associated with neoliberal processes of state restructuring: the denationalization of the state, the destatization of political systems, and the internationalization of policy regimes.[8] These three processes allow the analysis of the inner logic and workings of some of contemporary global capitalism's apparatuses – in particular the privatization of social goods and public assets, national resources, state institutions and industries – and show how these are orchestrated and made operative in a vast array of scales and domains. While the city, or the urban, is here the preferred dimension (scale) to explicate both the inevitability of neoliberal capitalism and its irreversible consequences, the connection to other scales, levels and domains is indispensable. In particular, the multiscalar analysis of the mechanics of subjectivization, the process by which ideology impregnates in the formation or deformation of subjects, allows approaching different social formations and institutional configurations (understood as potential agents), as well as different forms of governance and governmentality (understood as processes), while analysing the changes that have been registered in those periods in which neoliberal capitalism was introduced in different regions across the world.

In very summarized terms, the issue that interests me here is the process of denationalization and its link to privatization, namely as the apparatuses and dynamics that set in motion the dissolution of the imaginary of the nation – and specifically the transformation of the idea of nation as the locus and guardian of social property, of social, public, collective and common good – through the coercion of the state as the auctioneer of these public or common assets. Furthermore, the process of denationalization encompasses more than the 'hollowing out' of state activity, as much of neoliberal literature sustains, but it also marks the shift in territorial scales as it signals the rise of 'new' scalar units, in particular the regional, local, and urban, all of which help to by-pass the nation-state.[9]

Specifically relevant for this chapter is the case of the Latin American region, where neoliberalism was first introduced and tested in the early 1970s. Using the example of Mexico's transition into neoliberal capitalism during the mid-1970s and early 1980s I hope to show how the piecemeal and

**5** Peter McLaren, **Capitalists and Conquerors: A Critical Pedagogy Against Empire** (Oxford: Rowman and Littlefield Publishers, 2005), p. 22.
**6** Ernesto Laclau, quoted in Simon Critchley, **Infinitely Demanding: Ethics of Commitment, Politics of Resistance** (London: Verso), p. 100.
**7** Neil Smith (2007).
**8** Gordon MacLeod and Mark Goodwin, 'Space, Scale and State Strategy: rethinking urban and regional governance', in **Progress in Human Geography** (1999), 23:503.
**9** MacLeod, Goodwin (1999), p. 505.

surreptitious, or sudden implementation of reforms, privatization waves and re-regulations at national (federal and state) levels, has debilitated the social imaginary of the nation-state, systematically eroding many pre-neoliberal forms and constituencies of nation and citizenship, and thus contributing to the dismantling of the revolutionary state project, the weakening of politics and political participation, and the enforcement of an a-political culture of individualism based on the pursuit of private property and individual ownership. This view largely stands in opposition to the more accepted perspective that regards the nation-state as artificially constructed, 'relatively fixed, self-enclosed geographical containers of social, economic, political and cultural relations'[10] exerting an 'iron-grip' on social imagination.[11] And further, it also suggest that the view that sees a transformation of the nation rather than its erosion as the locus of new emerging spaces and scales, some of which are potentially emancipatory or empowering, can itself be misleading. These concepts, especially as they refer to state project or state strategy have to be seen together with other 'politico-economic and socio-spatial activities as a series of situated context specific… processes'.[12] The interrelationship between different scalar and analytical units, as well as a deep and careful look at the notion of scale itself, is crucial at this juncture. As Swyngedouw shows, the politics of scale (and their metaphorical and material production and transformation) have manifested themselves 'in a profound reworking of geographical scales in the regulation of production, money, consumption and welfare'.[13] The process of denationalization in Mexico has produced the loosening of the conventional 'spatial-fix' associated with the nation, and this in turn has had implications for cities and regions and the way these are governed. This 'relativization of scale'[14] may be interpreted and explained from a variety of angles when looking at the Mexican case: from the blurring of national boundaries into economic regions such as GATT, NAFTA, PPP, and the contradictory intensification of the problem of borderlines and national sovereignty, to the very specific case of Mexico City's transformations in terms of urban politics and governance since the 1970s. But it can also be read from a sociological perspective.

Taking the convoluted case of contemporary Mexico City as the context for this analysis (which will per force have to remain reductive and limited) the final part of this chapter will explicate the conceptual model mentioned at the outset of this paper using as an example the research and design work produced by the Urban Asymmetries Mexico City study group. The aim is to offer a normative vision of a possible urban politics defined by the integration of theoretical ethics and strategic urban politics as the locus for a 'new' form of political subjectivity, which when set into motion, may act as a radical means to resist and counter the forces and affects of the neoliberal urban machinery, while proposing alternatives to changing it. This new urban political subjectivity is given, among other understandings of governance, by a contemporary reinterpretation of the 'spectre of collectivism'.[15]

## 2 Nationalization, denationalization and privatization of the Mexican nation state

Mexico is an extremely complicated and variegated case in the context of global capitalism and the introduction of neoliberalism into Latin America during the 1970s. Not only has it been key in this historically and geographically, but politically and economically it has played a very important – if not all too well known – role as well.

Very generally, it may be argued that neoliberalism would not have spread as easily and as effectively across the region hadn't Mexico been coerced into this process at the time it was, and with the type of fine-tuned macro- and microeconomic mechanisms that were used, with for instance Mexico's forced participation in GATT (General Agreement on Tariffs and Trade) immediately following the 1982 crisis, and its subsequent entry into NAFTA (North American Free Trade Agreement) following the 1994/1995 crisis. More recently, under the illusion of national interest, Mexico's willingness to participate in the –until now – failed FTAA (Free Trade Area of the Americas), which is nothing less than the hyperextension of NAFTA, and its active engagement in the materialization of the related PPP (Plan Puebla-Panamá), a macro-development project that pretends to convert Mexico and parts of Central America into a giant *maquiladora* zone with nearly 60 million people,[16] shows the coercive pressure of external economic imperatives and foreign interests, in particular from the United States, upon national and state affairs. On the other hand, the less evident connections that may be established between these macroeconomic policies and reforms determined from outside and other issues occurring within the limits of the nation-state, as for example the very questionable engagement with the extremely violent – and even unconstitutional – 'war' on drug trafficking all along Mexico's northern border with the US[17], are evident

---

**10** John Agnew, 1996 quote in Neil Brenner, p. 29.
**11** Peter James Taylor, 'Embedded statism and the social sciences: opening up to new spaces' in **Environment and Planning A**, 28:1917-28, (1996) referenced in Neil Brenner, **New State Spaces: Urban governance and the rescaling of statehood** (Oxford: Oxford University Press, 2004), p. 29.
**12** MacLeod and Goodwin (1999), p. 505.
**13** Erik Swyngedouw, 'Neither Global nor Local: "glocalization" and the politics of scale', in K. Cox (ed.), **Spaces of Globalization: Reasserting the Power of the Local** (New York: Guilford, 1997), pp. 153-54 [137-166].
**14** See for instance Bob Jessop, 'The Political Economy of Scale and the Construction of Crossborder Microregions' available from http://socgeo.ruhosting.nl/colloquium/ConstructionOfCrossborderMicroregions.pdf (last accessed Oct. 2010).
As Bob Jessop explains, the relativization of scale may be understood as the pervasiveness of the national scale in spite of the fact that the processes accompanying the rise of neoliberal economies and the collapse of the post-war period have demoted the national scale as the basis for organizing economic, political and social relations. 'No other scale of economic and political organization (whether the "local" or the "global", the "urban" or the "triadic", the "regional" or the "supraregional") has yet won a similar primacy.'
See also Chris Collinge, 'Spatial Articulation of the State: Reworking Social Relations and Social Regulation Theory', in **Birmingham: Centre for Urban and Regional Studies** (1996) or Neil Brenner, **New State Spaces: Urban governance and the rescaling of statehood** (Oxford: Oxford University Press, 2004).
**15** Blake Stimson and Gregory Shollete, **Collectivism after Modernism: The Art of Social Imagination after 1945** (Minnesota: University of Minnesota Press, 2007).
**16** Peter McLaren and Nathalia E. Jaramillo, 'Alternative Globalizations: Toward a Critical Globalization Studies', in **Rizoma Freiriano**, Vol 1/2, 2008. Available online: http://www.rizoma-freireano.org/index.php/global-studies
**17** Since 2006, when president Felipe Calderón ordered military and federal police presence

indicators of a nation in peril and the symptoms of a state in a clear state of decomposition. But perhaps more importantly, these issues show how the absence of a clear national project with well-established state strategies has increased Mexico's propensity to uncritically adopt and adapt to imposed foreign 'development plans' regardless of the consequences that are infringed upon its own population, its sovereignty and its integrity. Unfortunately, these and many other of contemporary Mexico's malaises are a direct result of advancing neoliberal policies and reforms, which together with domestic or local vices, have managed to systematically erode the structural strongholds of the traditional nation-state construction since the 1970s.

Back in 1982, at the heart of the extremely dramatic economic meltdown that Mexico was suffering at the time as a consequence of the international oil crisis and due to the stratospheric foreign debt to which it had made itself subject, José López-Portillo (then Mexico's recently stepped down president) addressed the UN in a very eloquent discourse in which he – among many other things – warned against the impact of liberal economics on nation-states in the global south, referring to it quite factually as the process of denationalization.[18] The compromising of sovereignty as much of natural resources as of economic processes would lead, he claimed, to the dissolution and loss of sovereign states. The hollowing out of state activity was in this case intimately related to the destatization of the political system as well. This, as would become evident in subsequent decades, did not automatically signify positive outcomes for the country. In his speech, he mentioned other mechanisms of the neoliberal apparatus, and some related processes, which endangered the very existence of the nation-state via the internationalization of policy regimes: the interference of multinational companies, the growing concentration of financial capital, the subordination of banking systems to global metropolises, the massive expatriation of capital, and the imitation of foreign development models. In his address to the UN López-Portillo – who months earlier had nationalized the Mexican banking system in a desperate attempt to salvage the economic situation of the country – tacitly implied further, much more damaging measures that were to be taken in the aftermath of the 1982 crisis. Among them, draconic economic reforms, several waves of rampant privatizations of state-owned enterprises and the sell off of public interests more generally that would not stop until most – if not all – of Mexico's public assets had been either privatized, dissolved or auctioneered. López-Portillo's warning was more than metaphorical or purely political rhetoric. There was an important dose of material implications to his 'emotive' discourse.

It is well known today that as a bail-out to the excruciating foreign debt to which Mexico (and many other Latin American countries) had been subjected after the period of intense economic growth (and even boom) during the 1960s and early

1970s, and which had sent it to declare itself bankrupt in August 1982, it was obliged to comply with all sorts of economic and political reforms imposed by the IMF, the World Bank and the US Treasury, or more generally to conditions as disposed in the so-called Baker Plan.[19] Mexico's bankruptcy came at an extremely high cost. As Harvey says, the Baker Plan 'not only insisted on budgetary austerity... In 1984 the World Bank, for the first time in its history, granted a loan to a country in return for structural neoliberal reforms.' Needless to say 'the effects were wrenching'.[20] In addition to the economic and social costs, the political situation also deteriorated beyond repair, thus sending the post-revolutionary state project (or whatever was left of it at that point) far out of reach.[21]

Looking back, the causes for the turbulent decades of the 1970s and 1980s and many of the hardships and economic adjustments of the time lay at the core of the global collapse of production and the rise of speculation as a mode of development. The Latin American equivalent of the crisis of post-war Keynesian economics was the demise of the so-called autonomous industrialization model, also termed ISI – or import substitution industrialization – which dominated the Latin American economies during much of the second half of the twentieth century. The ISI model allowed states to enforce tariff barriers in order to promote sustained economic growth based on employment within the boundaries of the nation-state. In Mexico, the ISI model is commonly associated with wide state intervention still reminiscent of post-revolutionary policies and the political styles of a largely interventionist and corporativist state with strong anti-market traits. Its objectives were to sustain and strengthen the import-substitution strategy, thus guaranteeing political and economic arrangements that were favourable to this and other development strategies and macroeconomic policies. In spite of its own vices, policies were generally aimed at impeding the accumulation of wealth in the hands of individuals (usually understood as 'private hands') and foreign enterprises. Privatization was not a common measure as it was considered to weaken state and political power. In fact, after the global economic crisis of the 1970s the response of the government was 'to extend the public sector by taking over failing private enterprises, maintaining

in the border areas with the US to 'control' the drug cartels, the violence has escalated to unprecedented levels, involving massive casualties of civilians. More than 30,000 deaths have been registered in this conflict. For a recent insight on the conflict see: 'Mexico: a failed state', in **La Jornada**, November 6, 2010. Available online: http://www.jornada.unam.mx/2010/11/06/index.php?section=politica&article=002n1pol

**18** See José López-Portillo's address to the United Nations on October 1, 1982. Available in two parts from YouTube (last accessed October 27, 2010):
http://www.youtube.com/watch?v=_tpwZaFlP04&feature=related
http://www.youtube.com/watch?v=_tpwZaFlP04&feature=related

**19** Mexico's foreign debt rose from $6.8 billion in 1972 to $58 billion by 1982. Ian Vásquez, 'The Brady Plan and Market-Based Solutions to Debt Crisis', in **The Cato Journal**, 16/2 (available online: http://www.cato.org/pubs/journal/cj16n2-4.html) referenced in David Harvey (2005), p. 99.

**20** David Harvey (2005), pp. 99-100.

**21** As a direct outcome of the Revolution of 1910, Mexico's power elites at the time –united under the political patronage of the PRI – formulated a solid political project for the Mexican nation-state that reunited political, cultural, social and economic visions of a modern, but highly nationalistic Mexico. The post-revolutionary political project among many other strongholds, stipulated the parameters and criteria for the exploitation of national resources, human capital and economic self-regulation. See for instance: Luis Barrón, 'La Constitución: proyecto político surgido de la Revolución de 1910-1917', in Enrique Florescano (ed.). **La Política en México** (México: Taurus, 2007).

them as sources of employment to stave off the threat of working class unrest. The number of state enterprises more than doubled between 1970 and 1980'.[22] This widely accepted model registered significant economic successes during its early decades, but was gradually compromised by several factors – bad management in short term economic policies and the breakdown of the corporativist political system – until its demise in the 1980s.

Arguably, the Mexican reaction to economic globalization and its related crises serves as the milestone to the swift shift in the modes of production and development of the whole region. During the 1980s and 1990s in country after country the ISI model gave way to a varying extent to the free market model, the privatization of state enterprises and public assets, and the reduction of the state's directive role in the economy. In other words, the demise of the ISI model reflects in all clarity the confluence of the three trends of denationalization, destatization and internationalization, and signals at the same time the transformations and changes in the structures of *government* and their abrupt transition into other forms of *governance*, which not only tolerated or accepted a new model but which in fact sustained and enforced it. The new model that was implemented under the influence and with the guidance of the usual global institutions (IMF, WB, etc) had momentous effects on the societies, political systems, and class structures of the region,[23] few of which were positive, liberating or emancipatory in the long run. In Mexico, the main effect was the substitution of one regime for another one, which needless to say was less socially concerned, and which produced more than uneven development, it enforced an extremely uneven distribution of justice, welfare and wealth.

What was left after the so-called 'lost decade' of the 1980s was an eroded nation-state with a very debilitated public and social government programme; weak political parties and a loss of faith and disenchantment in electoral politics; a country with few options but to attempt its recovery by consolidating the neoliberal model with further structural adjustments, including commercial liberalization and the disincorporation of the public sector, and widespread acceptance of privatization as a viable political and economic practice of the state, as stipulated in the different phases of the Brady Plan. Under the slogan of allowing 'access to modernity' and promising 'greater welfare and social justice',[24] the following two administrations – de la Madrid and Salinas de Gortari – used the position of the state as the main agent of change, as the actor in charge of opening the system to the free market, and in a way also as the executioner of the nation-state proper. This moment heralds the confluence of internal interest groups and external forces, and also exemplifies how nation states are – 'through the actions of constituent properties (governments, courts, bureaucracies) *active agents* in the structuration of globalization, "glocalization", post-Fordism and "hollowing-out"'.[25] Especially from 1988 onwards, Mexico enters a stage that clearly shifts the efforts of the nation state to achieve a 'well balanced' domestic *performance* of the national economy towards its overall international *competitiveness*.[26] This process of change entailed dire challenges for the country, and generally, conveyed two dimensions: the political one, which strove towards the ideal of democratization, and the economic one, aimed at achieving macroeconomic and fiscal balance, as well as liberating internal and external market forces. Not uninterestingly, both these dimensions represent a dual set of policies, which are not without their inner conflicts: those to achieve *equilibrium or stabilization*, and those to achieve *structural change*.[27] The best way to pursue equilibrium was, most probably, through invented social programmes inflamed with welfare rhetoric (and which ultimately had marginal successes). But structural change could not be achieved without setting the neoliberal apparatus into motion. Through a vast host of re-regulation programmes, profound institutional reforms, and in particular through a process of rampant privatizations, which was aimed at the massive sell-off (auctioneering) of so-called SOE's or state-owned enterprises (also referred to as '*para-estatales*', many of which had been acquired during the 1970s crisis), and/or the privatization of property rights and activities, especially of the public sector and the transformation of common good into private property, Mexico transitioned from a post-revolutionary, populist and interventionist state gone bankrupt in many respects, to a text-book example of a neoliberal state.

## 3 Neoliberal urbanization

The processes of denationalization – whether as the demise of the nation-state or as its transformation – destatization and internationalization signify the rise of other 'scales' including the regional and the urban, and while it is true that none of these scales has taken hegemonic position or importance over the other, it is also clear that new geographies of governance have emerged as a result of the reorganization of state capacities.[28] In this sense, denationalization and destatization would then mean more than the hollowing out of the nation, or the simple retreat of the state from its social and politico-economic commitments. In fact, they would imply much more than the rise of other scalar units; they would signal the definitive transition from government to governance. Arguably, this is a radical shift in the regulation of social practices and the arrangements and practices of power, as well as in the emergence of new agents and 'actors'. Governance 'denotes the relationality of power as it flows through networks

**22** David Harvey (2005), p. 99.
**23** Alejandro Portes and Bryan Roberts, 'The Free-Market City: Latin American Urbanization in the Years of the Neoliberal Experiment', in **Studies in Comparative International Development**, Spring 2005, p. 44 [pp. 43-82].
**24** Carlos Bazdresch and Carlos Elizondo, 'Privatization: The Mexican Case', in **The Quarterly Review of Economics and Face**, Vol. 33, Special Issue, 1993, pp. 45-66.
**25** MacLeod and Goodwin (1999) p. 506. [their emphasis]
**26** Bob Jessop, 'The entrepreneurial city: re-imaging localities, re-designing economic governance, or re-structuring capital?', in N. Jewson and S. Macgregor (eds), **Transforming Cities: Contested governance and new spatial divisions** (London: Routledge, 1997) p. 37. [My emphasis] In 1988, then president Carlos Salinas de Gortari stressed the 'need to deepen the reforms with the aim of achieving a true transformation of the economy and society in order to adapt them to the market forces and enable the economy to compete successfully in the international market.'
**27** Bazdresch and Elizondo (1993).
**28** Bob Jessop in MacLeod & Goodwin.

between the state and institutional actors in the market and civil society'. Hence, governance 'is not a homogenous agent, but a morass of complex networks and arenas within which power dynamics are expressed and deployed'.[29] In practice, however, this also means the engagement of quasi and non-state actors in private-public partnerships and other types of networks over a large variety of functions and responsibilities formerly assigned to the state. But just what do these 'new geographies of governance' entail under a climate of widespread neoliberalism, and specifically under neoliberal urbanization, in the Mexican context?

A good point of departure to address this question would be to look at the capital city of the nation-state, the extremely complex urban formation we call Mexico City. From its fragmented and polarized 'nature' in political, social, economic and morphological terms, to its position as the seat of power of the country, Mexico City resists proper classification. Today it is almost impossible to refer to Mexico City without running into problems of definition, and inconsistencies or inaccuracies abound. Mexico City comprises the *Distrito Federal* (Federal District) with its 16 *delegaciones* (boroughs), as well as 62 adjacent municipalities pertaining to two federal states (*Estado de México* and *Hidalgo*), which have been absorbed by the capital from the onset of the industrialization and modernization of the city since the 1930s, but at an increased pace during the second half of the twentieth century. More than 20 million people are estimated to dwell in the ZMVM (*Zona Metropolitana del Valle de México* – Metropolitan Area of the 'Valley' of Mexico)[30] 56% of which live in the adjoining municipalities of the *Estado de México* and *Hidalgo*, and the remaining 44% in the city proper.[31] As the capital city, and due to its very particular political character, but also because of its sheer size, Mexico City is especially susceptible to political and economic crises. The debt crises and the politico-economic reforms of the early 1980s had a direct impact on the urban structure and morphology of most of the larger cities in the country, but were felt most strongly in the capital. One the first effects to be registered was a very significant decentralization of the population from the inner city into the peripheries, a phenomenon that because of its scale also evidenced the convoluted spatial and political situation of the periphery itself. Firstly, the eastern periphery of the city belongs to the *Estado de México* (State of Mexico), which traditionally has been governed by the PRI (*Partido Revolucionario Institucional*), and since the 1970s has been controlled by powerful industrial capitalist power groups,[32] while the Federal District has been the stronghold of leftist government PRD (*Partido de la Revolución Democrática*) since it was granted the right to democratic state elections in 1996.[33] However, and as the capital of the Federal Republic, it is also the seat of the Federal Powers, and the president elect – who has been from the conservative right wing party PAN (*Partido Acción Nacional*) since 2000 – also resides and governs from the capital. This has produced a very complex political landscape in and around Mexico City, as geopolitical boundaries have also become painful sites of contestation, struggle and conflict of government and governance between so much political entities, policies, planning and administration and other public and social institutions, which instead of producing constructive or productive exchanges, has only intensified the structural and systemic problems that historically have existed among the three different entities ruling over the same city.

In addition, in the eastern periphery – but not exclusively, as this is a national issue with territorial and spatial consequences everywhere – the problem of the privatization of the 'ejido' landholding system has also become patent, as will be dealt with more extensively in the final part of this chapter and in the following two contributions included in this section. Suffice it to say that from the mid-1970s onwards, but taking force after the entry of the neoliberal regime in the 1980s and 1990s, Mexico City has in its own contextual problematic, absorbed the effects of the crises of global capitalism. In that way, uneven urban development, polarization, a widespread system based on corruption and illegality, socio-spatial segregation according to income and class, have taken very spatial forms, dividing the city into two imaginary halves. The ZMVM materializes as a geopolitical map of uneven development and segregation, where the wealthier classes have moved to the west and the lower-income groups and urban poor have been forced to spread out into the east.

**29** Patsy Healy, 'Planning Theory and Urban and Regional Dynamics: A Comment on Yiftachel and Huxley', in **International Journal of Urban and Regional Research**, Vol. 24, No. 4, p. 919; cited in Edgar Pieterse, 'Working notes on a relational model of urban politics', conference paper, p. 3. Available online from: www.princeton.edu/~piirs/projects/Democracy&Development/papers/Pieterse,%20Relational%20Urban%20Politics.pdf

**30** Mexico City is located in the middle of an endorheic basin, not in a valley. This has been one of the pervasive geographical and geological misunderstandings of the city, and which has caused many of its environmental and urban problems along the centuries since the arrival of the Spanish conquistadors and the destruction of the Aztec city.

**31** Gustavo Garza, 'Ambitos de Expansión Territorial', in G. Garza (ed.), **La Ciudad de México en el Fin del Segundo Milenio** (Mexico City: Gobierno del Distrito Federal and El Colegio de México, 2000), pp. 237-46.

**32** The Estado de México (State of Mexico) is a doughnut shaped political entity that surrounds the Distrito Federal on three of its sides (north, west and east). It is a rich state with access to natural resources and is, of course, in proximity to the country's capital. During the 1970s and 1980s the State of Mexico was ruled by the Hank González family, a very strong political clan of the PRI 'dynasty', who took the state as its main source of investment and income. In this way it became a bastion for many of the most prominent political and industrial families in Mexico, as well as important business and corporate groups, such as Grupo Atenco, Campos Hermanos, etc. The State of Mexico has remained under the government of the PRI throughout the entire twentieth century and the first decade of the twenty-first. More than half of the population of Mexico City lives in the State of Mexico.

**33** The political history of contemporary Mexico City can be traced back to the beginning of Mexico's independent period following the Independence War of 1810-1821, when the city was declared capital of the Federal Republic (Unites States of Mexico) in 1824. As such, and following the example of Washington, Mexico City was a Federal District, not an autonomous state within the federation (**Unión**). For the next century, the status of the city did not change much, although there were several constitutional amendments, which slowly endowed the city with more political capacities and legal functions. In 1987/88 and probably as a result of changes in the nation-state, Mexico City underwent an important process of democratization that transformed its political and legal character. In general terms, the changes were aimed at changing the undemocratic system of direct selection of the city's **Regente** (mayor) by the president. These reforms to the structure of the Federal District took definitive shape with the political reform of 1996 in which direct elections were held for the first time. The election of the **Jefe de Gobierno** (governor) occurred in a climate in which the opposition party (PRD) achieved majority over the ruling national party (PRI). This political climate had many important consequences for the political and organizational structure of the city's government.

After the debt crisis of 1982 and the demise of the ISI model, Mexico City also mustered changes in the patterns of lifestyle and consumer preferences of both the wealthy and the poor, which clearly follow the generic neoliberal model of urbanization. In particular the diverse processes of privatization of common social and public goods – through policy-making, constitutional reforms and other legal frameworks, the restructuring of institutions, reforms in ownership and property rights, and sell-offs, but also and not unimportantly, through a generalized privatization of public space, and of the city itself – have transformed Mexico City in very significant ways. The promotion of global investments through the creation of so-called urban megaprojects, for instance, has led to the prevalence of trends that enforce social and spatial segregation.

While these projects originally were planned from an Anglo-Saxon perspective to cater the taste of the upper income groups, and conventionally include office spaces for transnational companies, shopping malls, private schools and hospitals and well as high-end residential areas in the form of either highly surveyed and controlled gated communities or high-rise apartment buildings, in Mexico (as in many other Latin American cities) this model has had several variants, including one for the urban poor and the lower income groups, as well as 'plug-in' projects such as privately developed and operated, yet publicly financed, traffic and transportation infrastructure that connects these 'private-cities' in the periphery to the central city.

The so-called 'common-interest developments' or CID's – regardless of whether for the rich or for the poor – have become the dominant form of residence and housing in the neoliberal city. The main characteristics are their peri-urban location, their private nature, and their exclusion / isolation from anything that slightly resembles public space. The fear of the city, the feeling of insecurity, a feeling that has been increasing over the last three decades in Mexico City as a direct result of the polarization of society and the rise of criminality and violence, explains why security has become almost a status symbol, which rich and poor value equally. Interesting is the terminology of these developments; no longer of 'social interest' (*interés social*) but of 'common interest', they represent several interconnected phenomena, all of which are related to the advance and encroachment of neoliberal urbanization trends: the retreat of the state and the government in urban governance, urban planning and urban administration, and the rise of private developers as the active agents in the making of the city.

Just like CBD's (Central Business Districts) in their time, the construction of CID's are today the favoured investment scheme for developers for very pragmatic reasons: they permit high density housing schemes (volume) with very high profit margins, regardless of the 'price-tag' on each dwelling unit. On the other hand, these developments are also interesting for local governments, as they take care of the problem of housing at minimal public expenditure.[34] This brings us back to the issue of privatization. In theory, and in contexts with more developed democracies and lower levels of corruption and inequality, privatization is based on the supposition that there are better and more efficient ways for governments to deliver goods and services to their citizens, while maintaining accountability and responsibility. Performance is key, and there is a culture of public involvement and scrutiny.[35] In Mexico, however, this is not the case. Privatization, on all scales, has resulted in a wild form of governance, or rather self-governance, in which the developer acquires the land 'dirt-cheap', determines the conditions of each development, fixes the ratio of functions and zoning of each development, invests in those parts of the scheme that are profitable, and leaves the rest to the municipalities or local authorities, who with the exception of high-end CID's, not often meet their responsibilities. The state has equally relinquished its role in the making of the city, and remains present only in the form of financing institutions such as FOVI or INFONAVIT. This leaves the dweller (now transformed in 'owner' of a life-long mortgage) virtually unprotected and therefore vulnerable to all sorts of risks. This is how the neoliberal model of urbanization operates in Mexico, and many other countries. But while this has produced outbursts of public protest elsewhere, as the public complains of double taxation and other forms of abuse, in Mexico, the surprising element is that it has not yet become a political and legal issue. There are many explanations to this, but what remains a fact is that the much acclaimed 'new agents' that emerged from the transition from government to governance – greedy private developers, weak and corrupt authorities, crony private, and public financial institutions catering to 'common interest' schemes – are hardly what the critics of the nation-state model expected as a positive contribution of the demise of the interventionist, populist welfare state.

The neoliberal regime in Mexico City has made two issues clear: the government has been incapable of meeting the challenge of competitiveness, performance or progress to which it subscribed when it joined the neoliberal wagon, and secondly, this transition has widened the gap between the haves and the have-nots, leaving the urban poor as well as the urban billionaires of the likes of Carlos Slim, to 'take matters into their own hands.' Whether this means purchasing half of the historical centre for land speculation; taking over the land of peasants at bottom prices and developing flashy CID's for the rich and sordid 'sleepburbs' for the poor; buying the remnants of bankrupt SOE's and turning these into multimillion corporations; or simply joining the infinite ranks of financial slaves that this system has produced, what is undeniable is that the situation will not be tenable in the long run. The social, political, economic and environmental consequences of the neoliberal urbanization model in Mexico are the result of the processes of denationalization, destatization or internationalization; of rampant privatization, of a culture of increasing individual-

**34** Evan McKenzie, 'Common-Interest Housing in the Communities of Tomorrow', in **Housing Policy Debate**, Vol. 14, Issues 1 and 2, 2007, [pp. 203-234]; p.207.
**35** Ibid.

ism, which instead of remedying ailing economies, only perpetuate and intensify the ongoing historical process of segregation, dispossession and disenfranchisement that have characterized the socio-spatial structure of Mexico City and of the whole country.

## 4 Towards the integration of theoretical ethics and strategic politics for the city
Probably the earliest sign of the unsustainability of the neoliberal model of urbanization in Mexico is the dwellers' need to improve the material conditions of the units almost as soon as they move in, and to modify and adapt – sometimes precariously – the common areas of the developments themselves to accommodate to the real needs of the inhabitants. These practices, differently from what we would like to believe, namely that the architecture of these complexes allows for user adaptability, are the result of utilitarian profit-making schemes and scams by the developers. But there is another, more interesting phenomenon developing today, which is related to the silenced, yet recurrent history of failure in occupancy rates of CID's on both ends of the socio-economic spectrum.

According to some developers, the rate of empty standing residential units (but also office and commercial spaces) has become a reason for concern; in 2009 it was estimated that close to 2.5 million dwelling units in recently built middle and lower-income massive CID's or gated communities were standing empty throughout the country; the number for Mexico City alone was estimated at an impressive 750,000 units.[36] The problem does not seem to be related to a slowing or decreasing demand for housing, since in the country and in Mexico City there still is a clear housing shortage. Most of the unoccupied dwellings have been leased or sold following accessible credit systems and subsidized financial schemes and hence have a legal owner; they simply are left uninhabited, or sublet informally to individuals who cannot access the formal housing market. It is believed that some of the reasons for this phenomenon range from small-scale practices of real estate speculation, to more tangible factors such as the inhospitable and anti-urban situation of these developments. To this one would have to add the extremely low quality of construction and execution of these housing developments, the lack or very low quality of basic urban services and infrastructure, the distance to the city and the lack of opportunities for employment, education and health, and the costs associated with commuting, the absence of public spaces and therefore the isolation from urban life, etc. In short, low occupancy, abandonment and the continuous modification of as much the structures as the functions not only evidence the shortcomings of the neoliberal urbanization model in this format; they are also changing the very nature of peri-urbanization. Given their anti-urban character, their massive scale, and their location, it is paramount to ask what are these changes going to entail, and what will be the consequences for the city in the long run? Paquette and Yescas, for one, claim that the most imminent danger is that – similarly to most peri-urban sprawl in Mexico and elsewhere – these developments will too transform into immense peripheral ghettoes, as the material conditions deteriorate over time.[37] Whatever the future may bring is uncertain, but it certainly will not be the outcomes of a development model based on qualitative criteria for the enhancement of social exchange and welfare, or on flexibility of inhabitation, but rather the multiplication of problems derived from a profit-driven, utilitarian and massive anti-urban approach.

Under this predicament it becomes urgent to acknowledge this emerging landscape and realize that although many of the problems of this model originate from the confluence of political, economic and social forces with little bearing on the tangible and spatial planes, it is precisely on these planes that real problems ultimately materialize, hindering the development of a healthy urbanity now, and especially in the future. In that sense, it is possible to think of the spatial disciplines, including architecture and urbanism, as relevant actors in the devising of alternatives to the dominant yet flawed model of urbanization. The question will then be how and on what terms.

If, as this elaboration has been trying to reveal, one of the effects of global capitalism and its neoliberal apparatus has been the deconstruction of fixed formations and understandings of scale and of territory in favour of more 'flexible' concepts of space and territoriality, it is almost obvious that our understanding of the spatial disciplines would also have to change and adapt to these 'new' realities. Hence, it becomes paramount to begin implementing a multiscalar and multidisciplinary approach that gives precedence to process over other understandings (over the 'fixity' of a plan or of a design). This brings us back to Laclau's propositions of devising other, non-capitalist alternatives, but which take into account the transformations brought about by this system; alternatives, which in their core-formulation would already convey what Boltanski and Chiapello refer to as 'the new spirit of capitalism'.[38] This would imply that alternatives to the dominant neoliberal urbanization model cannot be formal or even spatial in their scopes; they will require the confluence of a myriad of instances, including the political, the social and the economic dimensions.

In Mexico and in Mexico City, in which government has become synonymous with a denationalized, weak and inefficient state apparatus, and governance has been steered mostly by private interest groups and powerful politico-economic networks with little regard for the social, it is all the more important to question the ethical considerations of contemporary global capitalism, and in this context, of neoliberal urbanization, utilizing both a theoretical *and* an applied ethics. So

**36** In an informal presentation in Mexico City, Javier Sánchez Higuera estimated that close to 10% of the housing stock in the country and approximately 20% in Mexico City (ZMVM) privately built and sold between 2000-2009, remained unoccupied. According to the BBVA and Conavi during the period 2000-2009 the housing shortage was tackled at a rate of 650,000 units per year. Source: BBVA Research, **Reporte Annual 2009**. Available online: http://inversores.bbva.com/TLBB/fbin/120310_annual_report_tcm240-216439.pdf
**37** Catherine Paquette and Mabel Yescas Sánchez, 'Producción masiva de vivienda en Cuidad de México: dos políticas en debate', in **Centro-h, Revista de la Organización Latinoamericana y del Caribe de Centros Históricos**, No. 3, April 2009, pp. 15-26.
**38** Luc Boltanski and Eve Chiapello, **The New Spirit of Capitalism** (London: Verso, 2005).

that the question shifts from what constitutes distributive injustice, or uneven development, for instance, to the application and evaluation of principles and norms that guide practice in these particular domains. The focus is then placed on issues and problems specific to the urban dimension, through a combination of theory and practice.[39] In other words, what is required is the search for methods to integrate theoretical ethics and strategic (urban) politics. Arguably, this is the prerequisite for the emergence of new political subjectivities, which may transcend the impasse of contemporary neoliberal urbanization.

## 5 Mexico City Study Group

*So where shall we start our revolutionary anti-capitalist movement? Mental conceptions? The relation to nature? Daily life and reproductive practices? Social relations? Technologies and organizational forms? Labour processes? The capture of institutions and their revolutionary transformation?*[40]

In his most recent publication, *The Enigma of Capital*, David Harvey develops the outline for a potent conceptual model – a socio-ecological totality – constituted by the dialectical relationship of seven activity spheres, which co-evolve with the historical evolution of capitalism. This evolutionary ecological system (something comparable to a Deleuzian assemblage) facilitates a much more complex, and therefore much more accurate interpretation of the real[41] and may therefore serve the wider purpose of devising alternative projects for a healthier human existence. Interestingly, he exemplifies this conceptual model using the case of an urban design competition for the new administrative city of Sejung in South Korea, and explains how this system – a co-evolutionary theory of social change – not only serves the purpose to propose revolutionary strategies, but also provides a framework 'that can have practical implications for thinking through everything from grand revolutionary strategies to redesign of urbanisation and city life.'[42]

This was also the main thematic of a workshop of the Mexico City study group with Prof. Harvey held at the DSD in February 2008.[43] Inspired by the outcome of this workshop the study group explored the implications and effects of the shift to neoliberal urbanization in Mexico in order to propose a series of theoretical strategies to counter this model and its related processes. The result is the collective strategic plan for the CID *Las Américas* in the municipality of *Ecatepec de Morelos*, an area in Mexico City's northeastern periphery, in which two opposing forms of undesirable urbanization exist in painful proximity and collide in dramatic ways. On the one hand, the informal city with all its spatial, social, political and environmental problems, and on the other, pervasive low-density, low-quality, uniform suburban housing developments for the working class, the 'formalized' sectors and the urban poor.

During the first stage of the project, the study group focused on the historical analysis of Mexico City from its founding as the capital of the Aztec Empire in 1325 to the present. This analysis revealed interesting connections between the morphological transformations of the city and the ideological and politico-economic shifts characteristic of each historical period. In this way, the study group found that Mexico City has been subjected to the interplay of both national and local power-relations as these adapt to impositions from the global arena, and which ultimately translate into dramatic urban transformation. The two most obvious and detrimental outcomes were the ones associated with the period of Conquest in the sixteenth century, and the contemporary period. The latter is a relatively brief, but very intense period of dynamic change, in which Mexico City turned into a megalopolis, and which is often reduced to simplistic descriptions of the city's growth or expansion, dealing with this as if it were the outcome of a natural process, in spite of there not being anything natural about this phenomenon. The rampant urban sprawl that began in the mid-1950s was facilitated by the establishment of a series of political mechanisms, which preceded the arrival of neoliberalism proper, but which nevertheless lubricated its entry and consolidation during the 1980s and 1990s.

The widespread wave of privatizations that began shortly before and during the regime of Carlos Salinas de Gortari in the late 1980s and all of the 1990s, and which have today become a common practice, are a good example of the complexity and wide-ranging effects of neoliberal capitalism on the production of space and of the city.

One of the most bizarre turns taken by de Gortari was the strategic reform to article 123 (labour reforms) and article 27 (privatization of *ejido* land) of the Mexican Constitution of 1917. This political manoeuvre managed to disintegrate several foundational collective and individual rights and guarantees achieved during the Mexican Revolution of 1910-1921; in particular the amendments to article 27 had enormous consequences for the entire country, but proved especially disastrous for Mexico City. Article 27 established the *ejido* system, one of the victories of the Revolution that had been won under the slogan *Tierra y Libertad*.[44] In very summarized terms the *ejido* system prescribed a form of land-use or usufruct derived from pre-Hispanic times in which agricultural land was understood as the means to guarantee produce from agriculture, and hence to ward the sustenance for millions of Mexicans. This entitled the farmer to the right to cultivate and inhabit a plot for life. The *ejidos* were not liable to a capitalist understanding of property or ownership, as these could not be sold or bought, but were assigned to a single or extended family, a cooperative or organization, and the plot could be inherited over generations as long as it was cultivated. This

**39** Stephen Ward, 'Researching Ethics'. Available online from: http://www.journalismethics.ca/
research_ethics/approaches_to_ethics.htm
**40** David Harvey, **The Enigma of Capital and the Crises of Capitalism** (London: Profile Books, 2010) p. 138.
**41** Ibid., pp. 119-39.
**42** Ibid., p. 137.
**43** February 22-23, 2008, DSD, Delft.
**44** **'Tierra y Libertad'** ('Land and Liberty') was used by the Mexican revolutionaries (especially Emiliano Zapata and Francisco Villa) to represent the main objective of the rural revolutionary movement in Mexico: the right to land. Today this is a political slogan associated with anarchism.

system was especially important in the countryside, but as in most developing countries, the line separating the countryside from the city is always blurry.

The case of Mexico City was no different: its periphery, which had been subject to informal urbanization since the 1960s, consisted entirely of *ejidos*. Triggered by a previous ban to subdivide plots in the inner city, the poor were forced to seek shelter on the city's edge, which to complicate things even more is part of a different political entity (*Estado de México*), and hence subject to different urban policies than Mexico D.F. – this fact producing one of the most important asymmetrical conditions of the megalopolis. But since the reforms to article 27 the country – and Mexico City – has experienced a massive sell-off of communal agricultural land, and its transformation into land readily available for massive, cheap urbanization. But to these urban problems, one would have to add several other issues that have contributed to the worsening of Mexico City's urban condition: a brew of environmental and natural catastrophes, ongoing cycles of crises, political instability, economic meltdowns, and growing polarization, all of which have had a direct impact on the situation of social housing in the megalopolis. This was one of the main items that the study group analysed in depth: the transformation of public social housing initiatives into profitable business for private investment.

Following the *problématique* of the overall research and design project the study group focused on the shifts that lead to the dissolution of the state-led programme for the construction of low income housing (workers' housing or 'social interest housing') and the mutations undergone within INFONAVIT (National Institute for Workers Housing) into a financial organ with little power over the production of social housing. It focused on both the motives (political and economic) of this mutation, and its consequences on spatial and social levels, and emphasized the situation developing in the study area.

Based on these findings, the study group then developed the proposal of a collective strategic intervention for the site, consisting of a set of urban and architectural projects: 'reconnecting the social'; 'making wastelands productive'; and 'alternative urbanization'.

The relational project proposals emphasize the need for integration in both spatial and social terms of the area, and the necessity to address the wider planning problem of Mexico City, while generating moments of possibility where dispossessed, deprived or powerless communities may find the motives for empowerment, thus fostering a sense of struggle to regain the right to the city. More than programmatic and compositional items alone, the projects carefully contemplate the possibility of proposing new social, spatial, financial and economic models that adapt to the actual conditions of the population, allowing the possibility for different form of 'urbanity' to emerge from these proposals. They include a process-based, relational understanding of 'project' and integrate the notion of phasing as a central design parameter.

An essential aspect in the project proposals is the emphasis on alternative social formations tied to the materiality of the site via the architectural or urban interventions. These social formations are based on small-scaled forms of autonomous self-governance and administration; sophisticated mechanisms of affinity-building among different groups at various scales and levels of participation and shareholding; several alternative models for cooperative ownership, property relations, and construction; community building and other schemes of social organization, all of which are designed to challenge and counter the individualistic approach conventionally associated with free market logics. This liberates the potentials of social and political agency as a significant element of change, and fosters a vision of strong social interaction based on collectivity, thus nurturing the possibilities of new political subjectivities that may once again trigger the spark for an engaged urban politics.

**Acknowledgements**   This article is a result of the collective research carried out during 2008 and 2009 by the Urban Asymmetries Ecatepec, Mexico City Study Group (MCSG) at the Delft School of Design. The study group was directed by H. Sohn and M. Robles-Durán. I wish to acknowledge the collective dedication, the tireless commitment to this project, and the valuable contributions of our dear 'asymmetricals': L. Asabashvili, Y. Bey, S. Bizzarri, C. García-Sancho, T. Guerrero, T. Jaskari, T. Kolnaar, P. Lühl, T. ter Weel, S. Voogt, W. van der Veen and I. Zveibil. In more ways than one and on countless occasions they inspired me to believe in the powers of collectivism to transform reality through directed action.

The study group wishes to thank the different scholars, activists, politicians, architects and urbanists and citizens who supported the project with their time and knowledge, and particularly Prof. David Harvey, the officials at the municipality of Ecatepec, State of Mexico, Roberto Eibenschutz and his team of researchers and students at the UEM-UAM Xochimilco, Jose Castillo, and Gustavo Lipkau.

# The Growth of Cities in Mexico

**Roberto Eibenschutz and Laura O. Carrillo**

This work reviews the way in which the expansion of cities in Mexico has come about, identifying, on the one hand, the characteristics of the formal process, supported and instigated by the national home loan institutions, seemingly in compliance with established regulations, and on the other, the informal and irregular settlements which follow the initiative of the poorer populace, who have no other solution to their housing situation in the formal housing market, nor rights to institutional housing support. Also suggested are some measures and tools which may be instrumental in breaking the vicious cycle of informal settlement,[1] originating in an unjust urban planning model driven by land speculation.

## Introduction

Historically, Mexico has seen a rapid and complex urbanization process subject to economic, social and political decisions both internal and external, which together have impeded the establishment of an institutional system of coordinated work amongst those involved in national land organization.

The war-oriented world economy of the 1940s gave Mexico the chance to begin a period of internal industrial development and growth, which had been programmed since the 1930s, when the first Six-Year Plan was approved. This plan started by considering the need to create adequate urban conditions in order to achieve a final outcome. During the subsequent two decades the focus was on reaching objectives without regard for the consequences that this would entail. Priority was given to creating the conditions in which industry could be established in the main cities: Mexico City, Guadalajara and Monterrey, with the population of Mexico City in 1940 reaching 40% of the national total, in contrast to 6% in Guadalajara and 5% of the national registered population in Monterrey, as Table 1 shows [see fig. 1].[2]

During the 1950s, the population percentage in Mexico City grew to equal the percentage of population based in the three main cities represented in the preceding decade; the relevant point being that industrial growth was so great during this period in Mexico City that for the first time a conurbation was formed between the Federal District (*Distrito Federal*) and several municipalities in the State of Mexico (*Estado de México*). In the following decade, this phenomenon came to be known as Metropolitan Zones, the largest of which was the Metropolitan Zone of Mexico City (MZMC), comprising the 16 boroughs (*delegaciones*) of the Federal District and 19 adjoining municipalities of the State of Mexico.[3] This period was marked by the so-called import substitution industries (ISI).[4]

Government action during these periods, and up until 1960, was basically focused on two priorities. The first was to complete the distribution of land and regulate production in the Mexican

---

1 Alfonso Iracheta and Martim Smolka, **Los Pobres de la Ciudad y la Tierra** (Mexico: Ed. Lincoln Institute of Land Policy and El Colegio Mexiquense, 2000).
2 Gustavo Garza, **La Urbanización de México en el Siglo XX** (Mexico: Colegio de México, 2005).
3 Luis Unikel, **El Desarrollo Urbano en México** (Mexico: El Colegio de México, 1976), p. 28.
4 Gobierno del Distrito Federal, **Atlas de la Ciudad de México** (Mexico: El Colegio de México, 1988).

countryside, pending from the Mexican Revolution. The second was industrial development.

The manner in which urban growth and expansion took place was a result of not taking into consideration the immediate impact on the land of both governmental priorities, which generated the so-called demographic explosion owing to the high reproductive rates characteristic of rural societies, and a drastic reduction in mortality thanks to advances in public health procedures, combined with an accelerated process of urbanization fed by the attraction of employment in the cities and the exodus of surplus population from the countryside.

Mexican cities were unprepared to face this situation and soon were unable to keep up with the demand for the infrastructure and equipment needed to support the urbanization process, as their regulatory ability was limited to existing construction codes, and urban developments with no solid legal base, which left the issuing of licenses and building permits, and urban development in general, to the discretion of the authorities.

This situation led to an awareness of the state of human settlements, also addressed by the United Nations conference in Vancouver, together with internal pressure exerted by some academics headed by Luis Unikel and planners organized by the Mexican Planning Society. This awareness led president Luis Echeverría in 1976 to bring about the institutionalization of Urban Planning through modifications to articles 27, 73 and 115 of the Mexican Constitution, establishing as a main clause the ability of the state to 'impose modalities on property' for reasons of public utility.

Following the constitutional changes, the General Human Settlement Law was issued, in which a national urban planning system was established, requiring the states of the Republic to pass laws on the subject and to draw up urban development plans for the country's main cities. From this moment it is possible to confirm that it is precisely urban planning that defines what is formal and informal when determining land limits for authorized urban use, taking into account such criteria as the land's characteristics (presence of water, forested or productive areas, established infrastructure, proximity to urban areas, topography, hazards, etc.). In this way, areas unsuitable for urbanization are assessed for their agricultural, forestry and environmental value. This classification often leads to 'informal' or unauthorized activity, since the owners of lands outside these boundaries, unable to develop them legally, organize the sale of land at rates well below those established by the authorized market, offering them up for sale at affordable prices to those with low incomes.[5]

Thus we can nowadays refer to two processes of settlement on urban soil in Mexico: the 'formal' or authorized settlement, so-called because it supposedly complies with regulations established by the three areas of government, and is legally recognized through corresponding planning approval, and 'informal' or unauthorized settlement, which does not respect the legal regulatory framework and conforms in only a basic and insufficient way to the social dynamic, originating in the migratory process from the countryside to the city which is characteristic of Latin-American cities and other places in the underdeveloped world.

The difference between the two types of Mexican urbanization has been recognized since 1950, when for the first time it was officially considered necessary to deal with the proletarian communities made up of rural migrants settling on land which did not belong to them. From there arose first the idea of 'invaders' and then of 'irregulars', who occupy land using various illegal means.[6] Using this logic, 'formal', authorized land can be defined as that which is legally owned, where the use of the land corresponds to that established in urban development plans and complies with fiscal obligations.

The classification of this type of land organization has various drawbacks, principally with respect to land ownership, as this determines the direction of urban development and consequently the structure of cities. At this point it is useful to mention that originating in the revolutionary movement (1910-1917), the large estates (*haciendas*) and ranches were divided up and given to landless peasants, which resulted in the subdivision of large productive entities and the creation of small agrarian groups, to whom was awarded collective ownership of the land, or *ejido*, assigning parcels for the usufruct of each of the members of the cooperative, the *ejidatarios* and the *comuneros*. Thus the main revolutionary demand was satisfied: reclamation of the land for those who worked on it, for habitation and farming, the fundamental aims of the armed movement.

Distribution of agrarian land continued until the 1940s and 1950s, when the country entered a period of accelerated urbanization as a result of the policy of import substitution, which gave great impetus to the development of manufacturing processes and as a consequence the creation of urban employment. The prospect of improving conditions for survival, added to the lack of rural productivity, stimulated the continual influx of people into the cities, and since then the *ejido* and communal lands have been the favoured areas for urban expansion, both authorized, and, to a greater extent, unauthorized.

Among the constant obstacles we are faced with in Mexico is the conflict between the agrarian

**5** Eduardo Ramirez Favela, 'Origenes, mediciòn, mecanismos de captura y aplicación de plus-valia', in Iracheta and Smolka, **Los Pobres de la Ciudad y la Tierra** (Mexico: Ed. Lincoln Institute of Land Policy and El Colegio Mexiquense, 2000), p. 198.
**6** Antonio Azuela, **La Ciudad, la Propiedad y el Derecho** (Mexico: El Colegio de México, 1989), pp. 221-31.

and urban views, the first being concerned with upholding the rights of the land-owning groups (*ejidatarios* and *comuneros*), who are seen as dispossessed and mistreated, and the second focusing on offering alternative settlement options to the large numbers of migrants who are living illegally on these lands.

In 1993, during the administration of Carlos Salinas, in keeping with the neoliberal views fashionable at the time, article 27 of the Constitution and the Agrarian Law that emerged from it were modified, granting the collective landowners, *ejidatarios* and *comuneros* the opportunity to have their land freely at their disposal and thus incorporate it directly into the property market. Prior to this modification agrarian land was nonseizable, imprescriptible and inalienable, which meant that it was prohibited from participating in the property market, in order to prevent the *ejido* members from losing their land, which gave them guaranteed security and income, and to stop the land from being concentrated again in the hands of a few owners. By that time the sale and purchase of *ejido* lands in the unauthorized market was widespread and in the 1970s the Commission for the Regularization of Land Ownership was established, charged with bringing about the expropriation of illegally occupied *ejidos* and community-held lands in order to give ownership titles to their occupiers.

After 1993 *ejidatarios* and *comuneros* took part freely in the market and the expropriations ceased to be relevant, which explains the increase in commercial value of the *ejido* lands neighbouring the cities, and also the greater diffusion of both new housing developments and unauthorized settlements always looking for the lowest land prices. It is these empowered players, together with an aggressive real-estate business class which also grew from the same neoliberal policies, who have generated a large-scale process of land speculation, which is reflected in the scattered growth around the urban periphery on the fringe of urban development plans or in their absence.

An additional factor, which brings even more complexity to the situation, originates in the constitutional stipulations that grant extensive powers to municipal authorities regarding the authorization of land usage and in general all activities inherent to urban management, regardless of their technical and organizational abilities, ignoring both the regional disparities and historical, social, economic and territorial diversity in the structure of Mexican municipalities.

The outcome is diametrically opposed to the compact city that was needed, one in which diverse activities and social groups mix and where the richness of the components produces a synergy that should translate into well-being, freedom of movement and efficient provision of public services, as well as reduced distances for transport, resulting in fuel savings and decreased pollution.

The *ejido* landowning groups have become real estate experts; the construction companies and developers have improved efficiency and greatly increased their profits and the authorities have relaxed the regulations and control of the processes. Corruption has become the means which permits a balance between the interests of the urban players, and the low-income population have to pay the price of the process, which for them implies longer travel times, higher costs of transportation and urban services, reduced living space, less public safety, fewer employment opportunities, greater distances to travel and inferior quality of education and health services.

In this environment urban planning is perceived as a limiting factor that impedes the growth of business, opposes market forces and puts the freedom of the individual at risk. We are faced with a short-term vision whose only parameter for evaluation is the maximization of profits, and which assumes that medium and long-term development is the responsibility of local authorities, who have neither sufficient training, resources nor interest in following up procedures and guaranteeing the minimum conditions of governability.

Returning to our central theme, and following on from the previous perspective, it should be pointed out that neither of the two ways in which urban expansion in Mexico has developed offers acceptable results for human coexistence, and in neither case is the issue of the absence of *city* resolved. So the following questions arise: Which is the best way for our cities to grow? How can the inhabitants' real needs be met? The starting point should be finding a solution to the lack of a *city project*, this being understood as a failure to create a vision of the physical, social and economic dimensions of a sustainable future, a future which offers conditions for a more equal coexistence and opportunities for a better quality of life for the majority.

It is important not to forget the assessment of recent experience and investigation into the two forms of Mexican land occupation, which appear to correspond to the characteristics of a polarized society, where the values of coexistence, cohesion, identity, and feeling of belonging have ceased to be a priority and have been replaced with others, such as the need to own property, competing in order to 'get ahead', and self-imposed segregation in the interests of so-called personal safety.

The main urban problem then lies not simply in the manner in which land is occupied, but in how to solve the structural issues within society, the economy and the environment. These problems generate conflict and social deficiency, whose effects can be observed in the unauthorized settlements as well as in the institutionally built housing developments, both of which are widely dispersed, lack security, facilities and infrastructure, have inadequate living space and insufficient basic services, and suffer social segregation. These areas are forcing the urban boundaries and in some cases precipitating future uncontrollable urbanization, which together with other urban conflicts is the result of current urban expansion in Mexican cities.

## Authorized and unauthorized urban expansion: problem or a solution?

Let us examine more closely the solutions that are offered by the institutions in order to avoid unauthorized settlement of land. The national lending institutions for housing, principally INFONAVIT (National Workers' Housing Fund) and FOVISSTE (Housing Fund for State Workers) offer credit to their contributors so they may purchase housing, having established certain regulations with regard to size of property and sale price to which those businesses interested in producing the housing must adhere.

About ten large construction companies and developers have developed within this framework, whose efficiency and production capacity have increased dramatically. Each one produces between 10,000 and 50,000 houses per year, thus controlling the lion's share of the market. They begin their operation based on the parameters established regarding property size and sale price, which leaves as the only variable the optimization of land price, which explains why these housing developments are situated ever further away from urban areas; the extraordinary profits stem from land speculation, since the land is acquired as low-quality farmland, and is then 'processed' with the local authorities to authorize a change in land use. Once this is obtained, generally involving corrupt methods, the price of the land multiplies between eight and ten times its original purchase price.

Being situated so far away from urban centres not only implies increased transportation costs and more time daily spent travelling to and from work, school and health facilities, but also means a shortage of the services and equipment which over time would normally become the focal elements of cities. These housing developments are self-segregated walled complexes comprising thousands, sometimes tens of thousands of identical houses, which are not integrated into the urban social fabric and can only be used for housing purposes. One peculiarity of these locations is that generally speaking they are situated on productive agricultural or forested land, which, in addition to providing a source of economic survival for present and future settlers, also legally belongs to the cooperative and communal landholders. In short, the location of these housing complexes as part of the formal solution in fact answers exclusively to the price of the land, which can be acquired without overstepping the limits of the regulations set out by the credit institution, thereby guaranteeing significant profits.

By making these offers the formal housing market neglects the fact that the buyers have no guarantee that they will keep their jobs for the duration of their commitment to pay back the housing loan. Consequently, as Mexico has now been facing economic crisis for more than 20 years, if a worker loses his job he automatically loses his ability to pay back his loan. Unfortunately there are no studies available with which to gauge the number of homes that have been abandoned by buyers, but during the census of 2000, among housing developments, out of 22 million houses it was reported that 4.5 million were uninhabited. Some of these were surplus houses built by the construction companies that the developers were unable to sell as they exceeded demand, but many were also abandoned for various other reasons, and we now have a growing number of widespread uninhabited houses, while at the same time, an increase in unauthorized housing.[7]

Faced with this situation, and with the aim of reversing the abandonment and shortcomings occurring in the authorized housing development market, a cross-institutional group has been established, representing federal urban development, housing and environmental authorities as well as financial institutions and housing loan authorities. Their goal is to support the DUIS (Integral Sustainable Urban Developments) through federal regulations which facilitate the assessment of projects put forward by developers before they are approved.[8] This would appear to be an interesting step forward; however it loses its impact once we take into account the fact that if the developers are presenting their projects, it means that they have already acquired the land and therefore the location is no longer a point of discussion.

Recently the Metropolitan Studies Programme of the Universidad Autónoma Metropolitana (UAM) has conducted many studies supported by the Secretary for Social Development (SEDESOL). Two of the studies, entitled 'Costs and benefits for low income families of the authorized and unauthorized property markets'[9] and 'Study of urban and social integration during the recent expansion of Mexican cities, 1996-2006',[10] explore the characteristics of the ways in which the country's housing needs are met, and recognize the complications of the daily impact created by both housing situations.

Among the most significant findings of the studies, the fact that stands out is that for both types of housing projects, authorized and unauthorized, the location of the developments is in outlying areas, separated from the established urban centres. This distance, as previously mentioned, is owing to the price of land and not as a result of rigorously analysed, fair and planned urbanization or to the application of current urban development plans.

---

**7** Roberto Eibenschutz and Rino Torres, **La Producción Social de la Vivienda en México** (Mexico: SEDESOL, CONAFOVI, CONACYT, 2006).

**8** The participating public institutions, instances and organs are: Secretary for Social Development (SEDESOL), National Housing Commission (CONAVI), Secretary of the Treasury and Public Credit (SHCP), Secretary of the Environment and Natural Resources (SEMARNAT), Federal Mortgage Society (SHF), National Public Works Bank (BANOBRAS), Secretary of the Economy (SE).

**9** Roberto Eibenschutz and Pablo Benlliure, **Costos y Beneficios de los Mercados Formal e Informal de Suelo para Familias con Bajos Ingresos** (Mexico: Porrúa, UAM, SEDESOL, 2009).

**10** Roberto Eibenschutz and Carlos Goya, **Estudio de la Integración Urbana y Social en la Expansión Reciente de las Ciudades en México, 1996-2006** (Mexico: Porrúa, UAM, SEDESOL. 2009), p. 26.

According to a valid statistical sample for the National Urban System (SUN),[11] applied to 3,000 families in 100 housing developments built between 1996 and 2006 in 21 of the 396 SUN cities, the authorized housing solution has severe problems, as perceived by those who live in these complexes.

Within the process of land occupation, the location favours the landowners (*ejido* members, *comuneros* and small landowners) and the developers, and is detrimental to the house-buyer, obliging him to live in places from where it is extremely complicated to travel to and from places of employment and education.

- By building these large housing developments in stages over a long period the need for facilities, services and infrastructure adequate for the total number of dwellings is not taken into consideration. Instead, only the indispensable facilities as per the regulations for each stage are taken into account.
- The distances between the housing developments and the cities on which they depend are a cause of insecurity for the inhabitants, as they feel isolated from their social networks.
- The type of housing offered is legal, but unsafe. The houses themselves are unsturdy and deteriorate very rapidly thanks to the low-quality construction materials used, and lack of maintenance.
- The buyer is committed to a period of more than twenty years in which to complete the house payments, and from the beginning complaints arise as to the distance from the city and the transportation costs this implies, while at the same time the house begins to require remodelling due to its small size.
- The dynamics of urbanization leave planning and urban regulations out of the picture. Correct location studies are substituted for corrupt procedures which allow the issue of permits and licenses.
- The profits from these housing developments are distributed among the landowners (*ejidatarios*, *comuneros* or small landowners), the developers, who obtain the change in land use and sell the houses, and the surrounding landowners who gain from the increase in land value generated by the development.

The images included at the end of the article [see figs 2, 3, 4 and 5] correspond to some of the developments studied and illustrate the points made above.
The impact of these developments on the inhabitants' living conditions is evident, and there is an unquantified tendency to abandon acquired housing. Sometimes the owners return to their previous dwellings, which are in deplorable overcrowded and unsanitary conditions, leaving the houses in the developments empty, some structurally damaged, which results in unoccupied and isolated urbanizations.

In the case of unauthorized settlements, the situation is not too different [see fig. 6]. The process begins with an offer for the sale of the land, as there is a large demand for housing from low-income families who generally work in the informal or unauthorized sector and do not have access to the housing programmes offered by the institutions. According to the study 'Costs and benefits for low income families of the authorized and unauthorized property markets',[12] the owners define the price of the land – the study showed that they are well aware of their urban situation, for example that their land should not be developed due to its environmental value – and they develop mechanisms parallel to those in the 'formal' process, managing loans, payment periods of five to ten years, but in contrast to the institutional developments, they offer only the land with no building nor services, facilities or infrastructure. The inhabitants themselves have to act as political agents with the government authorities and they manage, over time, to urbanize their settlements, which strengthens the social networks that have historically been used as a means of control by the national political system.

In contrast to the authorized developments, in this type of unauthorized settlement, while equally inadequate and distanced from the city, without services or legal foundation, it is the land that is purchased rather than the house, and through existing social networks, the inhabitants create their own urban conditions with little or no help from government authorities. They work together to integrate into the nearby urban centres, plan road systems, and introduce basic services and after this is achieved, the authorities, under pressure from the inhabitants, come and install the facilities and services.

Another relevant point to be made is that the inhabitants do not feel isolated from the urban centres. In general they do not share the view of what is 'formal', authorized and 'informal' or unauthorized within the urban context. For them, from the moment they make a payment for the land and occupy it, they consider themselves part of the urban fabric, a feeling that grows stronger over time and which friends and family are invited to also be a part of.

Although, of the two urban expansion scenarios studied, unauthorized urbanizations appear to create more favourable conditions for society, in reality they do not, since both types of expansion bring conflict to the affected population and also to the surrounding society which resents the impact this expansion has on transport, traffic congestion, air pollution, and above all on the fragmentation of the city and the resulting loss of conditions for governance.

Graph 1 [see fig. 7] shows percentages attributable to the different factors affecting land price, according to the information obtained from the eight cities studied. The difference in entry price in the unauthorized land ($49.10 per m²) and the price obtained using the residual method in the authorized market ($602.00 per m²) should be noted. Although the difference at the end of the

**11** The National Urban System (SUN) is made up of the 396 cities in the country with more than 15,000 inhabitants, in which more than 70% of the population is concentrated. The remaining 30% is located in the almost 200,000 localities of less than 15,000 inhabitants, the vast majority of which are small hamlets dispersed throughout the country. Federal Government, SEDESOL, Federal Mortgage Society, BANOBRAS, CONAVI, FOVISSTE and FONATUR are components of the Integral Urban Sustainable Developments.
**12** See Roberto Eibenschutz and Pablo Benlliure (2009), **Costos y Beneficios.**

period studied is relatively small (from $490 to $602), the important point is that in the unauthorized market, the inhabitants have access to the land before it is affected by price increase factors, whereas in order to gain access to the authorized land people must wait until the process of price increase is complete.

When analysing the data it is worth remembering the statement made by Alberto Rébora who, in his doctoral work, takes up Morales' theme,[13] suggesting that 'the assumptions about the workings of the neoclassic land markets are not valid, because the land market is not perfect.... price is generated by demand.'[14]

**Some solutions**    Given the information presented here, it would be wrong to suppose that there is no government response. What is clear is that what has been done up until now is inadequate. There are contradictions between the authorities in charge of the territory, a property market lacking in means of control, unspecific and unsanctioned policies and regulations, an excessive voracity on the part of the developers, a culture of informality which is repeated among the settlers, and a permissive attitude from the authorities, who lack the necessary tools to be able to offer legal settlement options to the low-income population and are easy prey for the conflicting interested parties, who find a point of balance through various forms of corruption. In addition, there are also fragile environmental beliefs that permit settlements and developments of both types on environmentally valuable land.

Among the measures that could be used to confront the current situation are the following, all of which require strong political and social support if they are to be put into practice:
• Plan the city and build the basic infrastructure in advance, which will always work out cheaper, both socially and economically.
• Make use of the existing urban land available, offering land and housing alternatives for the low-income population, through densification, saturation and improvement incentives.
• Make legally available 'developable lots' at accessible prices and forms of payment to the low-income population.
• Promote sustainable development in conservation areas, particularly at the edge of urban zones, with productive uses such as tourism, farming, forestry, as well as scientific, sporting and recreational uses, to strengthen these lands' environmental and economic value and prevent them from being wrongly used.
• Incorporate land into the market through systematic revision of urban development plans and structured promotion of provision declarations when dealing with new population settlements.
• Redefine public policy with regard to irregular settlements. Zero new settlements, zero growth, zero regularization and zero public finding for urban

services in these areas.
- Apply property taxes as a tool of public policy; land price appreciation as payment for the land's expected development.
- Implement and certify regulations to determine the sustainability of new areas for urban use and housing development.
- Apply subsidies for the purchase of the most-needed land/housing, focusing on the size, the urban area and the national situation.

Putting these measures into practice implies overcoming the obstacles which stand in their way. Among these must be mentioned the little relevance given in the political arena to the subject of urban development, in a combination of ignorance and rejection of planning, which is considered as going against the vision of the state as facilitator of private investment. From this stems the lack of decisiveness to intervene more aggressively in the urban land market, which requires revising land taxation and establishing new methods of induction and control. Overcoming this situation implies a huge training programme for public officials at three levels of government: federal, state and municipal, and also for legislative and judicial authorities, as well as enforcing severe punitive measures for corruption.

Social participation must involve overcoming illegal leadership and the paternalism exercised by the political parties, in order to achieve an organization capable of understanding and defending the collective interest above those of a single group or individual. In other words, they must move on from protest to proposal, asserting not only their rights but also their obligations and responsibilities.

The role of academics in this situation can be a pivotal link between the different players, insofar as the social function of knowledge is understood.

13 Carlos Morales, **Políticas de Suelo Urbano, Accesibilidad a los Pobres y Recuperación de Plusvalías** (Mexico: LILP, 2005).
14 Alberto Rébora, **Bases Institucionales de la Gestión Urbana en México: un análisis comparativo internacional** (México: UNAM, 2009), p. 33.

| Total Population I 1940-1970 | | | |
|---|---|---|---|
| National Total | Mexico City | Guadalajara | Monterrey |
| 1940: 3 927 694 | 1 559 782 | 240 721 | 190 128 |
| 1950: 7 209 528 | 2 872 334 / DF & EdoMex | 401 283 | 354 114 |
| 1960: 13 511 717 | 4 993 871 / ZMCM | 867 035 / ZMG | 695 504 / ZMM |
| 1970: 22 730 651 | 8 623 157 / ZMCM | 1 480 472 / ZMG | 1 242 558 / ZMM |

[1]

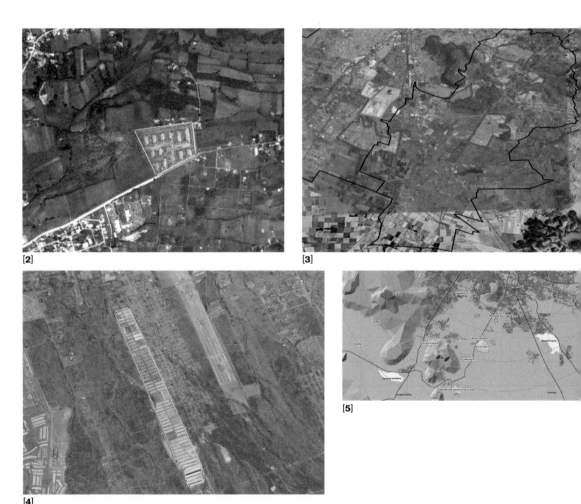

[2]

[3]

[4]

[5]

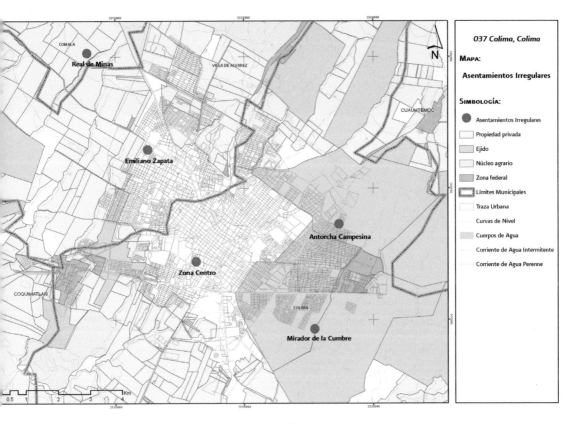

037 Colima, Colima

**MAPA:**

**Asentamientos Irregulares**

**SIMBOLOGÍA:**

⬤ Asentamientos Irregulares

☐ Propiedad privada

☐ Ejido

☐ Núcleo agrario

☐ Zona federal

Límites Municipales

Traza Urbana

Curvas de Nivel

Cuerpos de Agua

Corriente de Agua Intermitente

Corriente de Agua Perenne

COMALA

Real de Minas

VILLA DE ALVAREZ

CUAUHTEMOC

Emiliano Zapata

Antorcha Campesina

Zona Centro

COQUIMATLAN

COLIMA

Mirador de la Cumbre

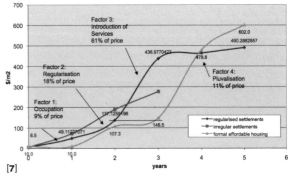

[7]

ments studied. The dotted circles are concentric, every 5 kilometres. There is clearly no connection nor infrastructure linking the developments to the city. Extensive areas of land in the vicinity of the developments, some as far out as 25 kilometres from the city centre, are open to urban speculation.

6  Location of five unauthorised settlements in Colima.

7  Formation of land price for formal (authorised) and informal (unauthorised) markets. Source: Eibenschutz, R. and P. Benlliure (2009), 'Costs and benefits for low income families of the authorised and unauthorised property markets'.

housing developments, randomly located over the terrain, with no structure linking them either to each other or to the urban municipal area. The size of the developments surpasses by far the operational capacity of the municipality to provide and maintain urban services.

4  Conjunto Loma Linda, Saltillo, Mexico. Total number of houses at time of study: 1,798. This image shows a development located on land which clearly was previously used for agricultural purposes. After obtaining the change in land use a housing development is built adapting to the shape of the terrain, but with no link to its surroundings.

5  Metropolitan Zone of Guadalajara. This image shows the urban area of the metropolitan zone, and the location of the housing develop-

tal population 1940-1970. Source: a, Gustavo, 2005.

llas San Miguel, Oaxaca, Mexico. Total es at time of study: 1,081.

is image is a high-density urban development in a rural zone, with no relation to the unding land use. It is self-segregated, no link to the road network, and controlled only one point of access.

ineral de la Reforma Municipality, Hidalgo e The Municipality of Mineral de la Reforma small municipal conurbation of the city of uca, the capital of the state of Hidalgo. As e observed, the municipal area, outlined ack, is very small and only contains a few settlements. The shapes shown in orange d lines correspond to recently approved

# Social Housing in Mexico: The Commodification and Peripheral Growth of the City

**Beatriz García Peralta**[I]

In Mexico today (2010), virtually half the population lives in poverty. Thus, 47.4% are unable to meet the most basic food, health, housing, education and public transport needs,[2] even if they assign their entire income to this. In principle, all these needs should be fulfilled. Guaranteeing social housing in areas with adequate urban services could help provide access to better opportunities for education and work, in order to meet other basic needs. This chapter looks at how – through an array of social housing programmes – various Mexican government administrations have attempted to solve this serious socio-economic and urban problem, while pointing out the obstacles the system faces in achieving this. Since the 1960s, as a result of policies promoted by the Alliance for Progress,[3] social housing was privatized, making it extremely difficult for the majority of the Mexican population to purchase homes. From the 1990s onwards, changes in Mexican economic and housing policy as well as proposals from multilateral organizations – through deregulation and privatization – facilitated access to the crucial resources of the workers' housing fund and large expanses of agricultural land. This encouraged the construction of large complexes of thousands of 'social' dwellings disconnected from the urban fabric, services and sources of work. However, although the various housing projects fail to meet the dwelling needs of most of the working population, they have been important to the development of the capitalist sector of housing production and the financial sector, which had led to the de-structuring of cities.

**First undertakings**    The 1910 Mexican Revolution led to profound changes in the political and legal structure of society and marked a radically new perspective for state intervention.[4] During the years immediately following the end of the Revolution, few possibilities existed in the country to build a modern nation. Although the legal basis was established for the modernization of the country's social and economic structure – particularly agricultural reform – , the right to collective labour contracts and to strike, these major aspects point out just some of the principles on which the new country would be constructed. However, from the 1920s onwards, they were only partially implemented within the framework of the institutions responsible for the new forms of social and state organization. The 1940s constituted a watershed between a rural society and the nascent urban society. The industrial sector was strengthened, and public policy oriented to further its growth through the construction of infrastructure and public works, which supported the consolidation of the national construction sector's relationship with the state and coincided with the emergence of the first major wave of the growth of labour associations. Taken as a whole, the process can be characterized by contradictions between social revolutionary rhetoric and the efforts regarding the modernization of the Mexican State to develop the structure of the country's capitalist economy, in order to meet the demands of the emerging industrial sector on the one hand and the needs of its own impoverished population on the other.

**1** This paper was produced during a research stay in Berlin in Autumn 2010, with the support of the Programa de Apoyos para la Superación del Personal Académico de la UNAM (PASPA).
**2** Consejo Nacional para la Evaluación de la Política Social (Coneval), 'Evolución de la Pobreza en México 2009', available online from: <www.coneval.gob.mx/contenido/med_pobreza/3967. pdf> [last accessed September 10, 2010].
**3** Alliance for Progress was a U.S. programme of economic and social assistance for Latin America with a 20 billion dollar loan, made between 1961 and 1970.
**4** The rise of the new middle class in Mexico is due partly to social policies in the fields of education and health and the revolutionary conception that recognized cultural diversity.

The various governments delegated the satisfaction of housing needs to society and individual economic conditions. Resources were restricted to providing housing for some of the workers in the government sector. This initial policy led to the construction of two multi-family housing complexes providing rented accommodation; as examples of the modernist architecture of the 1950s in Mexico City: the *Miguel Alemán* complex [fig. 1] and the *Benito Juárez* complex (later demolished due to damage caused by the 1985 earthquake) [fig. 2]. Although the housing supply was insufficient to meet demand, it provided new proposals for the urban fabric, which included green areas, sports infrastructure and urban services. It is important to mention two other housing projects from the 1960s: the *Independencia* housing unit, designed for workers from the public health sector and the *Tlatelolco* complex, the link between rented and privately-owned accommodation. Housing complexes at the time, then, were characterized by being the result of a search for new architectural and urban alternatives to house state workers.

## From social rented accommodation to private property

The 1960s were characterized by an increase in the direct participation of the state as an economic agent and as a controller, planner and regulator of the economic, financial and social spheres at the national level. These years were also known as Mexico's period of sustained growth, the main feature being sustained economic growth accompanied by stable prices, and an increase in average incomes, which in turn drove the demand for goods and services. Between 1959 and 1970, the country experienced unprecedented levels of urban population growth, particularly in the main cities: Mexico City (Federal District and neighbouring municipalities in the State of Mexico), Guadalajara and Monterrey.[5] Population growth throughout the period increased the demand for urban land, basic services, infrastructure and housing. As far as state housing actions are concerned, these were usually carried out through the complementary programmes of finance development institutions or social security institutions,[6] and were limited in scope and unable to meet the growing demand. Access to land for housing and finished housing located in the main urban areas built by the emerging private investors was severely restricted for the unemployed, under-employed and low-income groups, which together make up a significant portion of the urban population. New settlements began to emerge throughout the city, built by the social production methods used by low-income groups; more often than not, they were frequently located on land that was unsuitable for urbanization and often lacked infrastructure and urban services.

In 1961, President Kennedy launched the Alliance for Progress (Alpro). One of its main objectives was to block ideas in the region inspired by the triumph of the Cuban Revolution by attempting to promote economic improvements with an emphasis on supporting private property, even in social housing. The Alpro was signed in Punta del Este, Uruguay, by the representatives of Latin American governments, with the exception of Cuba. The negative repercussions this programme would have on Latin America's economic development were predicted by the then Cuban Minister of Economy (Ernesto 'Che' Guevara) and confirmed by the overwhelming economic haemorrhage caused by this devious loan disguised as economic aid. In a speech given at the University of Montevideo in 1967, Salvador Allende mentioned important data, such as the reduction of Latin American exports, the profits of US firms in the zone and the amount of debt payment.[7] As a result of the housing assistance programmes supported by the Alliance for Progress, incipient social rented accommodation programmes were cancelled and replaced by broad-ranging 'privately-owned social housing'.

The 'Nonoalco Tlatelolco' complex [fig.3], with its paradigmatic history,[8] embodied the transition from social rented accommodation to private property. Housing beneficiaries received a certificate of participation instead of a property deed. This housing unit had 15,000 dwellings, distributed among multi-family buildings of varying heights, with a density of a thousand inhabitants per hectare, 75% green areas and buildings fully equipped with all services. It was originally designed to provide housing for state workers and replace the precarious dwellings in the area. This last goal was never achieved, since it took place when the type of ownership of social housing was being rethought. To this end, the population living in the area was evicted with the promise that they would receive new housing there or be relocated. Nowadays this would be called a process of savage gentrification, although the process took place years before the term was coined, and on a larger scale. It was therefore a 'tlatelolcalization', testimonies of which can be heard on YouTube.[9]

This environment: sustained economic growth, Alpro principles and the impulse given to modern housing projects, served as fertile soil for the founding of the Housing Finance Programme (PFV), run by the Operating and Bank Discounts on Housing Fund (Fovi) in 1963; it also marked the beginning of large-scale private housing production for the salaried working class. The programme obtained its resources from a compulsory charge levied on banking institutions for resources they had obtained from public savings. A small initial financial loan was also received from the Inter-American Development Bank (IDB). In terms of income re-distribution, the combination of public and private capital operated by Fovi under the PFV had the perverse effect of protecting higher income groups rather than those on lower salary scales. However, Mexico's economic and political ups and downs – along with the systems established for the granting and the repayment

**5** Gustavo Garza, **La urbanización de México en el Siglo XX** (México: El Colegio de México, 2003).

**6** Banco Hipotecario Urbano y de Obras Públicas (Banhuopsa), the Civil Pensions Department, the Mexican Social Security Institute, (IMSS) and the National Housing Institute (INV).

**7** Salvador Allende, 'Critica a la Alianza para el Progreso: Discurso en la Universidad de Montevideo, 1967'. Archivo Salvador Allende available online: www.salvador-allende.cl/Documentos/1950/69/Critica%20a%20la%20Alianza%20para%20el%20Progreso.pdfCriticaAlianzaparaelProgreso.pdf> [accessed September 10, 2010]

**8** The construction began in 1960. In 1968 Tlatelolco was the scene of the killing of students and during the 1985 earthquake, the Nuevo León building collapsed. This type of architecture was also rejected by some Mexican architects.

**9** Nonoalco Tlatelolco, Mexico on YouTube, available online: www.youtube.com/watch?v=PKOYu5duu9Q> [accessed September 10, 2010].

of loans – led to the constant displacement of credits towards the higher paid sections of the manual workforce, independent professions and small businessmen. This led to a continuous trend to reduce the social coverage of the programme.

For the first time, state intervention guaranteed access to financial resources, which was a major factor that led to the emergence of a new agent on the housing production scene: the real estate promotion sector. Social housing construction companies emerged as a result of the financial support provided by the programme through the building of housing estates, some of which were on a large scale. These estates sometimes sought new design types that did not always consider the customs of the population intended to live in them. For example, some of the housing projects did away with the traditional feature whereby an area of the home is designated for hanging out the laundry.

## Social housing provision for workers: a (long) unfulfilled social right
In 1970, Mexico's urban population exceeded the rural population by a ratio of 58.7:41.3 respectively. Moreover, urban expansion mainly took place on the outskirts of the country's three largest cities. In 1972, a reform was carried out to implement part of employers' constitutional obligations established in 1917 regarding housing provision for workers. This reform specified that 5% of registered workers' salaries must be placed in 'solidarity' savings funds.[10] The latter were administered by three National Workers' Housing Funds (National Housing Funds for workers in private firms, state companies and the armed forces). The National Funding Institute for Workers' Housing (Infonavit) soon became the largest housing financing agency, since it had the highest number of affiliated members (private sector workers), meaning that it handled the greatest amount of money and had the capacity to finance more dwellings than any other institution in the country. One of its objectives was to establish itself as a support fund, in which the contributions of workers with the highest income would facilitate access to credit for those with the lowest income; in other words – the poorest workers.

The institution's initial idea of raffling dwellings in a transparent fashion in order to destroy the union's power, failed due to mistakes made in housing assignment as well as the vested interests of private sector agents, civil servants, and trade union leaders comprising Infonavit's tripartite commissions. After 1976, the distribution of housing loans was controlled through coordination mechanisms with trade unions and private sector companies that made up the fund. They took advantage of the situation and developed their own construction companies. This mechanism was prone to corruption due to the institution's economic and political power, closely linked to growing labour associations that had developed clientelistic relations, which ensured that every loan granted secured a vote for the 'right' political party.[11]

Infonavit invested workers' savings in purchasing urban land and the construction of large housing estates with hundreds of units sold to low and middle-income workers. In the beginning, these settlements followed modernist architectural typologies located in urban areas with a wide range of services. Early housing complexes were architecturally sound, with an area of approximately 75 square metres. They were built under the slogan 'Make a city' – in other words, with the necessary urban requirements. Due to political clientelism, however, as well as high inflation rates, the financial conditions were not properly examined. Those purchasing houses in 1987 paid 4% interest, when the inflation rate was 147%. This benefited those who were given housing and paid very little for it, while those that had failed to obtain housing lost the purchasing power of their savings. As a result, the original aim of providing housing to lower-income workers, which they would otherwise be unable to afford, was only marginally achieved. However, it should be acknowledged that until the 1980s, the lower-income salaried population's housing needs were at least partly met.

The rising price of urban land led to the construction of housing complexes in increasingly remote areas. The mainly row and court houses of Mexican cities were supplemented by multi-storey buildings. Traditional housing concepts embodied the need for security, in a threatening urban context, typically with a drastic separation between private and public space. The new settlements lacked this quality. Openness clashed with the need for security. This was particularly a problem for the relationship between ground-floor apartments and their surroundings, and entrances to buildings. Additionally, apartments were smaller and the lack of safe parking space led people to alter the surroundings of the blocks, through fences, garage buildings (sometimes, only steel cages).

## Crisis, financial deregulation and commodification of housing
The consolidation of the changes to Mexico's economic model that began in the late 1980s led to the intensification of efforts to increase the country's competitive position in international markets, which included proposals for the housing sector. In fact, the development of the housing sector was an essential part of the modernizing project for the Mexican economy during the early years of the country's new market approach. During this decade, social housing disappeared from political rhetoric.

This meant that the Mexican state rather than serving as a guarantor for solving the housing problem brazenly adopted the neoliberal model, whose economic vision sought to reduce government presence by expecting the market to distribute resources in keeping with the efficiency and productivity of the various economic sectors.

---

10  This was possible due to the reforms to Article 123 of the Constitution and to the Federal Labour Law (articles 136 to 153), under which such contribution was set forth.
11  Beatriz Garcia y Manuel Perló, 'Estado, sindicalismo oficial y políticas habitacionales: análisis de una década del Infonavit', in **El Obrero Mexicano. Condiciones de Trabajo 2** (México: Siglo XXI Editores, 1984).

This new approach by official rhetoric shifted the responsibility for providing housing to the business and social sector. For many people, this meant the end of a long unfulfilled promise. Although the previous system had not achieved its aim of substantially contributing to increasing housing for the working class, this aim was now ruled out. The state formally gave up including all social classes in its housing programmes, focusing instead on households that fitted into the credit schemes offered by market-oriented financial institutions.

The economic crisis and the rapid growth of external debt increased Mexico's financial dependence on the International Monetary Fund (IMF) and the World Bank (WB) which, in the last instance, promoted, designed, financed and controlled structural adjustments, as well as the institutional and organizational reforms in every sphere of economic life. The various loans received from the World Bank conditioned Mexican housing policy. The change in the economic development model – focused on free trade, financial deregulation, market orientation, as well as increased democracy and transparency – had a major impact on housing policy. As a result, most subsidies for social housing were eliminated; new funding methods and conditions for granting loans were designed; banks were no longer forced to contribute resources to low-income housing; the promotion and defence of property rights were strengthened; and new private financial intermediaries for the housing sector emerged. With this type of economic focus in all state policies, it is assumed that the market is the most efficient agent for distributing economic resources. Official Mexican rhetoric therefore sought to improve supply and demand and to remove obstacles to its establishment of policy priorities; to reinforce the financial role played by housing institutions; and to create selection mechanisms whereby the population that received a loan from the housing finance organizations could freely select the home it wished to buy on the market.

The changes imposed by the economic development model on the federal organization with the greatest financial resources in the housing sector, expressed themselves in a change of the law governing Infonavit in 1992, with the aim of promoting free-market criteria in order to improve the institution's efficiency, put an end to clientelistic practices and increase loan recovery rates. Infonavit – which had formerly purchased land and determined the location, architecture, price and target group of its investments – was turned into a purely financial, semi-state institution. One of the main goals of Infonavit was to provide a Soft Loan Fund through which the contributions of workers with the highest incomes would facilitate access to credit for the neediest groups. However, in 1992, the Institute lost one of its basic foci and was gradually transformed into a source of funds for workers with medium and medium-high incomes, now largely financed by the savings fund of a majority with lower incomes that had virtually no access to credits. However, this is one of the perverse effects of this policy.

Despite government rhetoric restricting housing institutions to acting within a purely financial role, their participation included actually facilitating the opening up of the market to the financial sector and foreign firms. Infonavit sold its territorial reserves in conveniently located urban zones because – according to purely commercial criteria – they should not be assigned for building social housing. Conversely, developers protected by the changes made to Article 27 of the Constitution, allowing communally-owned (*ejido*) agrarian land to be sold on the free market in the country, acquired millions of square metres of land on the edges of the country's main cities. The huge demand for land led to an increase in land prices and, therefore, to greater inequity. Firms can negotiate payment according to the progress of sales and can enter into commercial agreements, which private purchasers cannot. Moreover, although land prices have increased, firms usually obtain extraordinary profits in this area.

## Housing developers: the main beneficiaries of housing policy

The early 1990s seemed to confirm some of the benefits of the new housing policy. Private banks responded to deregulation by providing housing loans. Construction firms actively participated in public bids for the construction of social housing, and a larger number of houses were built with the participation of the private sector. This situation did not last long, since conditions were significantly altered by the financial crisis that took place at the end of 1994. From 1995 onwards, the only financial resources for the individualization of credits were largely provided by Infonavit and to a lesser extent by Fovi, which were crucial to the growth and consolidation of large housing developers as well as to the firms that struggled to adapt to the new conditions. Neither private banking nor capitalist developers contributed to the growth of the mortgage system through their own resources. In other words, unlike industrialized countries (in which, during the period of the welfare state, one sector was supported by the state and the other produced housing for the market with private, long-term resources and financing), in Mexico, capitalist housing construction firms have depended largely on resources administered and/or funded by public organizations.

As a consequence, restraint in public spending (combined with the financial crisis of 1995) had an impact on the construction sector – producing a sharp drop of 28.8% in GDP terms. However, the housing sector was not affected, as we found by analysing the only survey that provides access to information by construction firms during the period from 1995 to 2001. Due to their restricted classification, these data are not available in the Mexican Chamber of Construction (CMIC) or the National Institute of Geography and Statistic (INEGI). The indicator chosen was the amount of sales, by branch: housing, urbanization, environmental engineering, industrial works, road links and others. The sales of firms not involved in housing production stagnated from 1995 onwards, recovering in 1998 only to fall drastically from that year onwards. Sales of firms in the housing sector showed a growth curve from 1995 onwards, with a slight drop in 2001 caused by the transition of government [see fig. 4]. Growth was primarily due to Infonavit resources, since during that period, banks stopped providing mortgage credits. As one can see from figures 5 and 6, housing development firms joined the 'major leagues' as the two housing development firms (GEO Corporation and ARA) occupied third and fourth place, respectively.[12] This situation was consolidated during the National Action Party (PAN) administrations. In terms of quantity, the revised system of semi-state housing production was hailed by multilateral international organizations, financing firms, promoters and construction firms as being very successful. As a result, in 2008 a new 1.01 billion dollar loan from the WB and granted by the Mexican government was approved for the Federal Mortgage Society (SHF) created in 2002 (Fovi's successor), to develop the private housing financing market. It was designed to provide long-term credits in charge of specialized financial intermediaries (Sofoles) established in 1995, to expand the mortgage market for 'low-income groups' (those earning less than six minimum salaries);[13] the outcome being 'more of the same' [see fig. 7].

## An (im)possible city

The urban sprawl of the Metropolitan Area of Mexico City (MAMC) comprises 16 boroughs in the Federal District, which includes the city centre, 60 municipalities in the State of Mexico and one in the State of Hidalgo. It houses over 19.2 million inhabitants, 19% of the country's population, in an area of nearly 2,000 square kilometres with a density of 170.7 inhabitants per hectare. In 2000, it had 4.2 million dwellings whose distribution, according to census data, was as follows: 17% located in upper-middle and upper class areas; 39% in middle class areas; and 44% in lower class areas.[14]

The city was prey to financial market forces, which made it almost impossible for local governments to intervene effectively in planning the location of housing developments in the urban fabric. The state's opportunity to address the blatant lack of structure and functionality of Mexican cities (particularly Mexico City) was lost, and social housing was regarded primarily as a financial business. Thousands of miniscule houses were 'sown' on the edges of Mexico City, the area where most of these housing experiences have taken place. From 1999 to October 2010, the building of 548,690 houses had been authorized in the Mexico City Metropolitan Zone to house a population of 1,476,131 inhabitants. The authorized housing was for estates of different sizes where the benefits of closed communities are a progressively promoted feature [see fig. 8]. These 'new gated communities' are a clear result of Mexican housing policy in the context of the major new national focus on the neo-liberal model of development.[15] Nevertheless, policy makers and constructors of these communities fail to critically assess other issues such as the poor quality of the finished product, the over-crowded conditions or the socio-economic cost of living so far away from the workplace, as well as ecological problems, or the fact of being disconnected from the city. This style of housing increases the profits of construction companies. The large number of housing units (more than 1,000) rules them out of the traditional category of 'condominium' or 'housing estates' that is typically open to the surrounding neighbourhood and inserts them into a different category and creates artificial barriers between the different social groups, and even between those with similar social status in the surrounding communities.

The 'centre-left' mayor of the Democratic Revolutionary Party (PRD) government promoted a programme to provide social housing for state workers with Fovissste. This was a hopeless attempt in the 'city of hope'[16] to build housing within the urban fabric at affordable prices, with an area of 60 square metres used to counteract the trend towards peripherization, increased costs and the 'lilliputization' of housing. The market study carried out by Benlliure[17] shows the impact of this project on the location, price and size of housing in the market as a whole [fig. 9]. The complexes are located in the Gustavo A. Madero delegation. Four developers took part, offering dwellings in housing complexes containing from 1200 to 3340 apartments, sold between 2004 and 2006 [see fig. 10]. The developer in the smallest complex was the only one that maintained its prices; the other developers sold the same housing at a higher price. The extreme was a developer that sold 49% of the dwellings for 47% more than the original price. This example shows the limits of these actions in a national context where the rules of the market prevail.

This brief historical review shows how the commodification of housing has provided increasing profits for a particular sector. The figures achieved seem successful, if one ignores the living conditions of the population that has supposedly benefited from the credit obtained. Although this population is not the group with the lowest economic capacity, its new living conditions may turn the dream of being an owner into a nightmare. They have to wake up at dawn – 4 or 5 in the morning – in order to reach their workplaces and schools, because these real estate developments

**12** GEO Corporation, one of the largest developers, was founded in 1973 and in the 1990s entered the stock exchange market. By 2010 it had built 510,000 houses in Mexico. ARA Consortium was founded in 1977, entering the stock exchange market in 1996. By 2010 it had built 220,000 houses in Mexico and owned 38.5 millions of square metres of land.
**13** Banco Mundial, Comunicado de Prensa No. 137, 2009, available online from: <web.world-bank.org/WBSITE/EXTERNAL/BANCOMUNDIAL/EXTSPPAISES/LACINSPANISHEXT/ MEXICOINSPANISHEXT/0 Comunicado de prensa N.º 2009/134/LCR> [accessed September 10, 2010].
**14** Data taken from Conteo de Población y la Delimitación de las Zonas Metropolitanas (Population Census and Metropolitan Zone Limits), produced in 2005 by the Secretaria de Desarrollo Social, Consejo Nacional de Población and the Instituto Nacional de Estadistica y Geografia (Sedesol-Conapo-INEGI).
**15** Beatriz Garcia and Andreas Hofer, 'Housing for the working class on the periphery of Mexico City: A new version of gated communities', in **Social Justice**, San Francisco, vol. 33 no. 3 (2006), pp. 129-141.
**16** Slogan of Manuel López Obrador, former mayor of the Federal District.
**17** Pablo Benlliure et al., 'Estudio de mercado habitacional de la Zona Metropolitana de la Ciudad de México 1999-2009 / Survey on Housing Market Metropolitan Zone Mexico City 1999-2009', Pablo Benlliure & Beatriz García Peralta (coords.), research project: 'Social Housing Policies, 2000-2010' (Mexico: Social Research Institute, National Autonomous University of Mexico; begun: 2010; currently in progress), archivo México 2010.

are far away from such services. In the evening, they return home tired; and young and elderly people have no leisure facilities. Less qualified people have no chance of securing a well-paid job nearby. Private ownership ties them to a property that cannot be sold in favourable conditions because they compete with large companies that sell similar products. The possibility of having the house of their choice on the market is a fallacy, because their low incomes only allow them to buy a house in other cities. The possibility of choice is only available to well-paid employees, who have enough money to buy a second home so as to make the purchase profitable. Within such a model, the perversity of the process shows that the savings of lower paid workers improve opportunities both for well-paid employees and large housing developers' companies. One wonders, then, whether socioeconomic inequality is the actual outcome of this type of housing politics.

[2]

Multifamiliar Presidente Miguel
**Alemán**—President Miguel Aleman Housing
Complex, Mexico City, c. 1949
source: Edificio Multifamiliar Miguel Alemán
Centro Urbano, Colección Digital de la Fundación ICA, http://www.codifica.org.mx/fica/
popup_fotonvapal.php?x=../imagen/jpg/obl/
obl_sn_006176r.jpg&nick=&password=
[consulted: 15 November 2010].

**2 Multifamiliar Benito Juárez**– Benito
Juárez Housing Complex, Mexico City,
c. 1952
source: 'Multifamiliar del Estadio', Colección
Digital de la Fundación ICA, http://www.codifica.org.mx/fica/popup_fotonvapal.php?x../
imagen/jpg/obl/obl_sn_008773r.
jpg&nick=&password= – Multifamiliar del Estadio [consulted:
15 November 2010].

**3 Unidad Habitacional Nonoalco
Tlatelolco**–Nonoalco Tlatelolco Housing
Complex, Mexico City, c. 1968
source: 'Unidad Tlatelolco', Colección Digital
de la Fundación ICA, http://www.codifica.org.
mx/fica/popup_fotopal.php?x=../imagen/jpg/
obl/obl_sn_019634r.jpg&nick=&password=
[consulted: 15 November 2010].

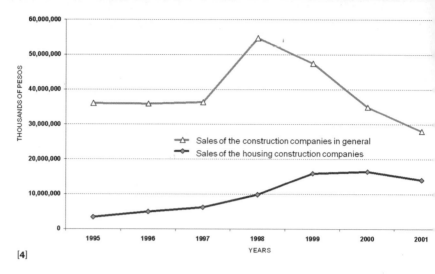

[4]

| Number | Housing construction companies | 1995-2001 Sales | Percentage |
|---|---|---|---|
| 1 | Consorcio Geo | 25,302,901 | 37.4 |
| 2 | Consorcio Ara y Cias. Subs. | 15,385,078 | 22.7 |
| 3 | Urbi Desarrollos Urbanos | 8,013,903 | 11.8 |
| 4 | Consorcio Hogar y Subs. / Constructora Consorcio Hogar | 6,089,876 | 9.0 |
| 5 | Consorcio de Ingeniería Integral | 5,325,364 | 7.9 |
| 6 | Desarrolladora Metropolitana | 3,427,108 | 5.1 |
| 7 | Grupo GP | 1,743,359 | 2.6 |
| 8 | Ingeniería y Obras | 704,425 | 1.0 |
| 9 | Inmobiliaria Ruba | 865,143 | 1.3 |
| 10 | Proyectos Inmobiliarios de Culiacán | 801,708 | 1.2 |
| | Total | 67,638,866 | 100 |

[5]

| Number | National construction companies | 1995-2001 Sales | Percentage |
|---|---|---|---|
| 1 | Empresa ICA Sociedad Controladora SA / Ingenieros Civiles y Asociados SA de CV | 90,971,762 | 36.84 |
| 2 | Bufete Industrial SA de CV / Bufete Industrial y Subs. / Bufete Indsutrial Construcciones SA de CV | 36,959,088 | 14.97 |
| 3 | Grupo Tribasa y Subs. SA de CV / Triturados Basalticos y Derivados SA de CV | 32,232,244 | 13.05 |
| 4 | Corporación Deo | 25,302,901 | 10.25 |
| 5 | Consorcio Ara y Cías. Subs. | 15,715,576 | 6.36 |
| 6 | Protexa Construcciones | 14,092,229 | 5.71 |
| 7 | Urbi Desarrollos Urbanos | 10,296,492 | 4.17 |
| 8 | Consorcio de Ingeniería Integral | 8,506,552 | 3.44 |
| 9 | Grupo Mexicano de Desarrollo SA de CV | 9,790,902 | 2.75 |
| 10 | Consorcio Hogar y Subs. / Constructora Consorcio Hogar | 6,089,876 | 2.47 |
| | Total | 246,957,622 | 100 |

[6]                                                        [7]

4  Sales of the housing construction companies and of the national construction sector in Mexico, 1995-2001 [base: 2000] source: own production according to the information published in 'The 100 Most Important Construction Companies in Mexico', **Obras Magazine**, Annual Report, several issues September from 1995 to 1997 and for 1998 to 2001, available online: http://www.obrasweb.com/informesanuales.asp [consulted: 15 November 2010].
5  The first ten housing construction companies in Mexico, 1995-2000 [in thousands of

pesos, Base 2000]
source: own production according to the information published in 'The 100 Most Important Construction Companies in Mexico', **Obras Magazine**, Annual Report, several issues September from 1995 to 1997 and for 1998 to 2001, available online: http://www.obrasweb.com/informesanuales.asp, [consulted: 15 November 2010].
6  First ten construction companies in Mexico, 1995-2000 [in thousands of pesos, Base 2000]
source: own production according to the infor-

mation published in 'The 100 most importan construction companies in Mexico', **Obras Magazine**, Annual Report, several issues S tember from 1995 to 1997 and for 1998 2001, available online: http://www.obraswe com/informesanuales.asp [consulted: 15 November 2010].
7  **Conjunto habitacional San Buenaver tura**, Ixtapaluca, Estado de México—Housin complex 'San Buenaventura', Ixtapaluca, Mexico State, Mexico City, c. 1998
source: Archive Michael Calderwood (autho [taken: November, 2005], website: http://

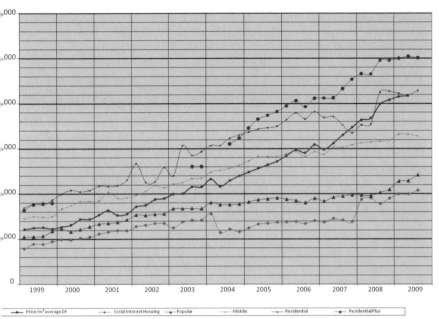

| | | | | | | | | | | |
|---|---|---|---|---|---|---|---|---|---|---|
| 1999 | 2000 | 2001 | 2002 | 2003 | 2004 | 2005 | 2006 | 2007 | 2008 | 2009 |

— Price/m² average DF   —▲— Social Interest Housing   —▲— Popular   —▼— Middle   —▲— Residential   —●— Residential Plus

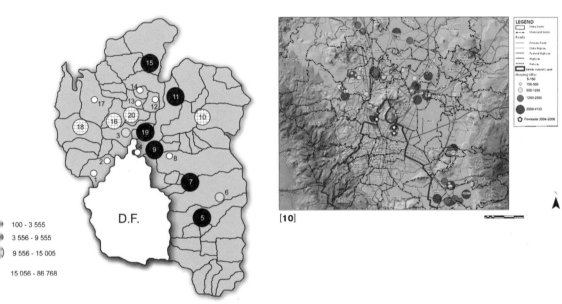

D.F.

[10]

● 100 - 3 555
● 3 556 - 9 555
) 9 556 - 15 005
   15 056 - 86 768

LEGEND

[10]

:.calderwoodphotos.com/
umber of dwellings authorized in housing
plexes, municipalities of the Mexico State
9-2005. Municipalities: 1. Huixquilucan;
aucalpan de Juárez; 3. Tultitlán; 4. Tlal-
antla de Baz; 5. Chalco; 6. Ixtapaluca;
xcoco; 8. Atenco; 9. Ecatepec; 10.
man; 11. Tecámac; 12. Jaltenco; 13.
pec; 14. Melchor Ocampo; 15.
pango; 16. Cuautitlán Izcalli; 17. Tepot-
án; 18. Nicolás Romero; 19. Coacalco;
Cuautitlán. Source: own production
rding to the information, available online:

http://www.edomex.gob.mx/sedur/estadisticas/
conjuntos-urbanos [consulted:
15 November 2010].
**9** Housing market prices per Square Meter
Federal District 1999-2009
source: Pablo Benlliure et al., Survey on
'Housing Market Metropolitan Zone Mexico
City 1999-2009', Pablo Benlliure & Beatriz
García Peralta (coords.), research project:
'Social Housing Policies, 2000-2010'
(Mexico: Social Research Institute, National
Autonomous University of Mexico; begun:
2010; currently in progress).

**10** Sales of housing developments in the met-
ropolitan zone of Mexico City, 2005—source:
Pablo Benlliure (coord.), Survey on 'Housing
Market Metropolitan Zone Mexico City
1999-2009', Pablo Benlliure & Beatriz García
Peralta (coords.), research project: 'Social
Housing Policies, 2000-2010' (Mexico:
Social Research Institute, National Autono-
mous University of Mexico; begun: 2010;
currently in progress).

# Ecatepec, Mexico City Project
# By the Mexico City Study Group

**Directed by** **H. Sohn and M. Robles-Durán**

**Participants** **L. Asabashvili, Y. Bai, S. Bizzarri, C. García-Sancho,**

**T. Guerrero, T. Kolnaar, P. Lühl, S. Voogt, T. ter Weel, I. Zveibil**

**Building technology adviser** **B. Gremmen**

**Urbanism adviser** **U. Hackauf**

## Incursions into the periphery of Mexico City

Contemporary Mexico City is a living example of the impact of neoliberal urbanization on the production of space. Much of its present day morphology and most of its urban problems are a direct result of nefarious or nonexistent urban policies, which in the advent of free market ideologies have incremented the speed of deterioration and thus determined the fate of its society as the socio-spatial and economic polarization of its citizens worsens day by day. This form of urbanization exposes the existing unbalanced relations of power between the makers of the city and its dwellers. While developers accumulate enormous monetary wealth and power, the city dwellers, especially the urban poor, have been gradually confined into far-away, serialized dormitory quarters, excluded from the production of their own environment. The asymmetrical or uneven development implicit in free-market logics has taken a material dimension in Mexico that will have lasting consequences.

Ecatepec de Morelos is a municipality in the north-east of Mexico City in which these asymmetries become evident. Home to approximately 2 million inhabitants, it displays some of the wealthiest groups living in painful proximity to the working class and the urban poor. This also manifests on the physical and morphological characteristics of the municipality. A large percentage of its built environment consists of irregular settlements, which have consolidated over the decades, as well as a sea of low-density, low-income more recent formal housing developments. Ecatepec, like most other peripheral municipalities, provides inexpensive land and laxer regulations than the Federal District. This, among other factors, has made this municipality and much of the eastern periphery of the city a good base for profit-driven housing developments. The model of neoliberal urbanization in Mexico conventionally materializes as a surrogate of the suburban middle-class 'gated community'; but in essence this model is nothing but uniform, low-density massive row housing, 'complimented' with a large-scale shopping mall, excessive vehicular space and a minimum of public facilities, thus straining existing urban infrastructure.

Politically, most of these massive housing developments are authorized at state level, effectively bypassing the local municipality. Furthermore, as forms of public-private partnerships, they enable developers to extract massive gains from the sale of housing while the public partner – the municipality – has to shoulder the long-term maintenance of the infrastructure. Another problem of these developments is that they rely on individual credit finance. This either creates long-term financial dependencies on individuals with marginal incomes and opportunities, or simply renders

[1] The confrontation of two spatial configurations: asymmetrical urban sprawl in Ecatepec de Morelos, Mexico City.

them inaccessible to a very significant sector of the population, namely the one engaged in the informal economy.

In these developments, sadly, architecture and urban design are reduced to merely decorative arts at the demand of capital. Design generates the fantasies and desires in the urban poor and the working class of belonging to middle class suburban urbanites, and thus contributes to the creation of false consciousness. It defines borders that cause further social fragmentation and segregation.

An exemplary case is the 'gated community' of Las Américas in Ecatepec, developed by Casas ARA, one of the ten largest Mexican housing development companies. This development consists of 14,000 housing units arranged in a mono-functional urban scheme of 'copy-paste' architecture of extremely low quality construction. But most dramatically it is an example of the complete disregard for the present and future urban and social needs of the inhabitants.

With this context in mind the main objectives of this project are to propose affordable alternatives to low-income housing, to raise density, to increase socio-economic semi-autonomy through local production and trade, to empower local skills and cultural consciousness, as well as to create possibilities of political manifestation through the strengthening of communal facilities. Raising density means not only increasing the density of built objects, but also increasing the density of social relations. In this context, housing can no longer be understood merely as the provision of dwellings. It is essential to provide alternatives that allow the inhabitants to sustain their livelihoods through local means of production and trade that are related to their habitat and their cultural and social production.

## Instances of urban history in Mexico City

Mexico City's contemporary urban condition reveals the incapacity of the urban and architectural practices to address the uneven development to which this city has been subjected in recent times. To overcome this a redefinition of urban research is required; one which considers the political, economic and social processes that shape the city rather than focusing exclusively on morphological hierarchies and formal aspects. In this research the socio-spatial production of Mexico City from its founding to the present was synthesized in nine historical periods and represented in a series of maps that relate these processes to the spatial formation of the city. Starting from Mexico's industrialization in the late nineteenth century the following pages present the last five stages of Mexico's urban historical development.

**Porfiriato 1876-1910**   Rapid industrialization during the dictatorship of Porfirio Diaz consolidated the centralization of the capital interests in the city in opposition to the rural areas. The city was drastically transformed in accordance with strong French cultural influences in urban planning and typology as well as in its cultural production. Transportation was revolutionized by electric tram and automobile, increasing the accessibility of peripheral country estates while the fast extending railroad network dramatically increased the city's economical reach enabling ever-stronger economical ties with the US.

**Revolution 1910-1940**   Latent social conflicts, inherited from colonial history and unresolved after independence from Spain in 1821, violently erupted in the Mexican Revolution of 1910. It culminated in the promulgation of the 1917 Constitution, stipulating restoration of peasants' rights to communal land ownership – the *ejido* – as well as wider recognition of labour rights while maintaining a capitalist mode of production. Cultural production saw the emergence of a national identity that recognized a shared cultural history, the social standing of the *mestizo* as the majority.

**Mexican Miracle 1940-1966**   Import-substitution and decentralization to curb massive rural-urban migration prepared the ground for the Mexican Miracle – the economic boom of the 1940s, 1950s and 1960s – that established Mexico as a modern economy. Consolidation of political power within the Institutionalized Revolutionary Party PRI increased its indifference towards the plight of the low-income classes. Enormous public spending on public infrastructure as well as large-scale collective housing projects within the Federal District (DF) favoured the middle class. The so-called VADO policy, which prohibited urban development at higher altitudes, successfully prevented further formal growth to the mountainous south of the city. In combination with a ban of industries from the DF it forced urban sprawl towards the north and east and beyond the limits of political responsibility of the DF. The labour force that shouldered the economic boom was accommodated in peripheral developments and informal settlements surrounding the industrial zones.

**Global Metropolis 1966-1985**   A short-lived oil boom initiated a credit-based public spending programme meant to regain the confidence of low-income classes in government. INFONAVIT, the National Housing Fund for Workers, realized numerous collective housing developments all over the city. During the Volcker Shock of 1979 the US drastically increased its interest rates and effectively doubled Mexico's foreign debt overnight and thereby enforced an end to the credit-

[2] 'Asimetrias Urbanas' – mural by Taufan ter Weel in the municipality of Ecatepec, commissioned by the local Institute of Youth. January 2009.

financed public spending. Subsequently the US and the International Monetary Fund imposed a shift towards neoliberalization of the Mexican economy including financial deregulation, privatization of government companies and cuts in public spending. A massive earthquake in 1985 destroyed large central parts of the city centre including 30,000 housing units, many of which were state-built housing complexes. The inefficient handling of the earthquake's aftermath further nurtured public scepticism towards government in the health and housing development sectors.

**Neoliberal City 1985-2008**    The turn to neoliberal politics of the early 1980s culminated with the signing of the North American Free Trade Agreement [NAFTA] in 1994, which opened up Mexican markets to foreign investment and fierce competition, most notably in the agricultural sector. The agreement stipulated amongst other things, the privatization of communal *ejido* lands which made inexpensive land available for urbanization in the periphery of Mexico City, consolidating the shift towards profit-oriented housing production. The development of lower-middle class gated communities in the periphery mimicked the exclusivity of their elite counterparts in the west of the city, revealing growing social inequalities. The business district of Santa Fe was built on a former dumpsite cleared of previous slum dwellers. With its concentration of multinational corporate headquarters, upscale apartment towers and dedicated infrastructure it became a bold example of the polarizing forces of capital. At the same time the renovation and beautification of the historical centre emphasized the government's legacy of servicing the city's core while neglecting the periphery.

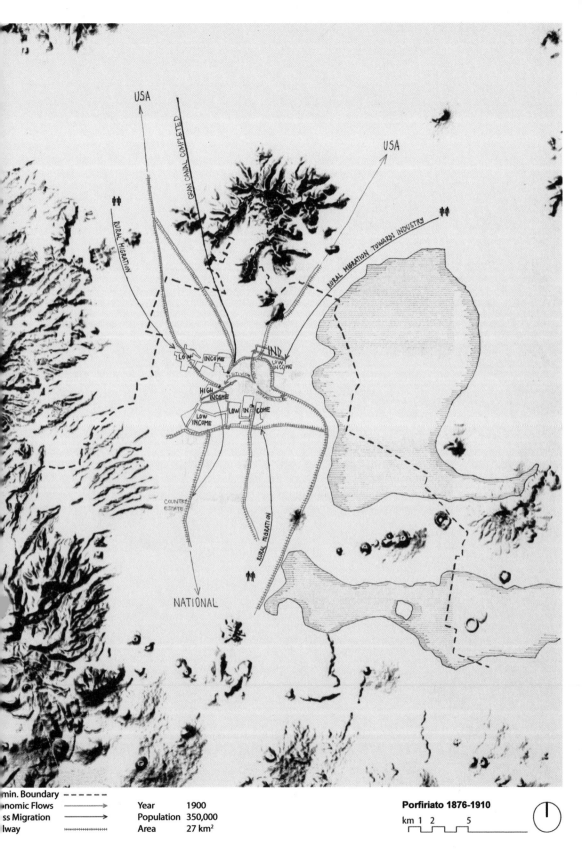

USA

GRAN CANAL COMPLETED

USA

RURAL MIGRATION

RURAL MIGRATION TOWARDS INDUSTRY

IND

LOW INCOME

LOW INCOME

HIGH INCOME

LOW INCOME

LOW IN COME

COUNTRY ESTATE

RURAL MIGRATION

NATIONAL

| Year | 1900 |
| Population | 350,000 |
| Area | 27 km² |

**Porfiriato 1876-1910**

km   1   2     5

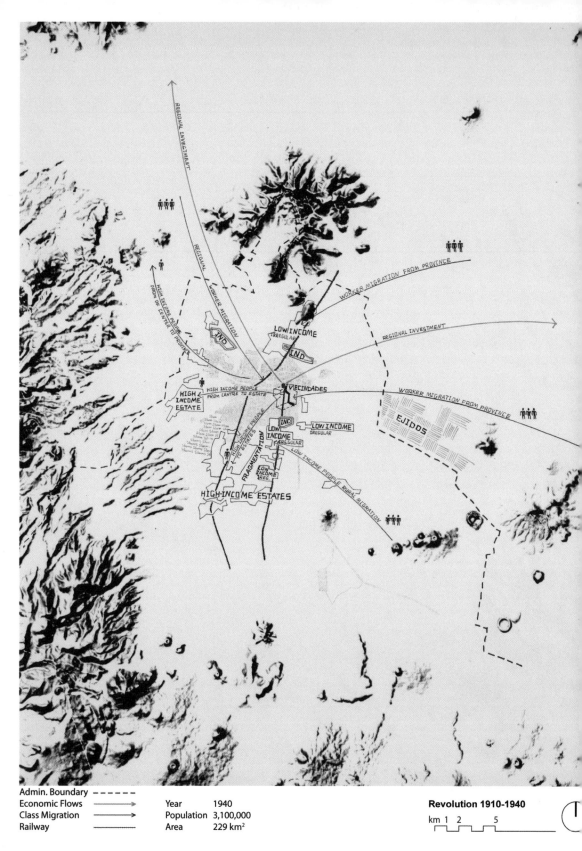

REGIONAL INVESTMENT

WORKER MIGRATION FROM PROVINCE

REGIONAL INVESTMENT

REGIONAL WORKER MIGRATION

HIGH INCOME PEOPLE PATH DE CENTRE TO PROVINCE

LOW INCOME IRREGULAR

IND

IND

VECINDADES

HIGH INCOME PEOPLE FROM CENTRE TO ESTATE

WORKER MIGRATION FROM PROVINCE

HIGH INCOME ESTATE

HIGH INCOME PEOPLE TO ESTATES

IND

LOW INCOME IRREGULAR

LOW INCOME IRREGULAR

EJIDOS

FRAGMENTATION

LOW INCOME IRREG.

LOW INCOME PEOPLE RURAL MIGRATION

HIGH-INCOME ESTATES

| Admin. Boundary | – – – – – |
| Economic Flows | ⟶ |
| Class Migration | ⟶ |
| Railway | ·········· |

| | |
|---|---|
| Year | 1940 |
| Population | 3,100,000 |
| Area | 229 km² |

**Revolution 1910-1940**

km 1 2 5

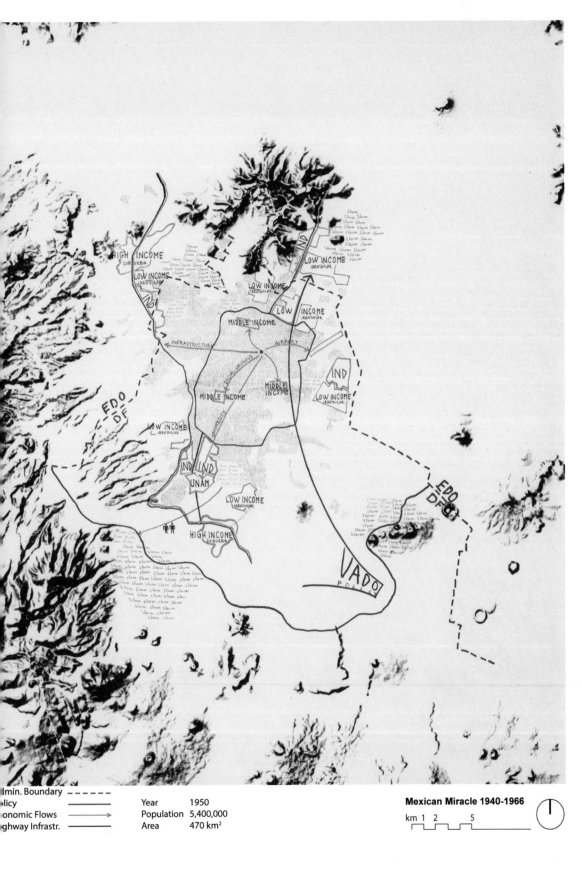

HIGH INCOME
SUBURBIA

LOW INCOME
IRREGULAR

IND

LOW INCOME
IRREGULAR

LOW INCOME
IRREGULAR

LOW INCOME
IRREGULAR

LOW
INCOME
IRREGULAR

MIDDLE INCOME

AIRPORT

INFRASTRUCTURE

SOCIAL HOUSING

MIDDLE INCOME

MIDDLE
INCOME

IND
LOW INCOME
IRREGULAR

EDO
DF

LOW INCOME
IRREGULAR

UNIVERSITY

IND IND

UNAM

LOW INCOME
IRREGULAR

EDO
DF

HIGH INCOME
SUBURBIA

VADO
POLICY

Admin. Boundary  - - - - -
Policy ——————
Economic Flows ——————→
Highway Infrastr. ——————

Year           1950
Population  5,400,000
Area           470 km²

**Mexican Miracle 1940-1966**

km  1   2          5

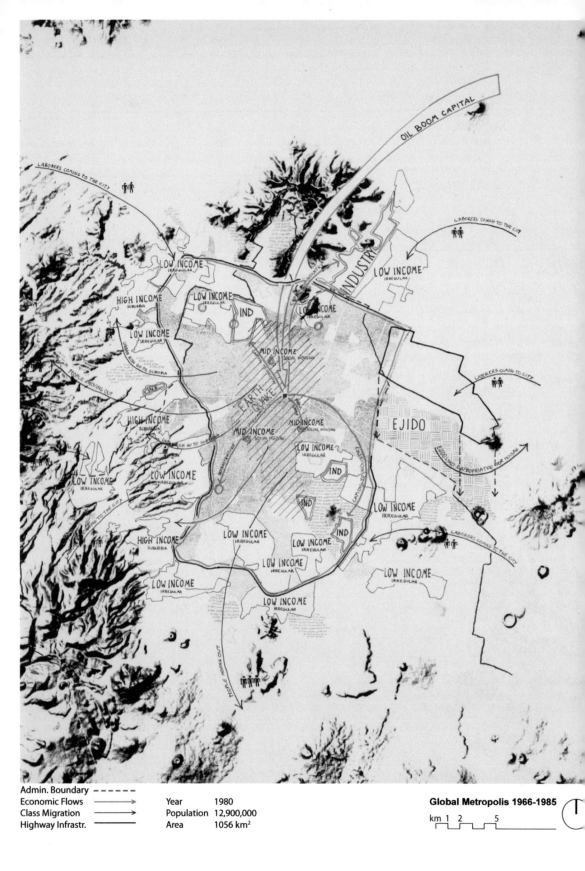

OIL BOOM CAPITAL

LABORERS COMING TO THE CITY

LABORERS COMING TO THE CITY

LABORERS COMING TO CITY

INDUSTRY

LOW INCOME
IRREGULAR

LOW INCOME
IRREGULAR

LOW INCOME
IRREGULAR

HIGH INCOME
SUBURBIA

IND

LOW INCOME
IRREGULAR

LOW INCOME
IRREGULAR

PEOPLE MOVING OUT

URBAN RICH GO TO SUBURBIA

MID INCOME
SOCIAL HOUSING

EARTH
QUAKE

HIGH INCOME
SUBURBIA

MID INCOME
SOCIAL HOUSING

MID INCOME
SOCIAL HOUSING

EJIDO

EJIDO LAND EXPROPRIATION FOR HOUSING

IND

LOW INCOME
IRREGULAR

INFRASTRUCTURE

CAPITAL-TECH INDUSTRY

LOW INCOME
IRREGULAR

LOW INCOME
IRREGULAR

IND

LOW INCOME
IRREGULAR

LABORERS COMING TO THE CITY

HIGH INCOME
SUBURBIA

LOW INCOME
IRREGULAR

LOW INCOME
IRREGULAR

IND

LOW INCOME
IRREGULAR

LOW INCOME
IRREGULAR

LOW INCOME
IRREGULAR

LOW INCOME
IRREGULAR

PEOPLE MOVING OUT

Admin. Boundary    - - - - - -
Economic Flows    ⟶
Class Migration    ⟶
Highway Infrastr.    ⸻

Year    1980
Population    12,900,000
Area    1056 km²

**Global Metropolis 1966-1985**

km 1 2   5

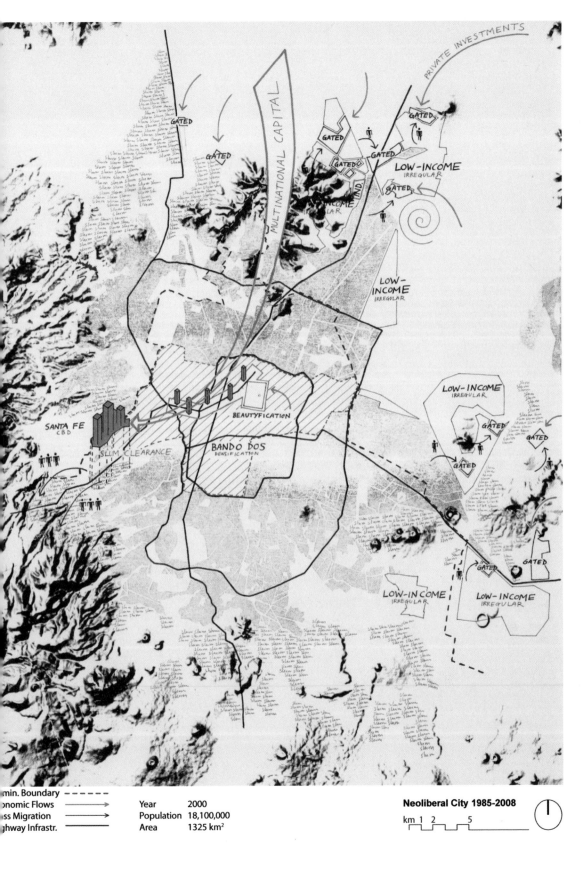

GATED

GATED

MULTINATIONAL CAPITAL

GATED

GATED

GATED

PRIVATE INVESTMENTS

GATED

LOW-INCOME
IRREGULAR

IND

INCOME
ULAR

GATED

LOW-
INCOME
IRREGULAR

LOW-INCOME
IRREGULAR

GATED

GATED

BEAUTYFICATION

SANTA FE
CBD

SLUM CLEARANCE

BANDO DOS
DENSIFICATION

GATED

GATED

LOW-INCOME
IRREGULAR

LOW-INCOME
IRREGULAR

LOW-INCOME
IRREGULAR

min. Boundary   – – – –
onomic Flows   ⟶
ss Migration    ⟶
ghway Infrastr.  ⟶

Year          2000
Population   18,100,000
Area          1325 km²

**Neoliberal City 1985-2008**

km 1  2          5

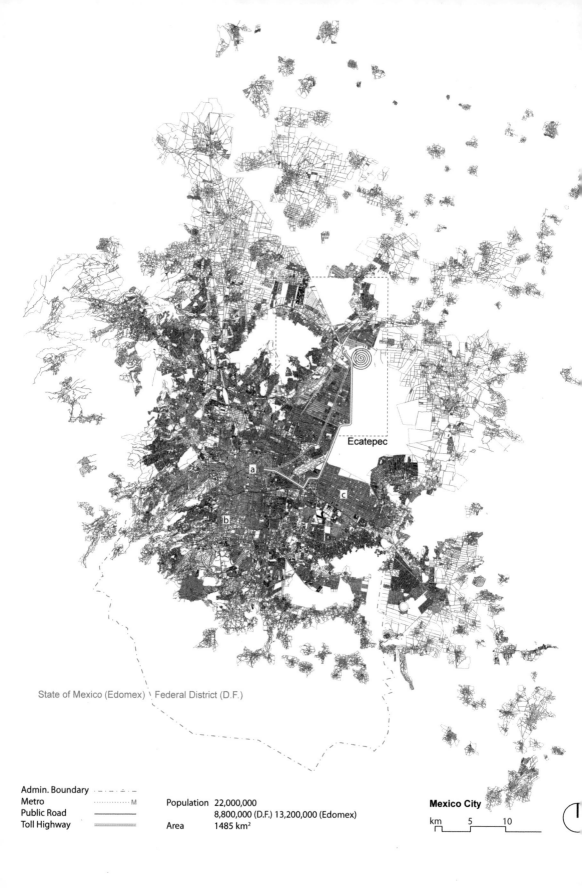

Ecatepec

State of Mexico (Edomex) \ Federal District (D.F.)

Admin. Boundary  — · — · —
Metro           · · · · · · · M
Public Road     ————
Toll Highway    ══════

Population  22,000,000
           8,800,000 (D.F.) 13,200,000 (Edomex)
Area       1485 km²

**Mexico City**

km    5      10

**Dependency on the city core**   Over fifty per cent of Mexico City's population lives outside of the official boundaries of the Federal District, which is roughly formed by the dense inner city ('Bando Dos') [fig. 4] and the historical core and city centre. Traditionally, it has been in the Federal District where the most efficient and modern urban facilities – public transport-systems, urban infrastructure, etc – as well as employment opportunities in the second, third and quarterly sectors of the economy have been located.

The municipalities to the north and east are the largest and most marginalized of the metropolis due to their function as point of entrance to the city for rural populations, and as 'sleepburbs'. These municipalities subsequently are less privileged in terms of public investment [fig. 5]. Extreme commuting times become the standard, while huge investments in privatized infrastructure of highways exclude large parts of the population that cannot afford toll-highway costs.

**3** Beautification and centralization of services in the Historical Centre.
**4** The inner core or 'Bando Dos'.
**5** Massive low-density urban sprawl in working-class municipalities outside the Federal District, Nezahualcóyotl, Estado de México.

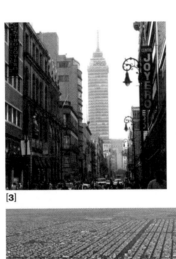

[3]

[4]

[5]

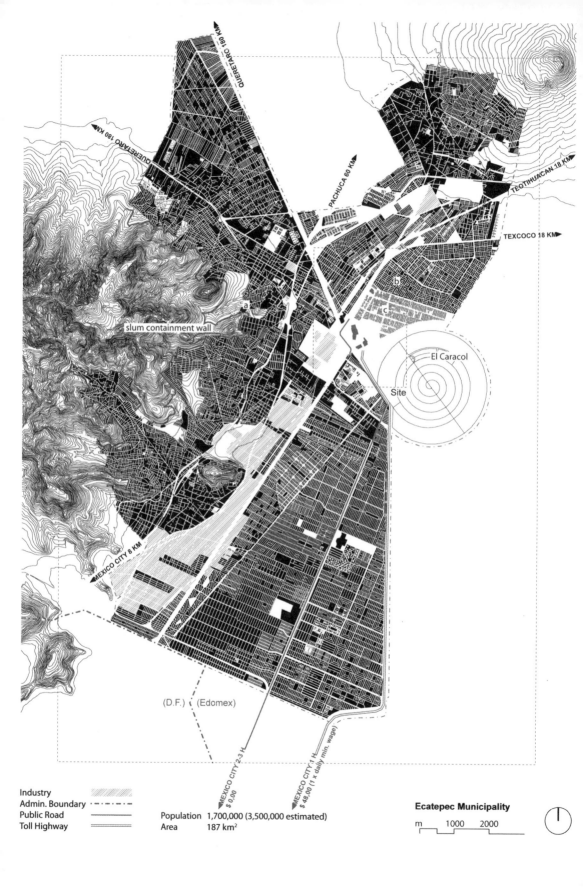

QUERETARO 180 KM

QUERETARO 180 KM

PACHUCA 60 KM

TEOTIHUACAN 18 KM

TEXCOCO 18 KM

a

b

c

slum containment wall

El Caracol

Site

MEXICO CITY 8 KM

(D.F.)   (Edomex)

MEXICO CITY 2-3 H.
$ 0,00

MEXICO CITY 1 H.
$ 48,00 (1 x daily min. wage)

Industry
Admin. Boundary
Public Road
Toll Highway

Population   1,700,000 (3,500,000 estimated)
Area           187 km²

**Ecatepec Municipality**

m        1000      2000

**Las Américas: case study**  Developing along an industrial corridor towards Pachuca since the late 1950s, Ecatepec is one of the municipalities where migrants to Mexico City first settled, resulting in continuously growing informal settlements in the Sierra de Guadalupe [fig. 6]. The municipality attempts to halt the spread of informality by means of a containment wall along the entire sierra.

Most of the urban fabric consists of irregular, self-built single-family housing [fig. 7] while new gated community housing developments have sprouted, most noticeably the case study Las Américas with its 14,000 units [fig. 8] and regional shopping mall. Las Américas is spatially and socially – intentionally – isolated from the surrounding urban fabric. It is also environmentally very unsustainable, as it is built on contaminated soil of the former caustic soda plant Sosa Texcoco, 'El Caracol', of which the 3 km wide spiral imprint is still clearly visible in the landscape.

**6** Informal settlements in the Sierra de Guadalupe.
**7** The largest portion of the municipality consists of self-built, single-family housing.
**8** Las Américas gated community: a profit-based development of 14,000 low-density, single-family units built by Casas ARA from 2004-2008.

[6]

[7]

[8]

Jardines de Morelos

a

c

Las Americas

b

El Caracol

Railway
Public Road
Toll Highway
Urban Void

**Las Americas Site**

m   100   200                    500

## Socio-spatial fragmentation

The extremely rapid urbanization process has left indelible traces in the urban fabric which remains heavily fragmented by large regional infrastructures such as gas pipelines, high voltage transmission lines, a notorious open-air sewage system as well as railways and highways. These have produced a series of urban voids that are largely unfit for human settlement and construction, and which often pose important health hazards. At the same time, the insertion of a large-scale shopping mall [fig. 10] in this urban bottleneck causes large congestion problems in the area. The spatial isolation of Las Américas by a continuous wall in the north [fig. 11] leads to an array of problems related to the discontinuity of infrastructure and urban facilities. It is also the spatial materialization of an imaginary class boundary between the inhabitants on both sides of the fence, so to speak, a line between 'mortgage-slaves' and 'informal settlers'.

**9** Fragmentation and urban voids left by rapid urbanization.
**10** Las Américas Shopping Mall centralizing regional consumption patterns.
**11** Physical and social segregation of urban fabric on the border of Las Américas and Jardines de Morelos neighbourhood.

[9]

[10]

[11]

96
m²

119
96
m²

119
96
m²

144
96
m²

96
m²

108
96
m²

120
96
m²

96
m²

116
96
m²

144
96
m²

**Modifications of mono-functionality in Las Américas** The failure and
inadequate design of Las Américas becomes patent in the tendency of owners and inhabitants to
modify and transform the dwellings almost immediately after moving in. This is not due to positive
aspects of an architecture of adaptability, or flexible urban planning and design, but rather it is the
result of a utilitarian model of insufficient living spaces and a total disregard for the needs of
urban populations for mixed functions and a rich programme for social exchange, employment,
education, entertainment, etc. In particular the populations of peri-urban developments such as
Las Américas, because of their extreme distance from the city, and thus from significant places of
work and employment, they have a real need for alternative sources of income in their localities. The
neoliberal urban model, this 'gated *cul de sac*', does not consider or envision these transformations
in the conception of these developments at all. Transformation occurs a posteriori and often under
extremely inconvenient conditions for the owners, inhabitants and citizens in general.

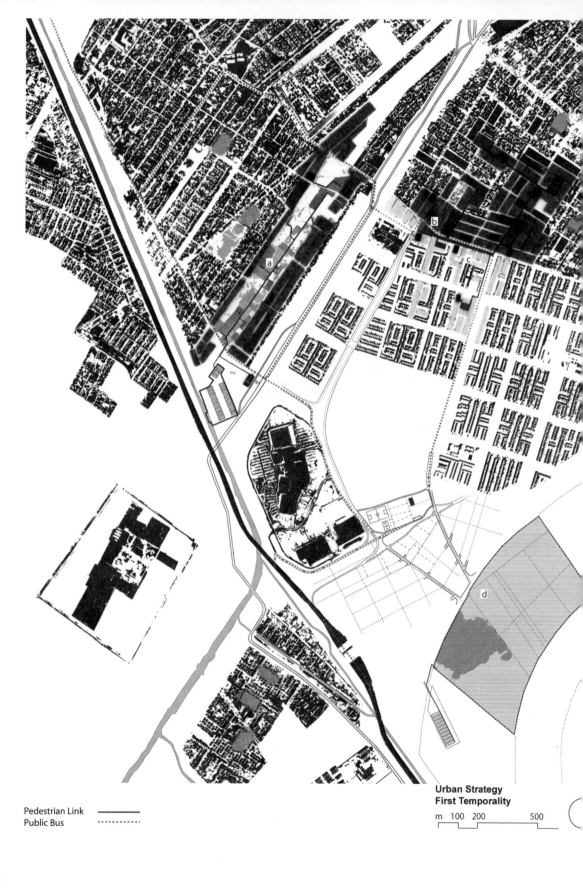

**Urban Strategy
First Temporality**

m  100  200          500

Pedestrian Link  ————
Public Bus       ············

**Contesting neoliberal urbanization**   The urban strategy for this project emerges from a close reading of marginal, local activities in the area, which may become the basis of a future urbanization, following these eight main aims:

1  Reducing dependency on the city core and strengthening local economies [fig. 12]. Existing gardens in urban voids under power lines will be transformed into plots for urban agriculture as a way to create places of gathering and interaction, which also enhance economic activities within the public domain.

2  Dismantling of physical urban borders. Social relations will be established through initiating public activities and encouraging social gathering [fig. 13].

3  Densification of existing urban fabric. By devising architectural strategies such as introducing shared spaces for work and commerce on both sides of the border its segregating character will be diminished [fig. 14].

4  Creating possibilities for alternative means of agricultural production. The proposed ecological recovery of the plant of 'El Caracol' will form the basis for the proposed experimental project to reclaim ancient knowledge of hydro-agriculture [overleaf].

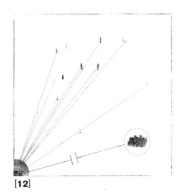

[12]

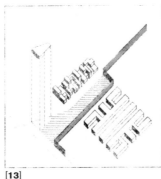

[13]

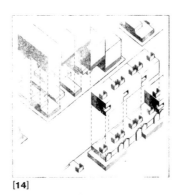

[14]

**12** Reducing dependency on Mexico City's centre by increasing local autonomy.
**13** Creating spaces of social interaction along the border wall of Las Américas.
**14** Densification of urban fabric and introduction of local means of production.

Pedestrian Link ——————
Suburban Train ··················
Public Bus -----------
Highway ==========

**Urban Strategy**
**Second Temporality**

m  100  200          500

5 Strengthening social alliances. The growing of *nopal* cacti will create the agency for developing collective facilities related to agricultural production and processing by using urban voids next to a highway with cooperative workshop facilities and housing [fig. 15].

6 Weaving of urban fragments. In cooperation with the federal government a series of pedestrian bridges are proposed which link Las Américas to its surroundings and plug into new systems of mass transport and public facilities [fig. 16].

7 Reclaiming of excessive vehicular space within Las Américas. A set of architectural strategies address this problem by building housing and collective and commercial facilities on partly reclaimed streets in cooperation with the municipality.

8 Creation of a unitary urban framework [see 'Visomex', overleaf]. Local communities are empowered to take control of the development and sustainability of their own habitat. The environmental recovery of 'El Caracol' with increasing production enables the formation of agricultural and housing cooperatives that give rise to a different kind of urbanization.

[15]   [16]

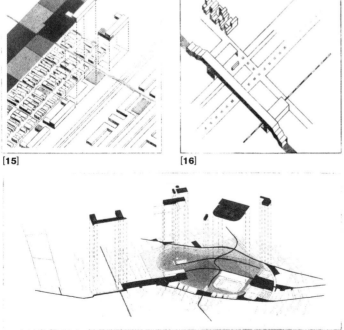

[17]

15 Cacti (**nopal**) agriculture as an economic base for cooperative production and housing.

16 Bridging urban voids with public facilities connected to public transportation.

17 Introducing modes of production connected to facilities for local trade as well as elaborating network of public spaces weaving disruptions in urban fabric.

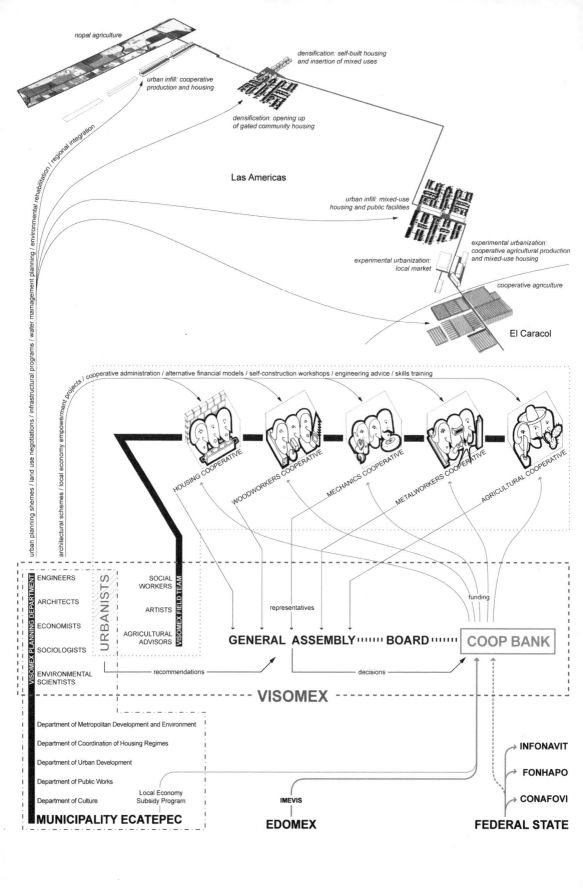

nopal agriculture

urban infill: cooperative production and housing

densification: self-built housing and insertion of mixed uses

densification: opening up of gated community housing

regional integration

environmental rehabilitation / regional integration

water managment planning / environmental rehabilitation / regional integration

infrastructural programs / water managment planning / environmental rehabilitation / regional integration

land use negotiations / infrastructural programs / water managment planning / environmental rehabilitation / regional integration

urban planning shemes / land use negotiations / infrastructural programs / water managment planning / environmental rehabilitation / regional integration

local economy empowerment projects / urban planning shemes / land use negotiations / infrastructural programs / water managment planning / environmental rehabilitation / regional integration

architectural schemes / local economy empowerment projects

Las Americas

urban infill: mixed-use housing and public facilities

experimental urbanization: cooperative agricultural production and mixed-use housing

experimental urbanization: local market

cooperative agriculture

El Caracol

cooperative administration / alternative financial models / self-construction workshops / engineering advice / skills training

HOUSING COOPERATIVE

WOODWORKERS COOPERATIVE

MECHANICS COOPERATIVE

METALWORKERS COOPERATIVE

AGRICULTURAL COOPERATIVE

ENGINEERS

ARCHITECTS

ECONOMISTS

SOCIOLOGISTS

ENVIRONMENTAL SCIENTISTS

VISOMEX PLANNING DEPARTMENT

URBANISTS

SOCIAL WORKERS

ARTISTS

AGRICULTURAL ADVISORS

VISOMEX FIELD TEAM

representatives

funding

recommendations

GENERAL ASSEMBLY ⋯⋯⋯ BOARD ⋯⋯⋯ COOP BANK

decisions

VISOMEX

Department of Metropolitan Development and Environment

Department of Coordination of Housing Regimes

Department of Urban Development

Department of Public Works

Department of Culture

Local Economy Subsidy Program

MUNICIPALITY ECATEPEC

IMEVIS

EDOMEX

INFONAVIT

FONHAPO

CONAFOVI

FEDERAL STATE

## Visomex (Vivienda Social de México): unitary urban framework

Visomex (*Vivienda Social de México*) is the key element of the unitary urban strategy devised in this project. It is intended as the legal and organizational framework within which a vast array of stakeholders and interest groups find their role as agents in the making of the city, in this case, in the transformation of Las Américas in Ecatepec. Visomex functions as a mediator between residents and municipalities, and is designed as a strategic devise for multidisciplinary planning. The basic unit is the resident, who in groups will form cooperatives applying for public funds for the development of local initiatives. Financial aid and funding is provided by redirecting sections of federal state funds of existing national housing institutions (Infonavit, Fonhapo, Conafovi etc.) as well as by the state housing budgets in this case of the State of Mexico (*Estado de México*), as well as from the municipal programme for local economic empowerment.

The cooperatives form the basis for a greater self-administration of local residents and the formulation of their collective needs. Cooperatives can take many shapes as their administrative form is decided upon by members and assisted by the Visomex Planning Department, which also joins in developing local urban and building projects and strategies, including communal land ownership models. Cooperatives can then apply for public funding for their initiatives, which can vary from housing to employment creation, specifically regarding urban agriculture and production. Other organs within Visomex are:

- General Assembly: will represent residents through cooperatives and will have the power of decision on all major Visomex issues, including the direction of Coop Bank.
- Coop Bank: Coop Bank is a financial institution that administers the public funding received by the government. Coop Bank will be directed by the Visomex General Assembly and will grant collective credits to cooperatives on a not-for-profit base.
- Visomex Planning Department: will gather professionals of varying disciplines to create a unitary urban strategy, both informed by and assisting the cooperatives. It will negotiate land rights and land use as well as develop strategies for the empowerment of local residents and cooperatives.
- Visomex Field Team: will be the direct link between the cooperatives and residents and Visomex. It will have a mainly educational character and will create projects and workshops where professional expertise and local knowledge converge to inform each other, mediated by urbanists.
- Municipality of Ecatepec de Morelos: will be directly involved in the formulation of the Visomex Urban Framework through its different municipal departments that form part of the Visomex Planning Department. It provides the general building regulations in line with the State of Mexico (*Estado de México*): and is also the main provider of subsidies for local economic empowerment as well as proprietor of large parts of unused land that will be made available in long-term leasehold agreements.

The State of Mexico provides the general legal framework regarding housing and urban development, implemented through IMEVIS (Mexican Institute for Social Housing).

The federal state will be the primary source of funding for Visomex, but it will not have direct regulatory powers.

1980

2010

2015

2020

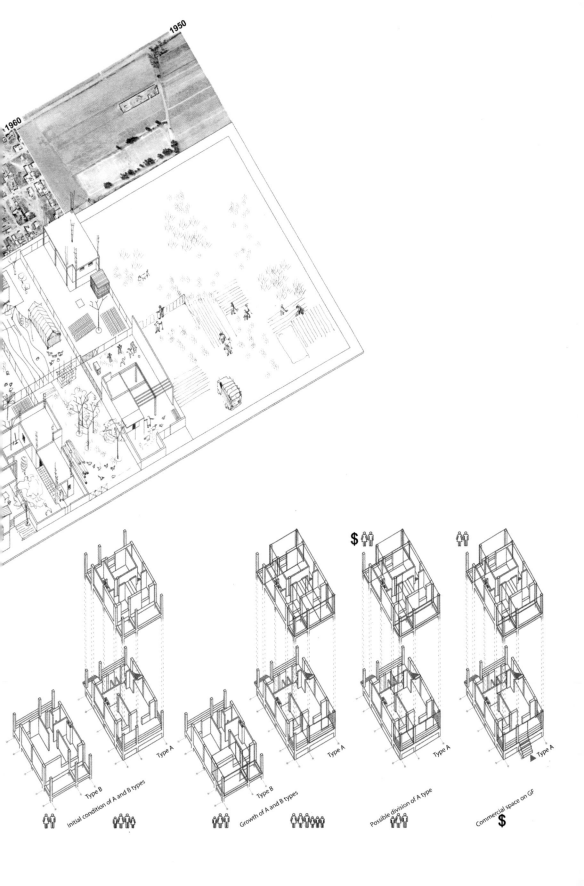

1950

1960

Type B

Type A

Type B

Type A

Type A

Type A

$

Initial condition of A and B types

Growth of A and B types

Possible division of A type

Commercial space on GF

$

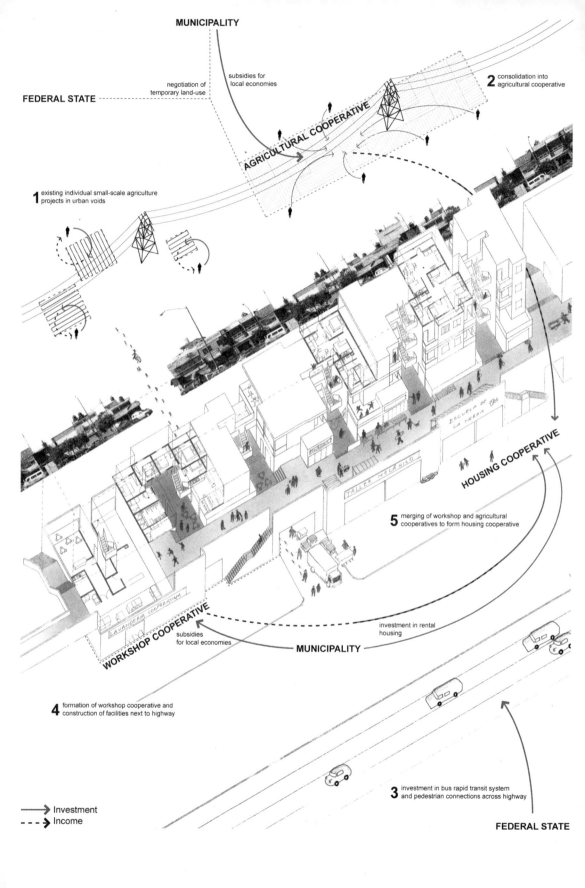

MUNICIPALITY

FEDERAL STATE

negotiation of
temporary land-use

subsidies for
local economies

**2** consolidation into
agricultural cooperative

AGRICULTURAL COOPERATIVE

**1** existing individual small-scale agriculture
projects in urban voids

HOUSING COOPERATIVE

**5** merging of workshop and agricultural
cooperatives to form housing cooperative

WORKSHOP COOPERATIVE

subsidies
for local economies

investment in rental
housing

MUNICIPALITY

**4** formation of workshop cooperative and
construction of facilities next to highway

**3** investment in bus rapid transit system
and pedestrian connections across highway

FEDERAL STATE

→ Investment
--→ Income

A part of the project develops alternative building systems which will gradually substitute existing buildings. The aim is to provide households with alternatives such as increased adaptability and flexible forms of inhabitation, including collective or communal patterns. While families keep living on the same plot of land in temporary shelters throughout the construction period, they are able to sustain their local economic activities and social relations [for project location see Urban Strategy First Temporality].

Small gardens in urban voids under high voltage transmission lines will be consolidated into a collective organization for cactus agriculture. This will encourage local means of production and strengthen the emerging community's capacity to build collective facilities for intensified production and processing, housing and other programmes. This process will be aided by government subsidies and collective credits [for project location see Urban Strategy First Temporality and Urban Strategy Second Temporality].

After the consolidation of an agricultural cooperative, other trades and means of production such as carpentry workshops, metal workshops, *adobe* brick-making and car repair centres will be initiated with municipal support. Other facilities will be built on empty land next to the highway [fig. 18] with good connections to the highway side as well as the neighbourhood side. Housing cooperatives are formed to realize housing projects, closely related to the workshop and to collective facilities and their owners [see project on next page].

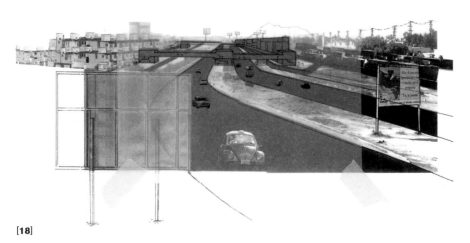

[18]

**18** The urban void of the highway is bridged by programmed pedestrian connections as well as workshop and commercial activities that relate to the side of the highway as well as to the neighbourhood.

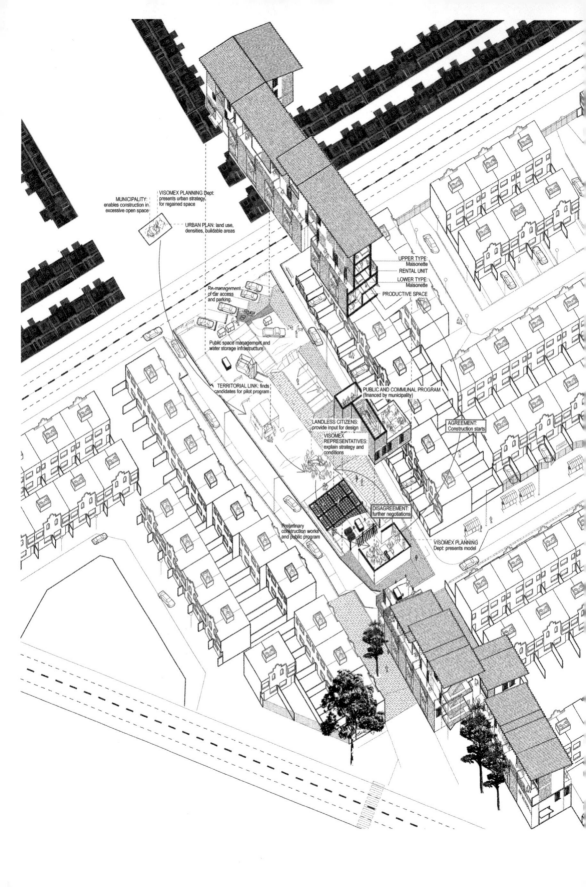

MUNICIPALITY:
enables construction in
excessive open space

VISOMEX PLANNING Dept:
presents urban strategy
for regained space

URBAN PLAN: land use,
densities, buildable areas

UPPER TYPE:
Maisonette

RENTAL UNIT

LOWER TYPE:
Maisonette

PRODUCTIVE SPACE

Re-management
of car access
and parking

Public space management and
water storage infrastructure

TERRITORIAL LINK: finds
candidates for pilot program

PUBLIC AND COMMUNAL PROGRAM
(financed by municipality)

AGREEMENT:
Construction starts

LANDLESS CITIZENS:
provide input for design

VISOMEX
REPRESENTATIVES:
explain strategy and
conditions

DISAGREEMENT:
further negotiations

Preliminary
construction works
and public program

VISOMEX PLANNING
Dept: presents model

The strategy of invading the excessively wide streets of Las Américas by retrofitting them with higher density mixed-use housing and public and collective facilities could become a basic strategy for similar kinds of urban developments [for location of project see Urban Strategy Second Temporality].

The urbanization of the wasteland adjacent to Las Américas is a pilot project for Visomex in cooperation with Casas ARA and the municipality of Ecatepec. Agricultural production will form the base of its economic and social formation and housing will be closely linked to agricultural and related production and processing facilities while offering spaces to establish other small-scale economies. The housing envisions a mixture of rent and private ownership in order to gain flexibility for enlargement of habitable spaces or the establishment of home economies [for location see Urban Strategy Second Temporality].

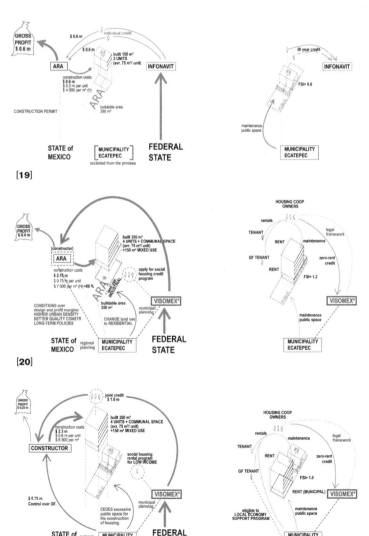

**19** Current profit-based model for the provision of 'social interest' housing: while developers profit even before construction starts, inhabitants and municipality suffer the consequences of bad planning.

**20** Proposed economic model based on collective credits received from Visomex for building on municipal land within Las Américas [see axonometric on the left].

**21** Proposed economic model for a pilot project for cooperative housing on restricted land owned by Casas ARA, the developer of Las Américas [see axonometric on next page].

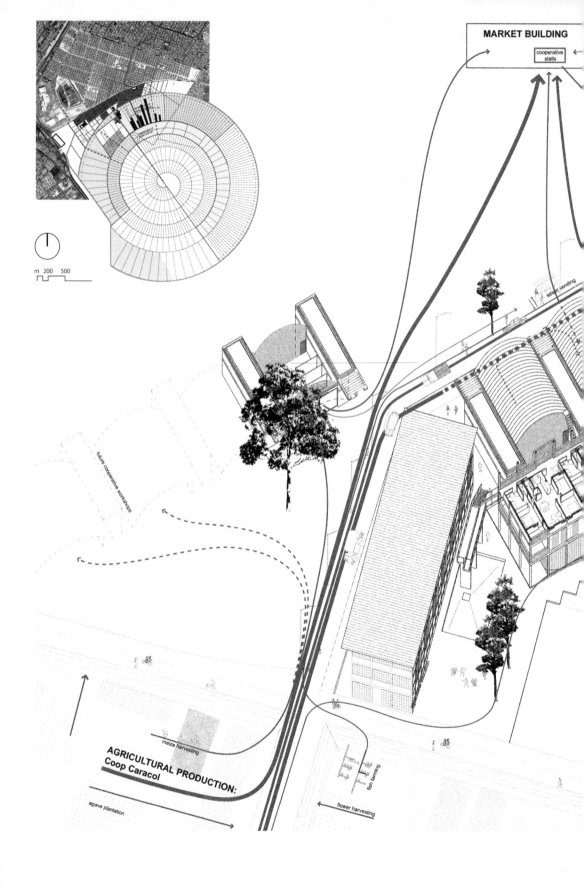

MARKET BUILDING

cooperative
stalls

street vending

future cooperative workshops

maize harvesting

AGRICULTURAL PRODUCTION:
Coop Caracol

agave plantation

fish farming

flower harvesting

m 200 500

WHOLESALE MARKET
AND DISTRIBUTION
CENTRE ECATEPEC

import non-local products

agricultural products

processing

housing cooperative meeting

manufacturing of building materials

# Santiago

# An Introduction to the Urbanization of Shock Therapy: Santiago

**Miguel Robles-Durán**

Throughout history, the process of urbanization has always been driven by the needs and wants of the economic regimes that have mandated the specific forms of surplus accumulation, market expansion, territorial control and social subjugation. This introduction is an attempt to present the urbanization of shock therapy in such terms, the very same terms defined by the capitalist logic of urbanization. Any urbanist lacking an understanding of capitalist processes is simply an instrument of an invisible hand. In this case, the invisible hand is the devastating neoliberal agenda.

Since the 1979 consolidation of neoliberalism as the new economic orthodoxy regulating public policy, and therefore urbanization, in the advanced capitalist world, three very distinct general forms of urbanization have dominated socio-spatial development in almost every major city of the globe. Strategies of inter-urban competition, surplus absorption and poly-central concentration have been the driving force of the development agenda of advanced capitalist cities, affecting not only the obvious global cities such as Paris, London and Tokyo, but mostly secondary and tertiary cities such as Melbourne, Lille, Cincinnati and Yokohama. Whereas in the third world, with the illusionary desire to join the standards of the developed world, the urban development strategies have been subject, on the one hand, to the mimicking of those considered advanced and, on the other, to the economic imposition of the international neoliberal regulatory bodies, whose main urban interest is in the production of a safe and open environment for foreign direct investment (FDI). The social theorist David Harvey explains the latter by arguing that 'the fundamental mission of the neoliberal state is to create a "good business climate" and therefore to optimize conditions for capital accumulation no matter what the consequences for employment or social well being'.[1] Demonstrating the dialectic of capitalist production, these parallel processes of urbanization have been dramatically unbalanced and heavily tilted in favour of the so-called advanced urbanities. The introduction of neoliberalism to the third world required a much bigger dose of shock therapy.

If the neoliberal agenda, as described by Harvey, 'proposes that human well being can best be advanced by liberating individual entrepreneurial freedoms and skills within an institutional framework characterized by strong private property rights, free markets, and free trade',[2] then it is clear that only those urbanities with developed economies and institutional frameworks would be able to successfully rebuild as power centres for capitalist accumulation and attract the massive amounts of surplus generated by the neoliberal exploitation of the weak, underdeveloped and emerging urbanities. More tangibly than in the previous two general capitalist modes of urbanization (Fordism and Keynesianism), the advanced neoliberal urbanization has made the parallel form of urbanization of the third world instrumental to its expansive growth, to an extent that it has become almost impossible to conceive any form of third world urbanization that does not submit to the aggressive ways and demands of the neoliberal agenda.

---

1 David Harvey, **Spaces of Global Capital: Towards a Theory of Uneven Geographical Development** (London: Verso, 2003), p. 25.
2 David Harvey, **A Brief History of Neoliberalism** (Oxford: Oxford University Press, 2005), p. 2.

The neoliberal regime has not expanded by the acquisition and ordering of weak territories, as many past regimes did after a conquest; instead, during its 29 years of domination, the global success of the neoliberal regime has been characterized by its violent penetration into any existing urban order or disorder. In the early 1970s, the American political scientist Samuel Huntington argued that expanding through penetration is in fact a mode of domination that is highly compatible with the multiplication of national sovereignties in the third world.[3] Indeed, the multiplication of sovereignties of the last three decades has not only facilitated the growth of multinational markets but more importantly, it has opened new territories to foreign direct investment, creating what Harvey calls 'fresh fields for capitalist accumulation'.[4] What characterized these 'fields' before the neoliberal penetration was a vulnerable economy, plus, in some cases, an existing or produced socio-political instability. This was the case with Chile in 1973, the famous first neoliberal state experiment, produced by a US supported military coup that ousted the democratically-elected socialist government of Salvador Allende, which was believed to be a threat to the capitalist elites of Chile and the big interests of foreign corporate capital investments.

The economic and socio-political instability brought by the coup allowed a group of government-supported American economists to penetrate and destroy any remnant of social policy and popular organization in favour of massive privatizations, foreign direct investment-led financial regulations, international loan programmes led by institutions such as the International Monetary Fund (IMF) and the 'freeing' of labour markets. The Chilean experiment, as Harvey points out, 'demonstrated that the benefits of revived capitalist accumulation were highly skewed under forced privatization. The country and the ruling elites, along with foreign investors, did extremely well in the early stages',[5] heralding the coming of a new world economic agenda. However, as with all capitalist experiments, the consequence of the drastic economic impositions did not bring much prosperity to the middle and low classes of society: 177,000 jobs were lost in the decade after 1973,[6] and by the mid 1980s the country was purposely in deep recession, coercing Chileans into a struggle to adapt and survive in a newly created world. This orchestrated economic shock was academically and politically propagated by the right, as an achievement of the theory of economic shock therapy, successfully demonstrating the triggering of a favourable condition for the fast penetration of the free market, along with all its policy, regulations, institutions, corporations and organizations. From 1973 until the end of Pinochet's regime in 1990, the population of the urban capital Santiago grew approximately from 2.5 million to 4.5 million,[7] mostly as a consequence of the massive rural migration heralded by the privatization of the farmlands and the poverty created by the economic shock.

Moreover, many people – about 28,000 between 1979 and 1984 – were transferred from illegal settlements by the authorities to low-income housing. The result was a further expansion of urbanization and an increase in the distances that people had to travel to work, look for work, or attend school.

In this early experiment, the urban impact of the shock therapy was not as well orchestrated as the economic policy that produced it. No real attention was paid to urbanization until 1979, when an amendment was made to the general urban plan of the city, proposing a large territorial extension. In principle, the objective of the shock was never spatial, although an important neoliberal prescription was the privatization of space. State property was offered to the market, and private concessions were sold to the building and management of public spaces and urban infrastructure. In a few years, most subsidized rental housing was converted to subsidized private housing; schools, hospitals and many public buildings were also offered to the market along with the state's construction industry; parks, transit infrastructure, utilities, urban management and services were given to private concession. In short, the production of the city, that since the late nineteenth century and throughout a large part of the twentieth century was the responsibility of a democratic social state, was now in the hands of a corrupt authoritarian regime, its collaborating developers, real estate speculators and international investors. The spatial consequences of such economic transformations were immense and possibly never predicted by the early neoliberal economists. I summarize in six general points the physical urban effect of the orchestrated economic shock:

1 The expansion of informal settlements, mostly in the peripheries, adding to the ones formed as a consequence of Chile's period of Industrialization.
2 The forced displacement of poor dwellers from central areas of the city towards housing settlements in the periphery, causing the multiplication of 'affordable' housing districts and the enclosing of middle–high class 'residential' areas.
3 The creation of what I call 'green zones',[8] a term inspired by the new American war terminology – urban fragments that are considered safe for direct foreign investment and tourism.
4 The building of central business districts (CBD) designed to concentrate in types of 'green zones' the administrative, commercial and financial operations of the fresh capital injection that came from privatization.
5 The introduction of poly-centrality as the main planning concept of the city. The making of central business districts and 'green zones' already followed such a conception.

3 Samuel P. Huntington, 'Transnational Organizations in World Politics', **World Politics**, vol. 25, no.3 (1973), p. 344.
4 Harvey, **Spaces of Global Capital: Towards a Theory of Uneven Geographical Development**, p. 25.
5 Harvey, **A Brief History of Neoliberalism**, p. 16.
6 A. Hirschman, 'The Political Economy of Latin American Development: Seven Exercises in Retrospection', **Latin American Review** 12, no. 3 (1987), p. 15.
7 Source: INE Censos de Población y Plan Regulador Metropolitano de Santiago, 1992.
8 The Green Zone is the common name given to the International Zone of Iraq, completely surrounded by high concrete blast walls, T-Walls and barbed wire and access was available through a handful of entry control points, all of which were controlled by Coalition troops. It is this security that makes the Green Zone the safest area of Baghdad. Consequently, the Green Zone is referred to colloquially as 'the bubble'.

6 The expansion of the main streets and avenues of the poly-centre network and the construction of new roads to reinforce the importance of the newly determined centralities. This goes together with the infrastructural and technological investment necessary to support such urban 'regeneration'.

These points exemplify, to my view, the most extreme urban territorial transformations produced by neoliberalism and by no means cover the total urban impact of shock therapy. Similar points can be made regarding the environmental disasters produced by the imposition of such rapid changes; the social pain caused by the dissolution of collective relations and economic exchange forms; and the radical alterations of patterns of daily life along with the mental conception of the city. It is also important to note that the urban processes under industrialization and the functionalist planning that typically accompanied it had already produced deep class divisions in the city, spatial concentration of capital, informal settlements and large infrastructural transformations. Neoliberal urbanization multiplied these effects and introduced new and better forms of penetration.

Neoliberal urbanization heralded the total social de-concentration of alienated dwellers and workers, by the indeterminate scattering of the means of production and their dependents into the outskirts, voids and peripheries of the city. While the nineteenth century showed the formation of peripheral concentrations of labour space and housing in determinate spaces inside or outside the city, the late twentieth and early twenty-first centuries evinced the splintering of the fragments and the submission of their economic autonomy to the urban centres of capital accumulation. Neoliberal urbanism created a radical division in the civic appropriation of the urban fabric, ultimately encouraging the worldwide-pronounced confidence in the idea of the polycentric city, defining the proliferation of urban centralities, as the main operative principle of neoliberal urbanization.

The following section includes excerpts from the work of the Santiago Study Group and a chapter by Rodrigo Hidalgo. Hidalgo studies the recent urban developments in Santiago's periphery, namely the constructing of subsidized housing and gated communities, whereas the work of the Santiago Study Group is focused on the area of La Victoria in Santiago. While offering only an introduction to the specific case of urbanization in the first nation to practise neoliberal policies, this section nevertheless enables a basic understanding of the forces which were later unleashed across the globe.
Observing not only Chile but also other third world nations which went through similar abrupt processes of urbanization in the 1980s, one cannot help notice how perfected the methodological frameworks of shock therapy have become.

**Acknowledgements**   The Santiago Study Group of the Delft School of Design was directed by H. Sohn, G. Bruyns and M. Robles-Durán; with the collaboration of D. Sepúlveda. The group included A. Distelbrink, T. Duinhoven, S. van den Heuvel, S. Jaffri, S. Kohut, A. Maessen, M. Marozas, N. Placella, D. Robers, V. Scheepers, E. Tijhuis, L. Verheul, K. Vervuurt and A. van Zweeden. The drawings and photographs included in this section were produced by the Santiago Study Group unless credited to others. The Santiago Study Group wishes to thank the scholars, activists, administrators and urbanists who supported the project with their time and knowledge.

# Socioterritorial Changes in Santiago de Chile and the New Outline for the Metropolitan Periphery: From State 'Precariopolis' to Real Estate 'Privatopolis'[1]

**Rodrigo Hidalgo**

One of the principal signs of change seen today in large Latin American cities, and of the Third World in general is related to recent modifications in the use of land in the urban peripheries. This work seeks to provide an empirical background and theoretical reading of the way in which the emerging territorial configurations are developing in the metropolitan periphery of Santiago de Chile, based upon analysis of the two main types of constructed residential areas: subsidized housing developments and gated communities. It is therefore useful to explore in depth the different dimensions and processes that give rise to the creation of a new socio-residential urban geography. Emphasis is placed on the resulting spatial forms and on the unequal roles played by the various agents involved, from private developers and the state to the actual residents.

**Introduction**  The spatial forms created by the expansion of large Latin American cities, and, in this particular case, found in the main urban areas of the Southern Cone (Chile, Argentina and Brazil), show symptoms of change and peculiarity that should be highlighted in an era of neoliberal globalization. In recent years, Latin American metropolitan cities have undergone an important transformation, represented, among other singularly important aspects, by the changes in socio-economic divisions in the cities and the development of new urban centres. Similarly, there has been an evident increase in gated communities, for the most part far away from the city centres, as well as in the construction of high-rise towers within built-up urban areas, linked to both big-business corporate buildings and to other uses, such as residential, office and hotel-related. For their part, these last are in direct relation to the need to rehabilitate the city centres and to renew financial strategies that focus on property development in search of profits giving more rapid returns. Many of these products are associated with what have been defined as artefacts of globalization:[2] large shopping centres, big chain hotels and exclusive housing developments, amongst others.

In addition to this emerging real-estate production, traditional areas designated for residence are marked by a new impulse stemming from the property development dynamic, which is becoming more aggressive and powerful owing to an increase in integration with financial capital.[3] This integration enables transformation from the urban into exclusive urbanization, exclusive above all for those who have no means to become a part of the production logic because they are not real

**1**  This work is a result of the research project financed by the National Fund for Science and Technology (Fondecyt) 1060759, entitled 'Expansión residencial en las comunas de la periferia de las áreas metropolitanas de Santiago y Valparaiso: efectos socio-espaciales y lectura de las relaciones de poder entre los agentes urbanos (1992-2005)', carried out between 2006 and 2008.

**2**  Carlos de Mattos, 'Santiago de Chile: metamorfosis bajo un nuevo impulso de modernización capitalista' in **Santiago en la globalización, ¿una nueva ciudad?**, ed. Carlos de Mattos, Maria Elena Ducci, Alfredo Rodriguez and Gloria Yáñez (Santiago: Ediciones SUR/EURE Libros, 2004) pp. 17-46.

**3**  See for example, Paulo Pereira, 'Reestruturação imobiliária em São Paulo (SP): especificidade y tendencia', in **Dinâmica imobiliária e reestruturação urbana na América Latina**, ed. Rogerio Lima Da Silveira, Paulo Pereira and Vanda Ueda (Santa Cruz do Sul: EDUNISC, 2006), pp. 43-63; or Carlos de Mattos, 'Globalización, negocios inmobiliarios y mercantilización del desarrollo urbano', in **Producción Inmobiliaria y reestructuración Metropolitana en América Latina**, by Paulo Pereira and Rodrigo Hidalgo (Santiago: Serie GEOlibros No. 11 and FAU/USP, 2008), pp. 23-40.

estate consumers. Within this urbanization there persist, and in some cases are amplified, the typical traditional Latin American housing scenarios whereby the concentration of income within certain social groups has always been significant. In this way, according to the United Nations Human Settlement Programme (UN-HABITAT), 130 million Latin Americans live in precarious and informal settlements, with no property ownership titles nor access to legal services.[4] There would seem to be no place in these settlements for a fulfilling existence, streets appearing only after people move in, giving the impression of an almost nomadic way of life.

This metropolitan restructuring, which in its urban and territorial dimension has references in current methods of real estate production, is changing the relation-ship between the public and the private, thereby influencing the administration of the means of metropolitan growth. So much so that, in some cases, it may be said that within the built-up areas, one or several private cities are in development, given the changes in the urban space and in the influence of the large real estate developers' actions. This scenario requires concrete action and new theoretical understanding on the part of the political powers, which can guide interpretations that are of service to society and to decision-makers, as there is practically nobody who is uninvolved in the divisions created by these socio-spatial tensions.

From a demographic point of view, one of the most important elements in this process of metropolitan change concerns the role played over recent years by migration and inter-city residential displacement, and by their determining forces.[5] In the case of Chile, a series of public works have notably influenced this evolution in recent times, especially in relation to main thoroughfares and highly transited roads, and in the residential mobility of medium and high-income sectors with their consequent changes to the urban and inter-urban landscape. In this way, within the framework of 'highway concessions', the private sector has begun to mobilize in search of attractive investment prospects, boosting the physical expansion of metropolitan areas and intermediate cities.

One of the manifestations of physical expansion of the Santiago de Chile Metro-politan Area (SMA) towards outlying areas is related to the construction of hori-zontal condominium developments and closed communities aimed at the middle, upper-middle and upper socio-economic classes. These groups migrate to the peri-urban areas in search of new, larger residential spaces, surrounded by an environment that is supposed to be the opposite of metropolitan modernity.

The coupling of residential developments with concessioned highways is the basis of what we have termed *real estate privatopolis*, which is related to the increase in area limits in the promotion and construction of closed residential communities, surrounded by protective walls and security, where progressive self-segregation has come about, not only in terms of the dwellings but also the services needed to support this function. This phenomenon, which began in earnest during the second half of the 1990s, now finds favourable space for expansion in the metropolitan outskirts: more square metres at a lower price than in the dense city, and often better connected than within the city in terms of road infrastructure, thanks to the aforementioned highways. In this way, real estate options in the rural outskirts are being increasingly made available to the middle and upper classes, these developments including supermarkets, schools, playgrounds and recreational areas for residents' exclusive use, similar to those services available within the SMA. The only excluded activity in these projects, up to the present time, concerns places of employment and work for potential owners.[6]

Another manifestation of the expansion process or of the outward growth of urbanization of the SMA is historically associated with the development of State-subsidized housing projects, aimed at lower and lower-middle class groups. These housing complexes have been traditionally built, especially during the second half of the twentieth century, on the immediate outskirts of the urban area. However, nowadays they are built far away, in municipalities mainly made up of rural land.

The results of this public housing initiative are what we have termed state *precariopolis* (precarious city), which refers to a mono-functional area, segregated and fragmented, defined by the presence of basic urban services – electricity, water, lighting and in some cases, paved roads. In these places, the inhabitants live in homes averaging no more than 45 square metres with an absence of other social classes and lack of some basic and most non-basic services and facilities such as schools, health centres, recreational areas and shopping centres, amongst others.[7]

This housing type makes up the majority of residential options offered within the metropolitan market, and in this way, its location pattern signifies diverse changes in the socio-economic profiles of the population and in the functions of the places where they are situated. This article aims to provide an empirical background and theoretical reading of the way in which the emerging territorial configurations are developing in the metropolitan periphery of Santiago de Chile, based upon analysis of the two main opposite types of residential construction: state-subsidized social housing developments and gated communities. It is therefore useful to explore in depth the dif-

**4** United Nations Development Programme (UNDP), **Human Development Report 2006. Beyond Scarcity: Power, poverty and the global water crisis** (New York: United Nations Development Programme, 2006).

**5** See for instance, Jorge Rodriguez, 'Paradojas y contrapuntos de dinámica demográfica metropolitana: algunas respuestas basadas en la explotación intensiva de microdatos censales', or Severino Escolano and Jorge Ortiz, 'Patrones espaciales de movilidad de la población: algunos efectos en la sociogeografía de Santiago', both in: **Santiago de Chile: movilidad espacial y reconfiguración metropolitana**, ed. Carlos de Mattos and Rodrigo Hidalgo (Santiago: Eure Libros y Geolibros, 2007), pp. 19-52.

**6** Rodrigo Hidalgo, Axel Borsdorf and Rafael Sánchez, 'Hacia un nuevo tejido rurbano. Los megaproyectos de ciudades valladas en la periferia de Santiago de Chile', in **Ciudad y Territorio. Estudios Territoriales**, 39, 151 (2007a), pp. 115-35.

**7** Rodrigo Hidalgo, '¿Se acabó el suelo en la gran ciudad?: Las nuevas periferias metropolitanas de la vivienda social en Santiago de Chile', **EURE**, 33, 98 (2007b), pp. 57-75.

ferent dimensions and processes that give rise to the creation of a new socio-residential urban geography in the periphery of SMA, and which relate to the unequal roles played by the agents involved, from the private developers and the State to the residents themselves.

## New residential spaces on the metropolitan outskirts: elements for interpretation
Using European and North American cities as reference, the evolution of the city from the nineteenth century to the present contains key moments which deserve to be highlighted from the perspective of this work. Firstly, the nineteenth-century metropolis was organized in a gravitational way: a functional economic centre around which there was a close and dependent periphery, where the boundary between the urban and the rural was clear and well defined. Influenced by industrialization and the proliferation of public transport – from urban and suburban railways to the motor car – this situation began to noticeably change. Strictly speaking this process gave rise to the creation of the suburbs, as an area of deliberate expansion of the city into the countryside, with mainly residential aspirations. With the passing of time this area has become more complex, uncontrolled and difficult to define and demarcate.[8]

In the twentieth century, owing to mutual interaction and growth, there was a continual process of spatial fusion between the less important centres surrounding the main cities and the cities' suburban areas. Centripetal and centrifugal forces overlapped, inducing a constant expansion of the city, leading to what is called the urban-rural continuum. Within this spatial fusion, the main cities maintained their role as cultural centres, but their polarizing force weakened. Towards the end of the century a new spatial pattern characterized the periphery, a structure made up of diverse and specialized spatial units, increasingly less dependent upon the traditional city and substituting old hierarchies. In this system, the relationship between the city and the country is no longer rational or unique in structure. Diversity and randomness are characteristics of what is termed *post-suburban*. In this context, and continuing the North American and Western European tradition, the *post-suburban* corresponds to a new urban structure which develops on the edges of a traditional city and functions practically independently of the established centralities within the city centre, having highly diverse activities, appearances and styles.[9]

Behind these phenomena are a series of transformations concerning modifications to production patterns resulting from global economic restructuring processes. Through changes in labour markets and their geographic diversification, this explains the appearance of this phenomenon in the majority of industrialized and developing nations and regions.[10]

The interpretation stemming from the European and Anglo-Saxon situation is different to that experienced in Latin American cities, which requires a permanent conceptual re-theorization that fits with empirical reality. From this we are able to formulate questions relating to the reality of the Latin American experiences and those upon which the analytical criteria is based, such as: are we really, in the cities of the region and in this case in Santiago de Chile, witnessing a *post-suburban* phenomenon? Can we mechanically apply the concepts of a diffuse or dispersed city in order to differentiate between various forms of metropolitan growth? What kind of functional decentralization is there on the outskirts of Santiago? In terms of constructed spaces, are there diverse and multi-functional areas or are we faced with mono-functional peripheral areas whose sole common characteristic with the *post-suburban* is the social fragmentation of land use?

## State precariopolis **and** real estate privatopolis: **what does this refer to in the metropolitan periphery of Santiago?** Analysis of demographic behaviour in the communities of the metropolitan area of Santiago (sma) and of those in the surrounding area shows that those in the central communities have lower growth rates than the peripheral communities, a relevant aspect of the metropolitanization of the sma and one which points to a tendency towards contra-urbanization,[11] also seen in other large cities in Chile.[12]

Within this general framework there are relevant considerations regarding the spaces under study, such as the historical dimension and the wide range of forms in which metropolitan expansion takes place. These are common to Chilean cities in general and to the sma in particular and help to establish specifics and the need to generate analytical categories which relate more closely with the events and realities that form them. This work intends to examine, firstly, how social housing, in its search for cheaper land, creates truly mono-functional, segregated and fragmented areas, which we will call '*state precariopolis*', defined, as mentioned, by the presence of basic urbanized services – electricity, water, lighting and some paved roads, but lacking in other aspects which

**8** Axel Borsdorf, 'On the way of post-suburbia? Changing structures in the outskirts of European cities', in **European cities. Insights on outskirts**, ed. Axel Borsdorf and Pierre Zembri (Paris: METL/PUCA, 2004), pp. 7-30.
**9** Ibid.
**10** Carlos de Mattos, 'Mercado metropolitano de trabajo y desigualdades sociales en el Gran Santiago: ¿Una ciudad dual?', **EURE,** 85 (2002), pp. 51-70.
See also: Carlos de Mattos (2004), pp. 17-46.
**11** This has been dealt with in the work of several experts such as: Mercedes Arroyo, 'La dinámica de las Áreas Metropolitanas en un contexto de desindustrialización', **Revista de Geografía Norte Grande**, 28 (2001), pp. 57-64; Brian Berry, 'The counterurbanization process: Urban America since 1970', in B. Berry, **Urbanization and Counterurbanization** (Beverly Hills, CA: Sage, 1976), pp. 17-30; or Carlos Ferrás, 'El enigma de la contraurbanización: Fenómeno empírico y concepto caótico', **EURE**, 33, 98 (2007), pp. 5-25.
**12** For Valparaiso see Rodrigo Hidalgo and Axel Borsdorf, 'Puerto abierto ¿ciudad cerrada? Transformaciones socio espaciales en la estructura urbana del área metropolitana de Valparaiso', in **Revista Geográfica de Valparaíso**, 36 (2005), pp. 189-206.
For Concepción see Leonel Pérez and Edison Salinas, 'Crecimiento urbano y globalización: transformaciones del Área Metropolitana de Concepción, Chile, 1992-2002'. **Scripta Nova. Revista Electrónica de Geografía y Ciencias Sociales**, XI, 251 (2007) http://www.ub.es/geocrit/sn/sn-251.htm [last accessed 25/09/2010].

create cities, such as the existence of other social classes and a variety of services and facilities, indispensable for the development of urban living.[13]

The logic behind social housing lies in the availability of lands whose surface value per unit is low. These are generally plentiful on the city's outskirts. These housing projects become a contributing factor in the development of socio-spatial segregation patterns promoted by urban agents with the aim of increasing their economic investments and raising political and class status, whilst they also become models of urban expansion in its broadest sense.[14] In spite of public efforts to diversify the geographic options offered to those with low incomes, the majority of these housing projects cause a concentration of low-income population in a few sectors of the city.[15]

Since the beginning, Santiago de Chile's social housing policy has been to locate public housing developments on the city's outskirts. This is shown in some studies,[16] which explain how, since the enactment of the Workers' Housing Law of 1906, administrations progressively built on the periphery of the city, either through direct or indirect action, building new houses, favouring accessible land or administering basic urban services enabling the creation of 'spontaneous' or 'irregular' settlements, which have adopted various forms and names throughout Latin America, such as the 'favelas' of Brazil, the 'young towns' of Peru, 'misery towns' in Argentina and 'encampments' in Chile, to name a few.[17]

However, since the second half of the nineties we have seen a large increase in public housing in the communities on the metropolitan periphery of Santiago, due to the growth and consolidation of free market policies, which has strong repercussions in the initiatives driven in all sectors by the State of Chile. Between 1978 and 2003 about 27,000 units were built on the metropolitan outskirts, almost half of these in the last decade.[18] Although many of these dwellings are for a population which does indeed reside in the areas associated with these communities, the figures unquestionably show that public housing is no longer located solely in the immediate periphery of the city, but that it is now moving into those spaces which join onto the metropolitan area itself.

The social changes experienced in the areas where this type of housing exists are reflected in the analysis of the variation in the Socioeconomic Development Index (SDI)[19] for the period 1992-2002, whose results indicate that the SDI dropped in areas of social housing, remained static and then rose slightly, which leads us to confirm that these social housing developments often lead to regressive social change in the area.

Consequently, it can be stated that the policy of commercialization in the use of urban land, imposed since the mid 1980s, forced public housing developments further and further away from the city. In this way, peri-urban communities began to receive new inhabitants who, because of their poverty, lowered the socio-economic status of the places to which they had moved. Empirical evidence shows a link between developing concentrations of poverty and the housing policies of the State [see fig.1].

So, are we really witnessing the creation of a *state precariopolis*, which, apart from having low objective indicators of living standards – as recorded by SDI – presents other problems seen in fig. 1, showing the association between public housing areas with functional dependence in terms of work and study-related activities? Specifically, public housing developments are situated in places which oblige the inhabitants to use services and sources of employment only available inside the metropolitan area or the established city, forcing them to travel great distances in order to fulfil their educational and employment needs.

Secondly, we aim to examine the other side of Santiago's residential expansion. This involves closed, gated communities and horizontal condominiums, which appear as products offered by private developers, who seek fast profits, taking advantage of diverse factors that help them to increase the value of land on the periphery. But these are not ubiquitous pieces of land that can be in any geographic position. They take advantage of the existing natural resources and landscape, 24-hour surveillance and high-speed access to the metropolitan mega-infrastructure, which help to instil a feeling of connection between the home and the heart of the city and all its services.

If we analyse the location of the gated communities of the type found on the outskirts of the city[20] that give rise to the *privatopolis*, the situation is different to that of the *precariopolis*, in that in the places there is a tendency for the area to be associated with an increasing or higher SDI. At

13  See for instance the work of Horacio Capel, 'La definición de lo urbano', in **Estudios Geográficos**, 138-139 (1975), pp. 265-301; or Horacio Capel, 'A modo de introducción. Los problemas de las ciudades: urbs, civitas y polis', in **Ciudades, arquitectura y espacio urbano** (Almeria: Instituto de Estudios de Cajamar, 2003), pp. 9-22.
14  See for instance, David Harvey, **Urbanismo y desigualdad social**. (Madrid: Siglo Veintiuno, 1977); or Henri Lefebvre, **El derecho a la ciudad** (Barcelona: Peninsula, 1978).
15  Rodrigo Hidalgo (2007b), pp. 57-75.
16  Ibid.
17  Rodrigo Hidalgo, **La vivienda social en Chile y la construcción del espacio urbano en el Santiago del siglo XX** (Santiago: DIBAM, 2005a).
18  Rodrigo Hidalgo, Hugo Zunino and Lily Alvarez, 'El emplazamiento periférico de la vivienda social en el área metropolitana de Santiago de Chile: consecuencias socio espaciales y sugerencias para modificar los criterios actuales de localización', **Scripta Nova. Revista Electrónica de Geografía y Ciencias Sociales**, XI, 245 (27) (2007c). <http://www.ub.es/geocrit/sn/sn-24527.htm> [accessed 20/08/2010]
19  The SDI was calculated using the Human Development Index (HDI), a methodology proposed by the United Nations Development Programme (UNDP) (UNDP/MIDEPLAN, 2000). The SDI was developed according to three indicators of factors: luxury assets, educational level of over 25s and quality of housing (Hidalgo and Borsdorf, 2005). The first of these took into account nine variables for 1992 and eleven for 2002. In the case of urban areas, the basis for analysis was the census zone; and for the rural areas, the census district. These last are administered by the National Statistics Institute (NSI) for the management, collection and treatment of census data.
20  For details see Rodrigo Hidalgo, 'De los pequeños condominios a la ciudad vallada: las urbanizaciones cerradas y la nueva geografia social en Santiago de Chile', **EURE**, XXX, No. 91 (2004), pp. 29–52.

the same time, we should consider the fact that in some places gated communities have been built in quite close proximity to public housing developments, reducing spatial but maintaining social segregation. In these cases, the figures may denote an increase in SDI, but this is not a consequence of an overall improvement in the standard of living in these places, but a result of the location of middle and upper-middle sectors who segregate themselves, both physically and symbolically, from the poorer population [see fig. 1].

In this context, the shape that the social geography of the outskirts of Santiago is taking can be seen as an example of interpreting differently the processes of expansion and re-configuration of these types of spaces in Latin America. Following on from this, the challenge lies in being able to create analytical categories, which break away from the European and North American models of metropolitan areas. Certainly our own references need to be created, whilst not forgetting that the experiences of Europe and North America may provide their own useful reference.

Therefore the modes of growth of Chilean cities and their metropolitan areas over the past decades are associated with a model comparable to dispersed and also *post-suburban* cities, but must not necessarily be interpreted as such. Neither *precariopolis* nor *privatopolis* fits the European and North American experiences, given that the basic circumstances for the creation of these spaces did not exist in these Southern cities as they did in the northern hemisphere. As mentioned, in the European and North American cities, growth and residential development of the metropolitan periphery and surrounding areas has come about together with the installation of facilities and services equivalent to those within the cities.[21] In the case of the SMA, it has been shown that the inhabitants of the peripheral areas of the SMA carry out their daily activities, study and work, principally within the SMA.

This means that the way of life of both the *precariopolis* and the *privatopolis* residents is based to a significant degree on a dependency on the intra-metropolitan offerings in terms of sources of employment and supply of goods and services. The migration of the inhabitants of the *privatopolis* towards peri-urban areas is principally associated with the search for new residential spaces, with some comparative benefits regarding the availability of existing real estate within the city. One of the theories that explain this is the accessibility of larger pieces of land and properties that offer a transition between a rural and an urban environment.[22] There are also subjective considerations taken into account by the new inhabitants, who are looking for open spaces evoking bucolic, rustic landscapes where they can participate in recreational activities surrounded by 'nature', as in golf clubs, equestrian centres and lakes for watersports [see figs 2 and 3].

So the *privatopolis* is formed from the change of residential location and does not develop in unison with most of the services and specialized facilities required by the residents in order to fulfil their needs. Although in many communities of the SMA periphery some primary and secondary educational institutions have been established,[23] the degree of centralization in these communities is considerably inferior to that within the city centre and therefore residents are forced to travel the same distances as those living in the *precariopolis*, but with the advantage of having their own means of transport.

Behind the dynamics of urbanization there are different interpretations of the effects caused by the *privatopolis* on the geographic environment. One estimate concerns the consumption of highly productive land, a natural resource for the native population's primary activities, in general agricultural. This situation must be clarified because the land market is not blind and makes available *parcelas de agrado* (rural plots of land developed for residence),[24] whose rent, often generated by agricultural use, is notably inferior to that of urban use. However, within the scenario of economic globalization, agricultural land competes with urban use and the land that is made available to the residential market is precisely that which is not sufficiently productive to enter into international agricultural markets. This occurs partly in the metropolitan periphery of Santiago where there is wine-growing activity, which is often the great obstacle facing residential expansion.

These dynamics have undeniable consequences for the creation and management of urban land beyond the traditional city limits and for the relationship with the socio-economic changes facing the municipalities involved. This situation has direct repercussions for the sustainability of the metropolitanization process, in other words, for the territorial harmony of metropolitan expansion, which is an enormous challenge for the governability of these areas, and for those who have a role in it, as much for the public sector as for the private and the community in general.

Therefore, the residential colonization of the external communities of the SMA provokes a domino effect on the provision of infrastructures, facilities and services.[25] And if the growth in migration

**21** See for example, Axel Borsdorf, 'La transformación urbana-rural en Europa. ¿Hacia una unificación espacial en "post-suburbia"?', in **Gobernanza, Competitividad y Redes: La gestión de las ciudades en el siglo XXI**, ed. Carlos de Mattos, Oscar Figueroa, Rafael Giménez i Capdevilla, Arturo Orellana and Gloria Yáñez (Santiago: Eurelibros, 2005), pp. 21-29; or Rodrigo Hidalgo and Axel Borsdorf, 'El crecimiento urbano en Europa: conceptos, tendencias y marco comparativo para el área metropolitana de Santiago de Chile', **Estudios Geográficos**, LXX, 266 (2009), pp. 181-203.
**22** Rodrigo Hidalgo, Alejandro Salazar, Rodrigo Lazcano, Francisco Roa, Lily Alvarez and Mario Calderón, 'Transformaciones socioterritoriales asociadas a proyectos residenciales de condominios en comunas de la periferia del área metropolitana de Santiago', **Revista INVI**, 20, 54 (2005b), pp. 104-33.
**23** See the work by Hidalgo, Borsdorf and Sánchez for the case of the megaprojects of Chicureo in Colina in the north of the SMA, in, for example, Rodrigo Hidalgo, Axel Borsdorf and Rafael Sánchez, (2007a), pp. 115-35.
**24** The **parcelas de agrado** refer to the division and development of rural land stemming from the Decreto con Fuerza de Ley 3.516 of 1980, which permits the obtaining of tracts of land up to 5000 m². 
**25** Rodrigo Hidalgo, Alejandro Salazar, Rodrigo Lazcano, Francisco Roa, Lily Alvarez and Mario Calderón, (2005b), pp. 104-33.

produces a substantial change in numbers of residents in these areas, this will have an impact on socio-political representation for these regions of urban-rural interface.[26]

One of the influencing factors in the metropolitan governability of the SMA is the administrative fragmentation of the 42 municipalities that make up the continuous urban belt of SMA. In Chile there are few examples of institutions trying to co-ordinate, between sectors, the policies and processes which affect the territorial configurations that make up the metropolitan areas.[27] The main tools are concerned with regional urban development plans and intercommunal regulation plans, by definition supposed to regulate urban land and its areas of expansion. This situation generates a series of problems and outsourcing in the process of Chilean urban development, because the existing channels are limited to regulating land use and determining the areas for urban expansion, whilst ignoring and having no power to deal with matters of great importance in urban management, such as transport services, waste collection and provision of certain products and basic services fundamental to achieve a minimum standard of comfort.[28]

The deregulatory and subsidiary framework that made way for neoliberal reform in Chile allowed the establishment of a method of land organization according to competing profitability of land use rather than the land's environmental and territorial capability. Neoliberal doctrine in Chile is associated with the establishment of General Pinochet's dictatorship, where economic growth was sought through the deregulation of the economy and opening the country to foreign trade. This led to a considerable reduction in import tariffs and an incentive for foreign capital to play a part in the economic activities of the country. Diversification of national exports was boosted using the principle of comparative advantage, and in this way, the exploitation of the country's natural resources became one of the most important ways in which Chile was able to begin participating competitively in the external market. This new development strategy affected many areas of life in Chile and its cities. The neoliberal reforms hit the urban land market and were the driving force behind the flexibilization of the urban planning system still in place today, having been established in 1953 with the enactment of the Construction and Urbanization Act. The greatest example of this situation came in 1979 with the National Urban Development Policy, which decreed that urban land was not in scarce supply and that its price should be fixed by the market forces. The effects of this initiative were felt as much in land prices as in the fragmentation of social spaces in Santiago. Greater land availability did not translate into a lesser value; on the contrary, land prices rose in response to the speculation process sparked by the freeing up of lands by the market. However, the increase in the limits of developable land made possible the accumulation of social housing developments in places offering cheaper land and this was targeted for this type of housing project. For the most part, these locations were far from the city centres, lacking in services and basic facilities, whose inhabitants had to travel great distances in order to reach their workplaces, schools and health centres, a situation which led to the social exclusion of families living in these housing developments. The Urban Development Policy of 1979 also resulted in the physical expansion of Santiago. Based on this policy, the area for potential urbanization was defined as 60,000 hectares, almost doubling the city's late 1970s area. The urban region grew by almost 3,000 hectares per year from 1980 to 1985, reaching an overall figure in 1985 of 46,000 hectares. In this free market environment the real estate sector became one of the protagonists of national economic development, particularly in the cities. The real estate business and its financial strength were viewed as a revitalizing element of the economy, considering the multiplying effect it had on other sectors in terms of labour and related services.[29]

In this sphere, the current residential picture of the metropolitan periphery is also affected by the role played by the businesses providing the installation of basic urban services for the housing built in these areas. This role is particularly important in the case of the *privatopolis*, in that these communities are created on the *parcelas de agrado* (rural plots of land for residential development). These are located beyond the boundaries of the regulatory plans and their development depends not on urban construction regulations but on what is feasible for the businesses providing the service. In other words, rural land that is not agriculturally profitable is used for residential purposes, and these developments are not made possible by Chilean urban territorial regulatory legislation, but by the ability of private businesses to provide the service.

Behind these processes there is a series of power struggles going on between the various agents involved in determining how the occupation of these territories takes shape. This power, defined here as the degree of influence held by the parties involved in the social construction of the area, can control the destiny of a determinate place, with the purpose of attaining specific previously defined objectives. This power is exercised by people who enjoy a position of privilege and are able to dominate the other players who, at first, appear subordinate to decisions taken outside their sphere of control. To decipher the mechanics of power in a specific case, it is useful to consider the elements operating on different geographic scales. As argued by Hugo Zunino,[30] on general as

**26** Alejandro Salazar, 'La periurbanización en la recomposición de los espacios rurales metro-politanos: Santiago de Chile', in **Santiago de Chile: movilidad espacial y reconfiguración metropolitana**, ed. Carlos de Mattos and Rodrigo Hidalgo (Santiago: Eure Libros y Geolibros, 2007), pp. 207-25.
**27** See Federico Arenas, 'Re-configuración espacial y adaptación institucional: un reajuste pendiente en el caso de los espacios metropolitanos chilenos', in **Santiago de Chile: movili-dad espacial y reconfiguración metropolitana**, ed. Carlos de Mattos and Rodrigo Hidalgo (Santiago: Eure Libros y Geolibros, 2007), pp. 177-88.
**28** All of the tools for urban and territorial regulation are controlled by the Ley General de Urbanismo y Construcciones (General Urban and Construction Law). See: Ministerio de Vivienda y Urbanismo (MINVU), 'Decreto Ley Nº 458 Ley General de Urbanismo y Construcciones' (Santiago: MINVU, 1975).
**29** See Rodrigo Hidalgo (2005a).
**30** Hugo Zunino, 'Formación institucional y poder: investigando la construcción social de la ciudad', in **EURE**, 28, 84 (2002), pp. 103-16.

well as on specific scales, there are different strategies to enforce authority (for example, laws and regulations) or the ability to change courses of action defined by agents operating on different levels than their own (for example, local or national authorities can have their decisions affected by local entities and vice-versa).

The formal authority behind the laws, current regulations and cost criteria for the construction of public housing which make up the *precariopolis*, outlines a situation in which property developers have ample powers over decisions concerning where to locate the developments aimed at the poorest inhabitants, their architectural design and the quality of the infrastructure and facilities offered to the purchasers. Given that the housing policy in Chile encourages either application as an individual or through housing committees which group together a limited number of families living in a specific community, this policy has strong bias towards the individual, which severely limits the benefiting group's ability to organize itself and put pressure on the formal organisms such as the municipalities or the property developers. In this way, the supposed beneficiaries of social housing programmes remain subjugated by the fact that they possess scant resources to question and change the decisions already made and approved by the formal authority in place. As a consequence, the *population movement* in Chile, which played an influential role from the fifties to the mid eighties, has disappeared. This movement was a strong example of how the most needy urban classes made the political elite aware, during a large part of the twentieth century, of their inconformity with the difficulties they faced regarding access to housing and urban services in general. This was widely expressed in Chilean cities until the start of the military regime in 1973, and gave rise to the large expansion of informal marginal settlements which were home to the poorest classes for many years, and where inequality and exclusion, symbols of Latin American society, were the overriding characteristics.[31] Currently, the ability of inhabitants to influence a project after the event depends on their capacity for organization and their execution of strategies to bring about change.

The situation is different for the *privatopolis*. In this case, property developers take advantage of legal loopholes in order to urbanize areas beyond the city limits, or they at least exert their influence – boosted by the formal authorities' need to attract investment and development – to modify existing planning tools in order to give specific projects a legal base. During the pre-project phase they hold direct talks with municipal authorities. Decisions regarding the feasibility of these undertakings come about as a result of these meetings and in many cases there are informal instances of decision-making.[32] In the case of sub-division of land beyond the city limits, the purchasers of the land and/or housing are in a vulnerable position, since they cannot demand services, facilities and infrastructure from the municipality because the land is not subject to the same protection given to subdivided land within the urban area. The relationship established between developers and purchasers is based on agreements that frequently give rise to numerous conflicts. For this type of housing within the urban area, development must exist within the framework of current formal urban planning regulations.

**Final considerations**    Both the *privatopolis* and the *precariopolis* are territorial forms resulting from a specific time and place, which, in large terms, are linked with actions occurring within the context of the neoliberal State. Both are related to the flexibilization of the land market, a process that takes place on different levels and scales of decision-making.

Within the same dimension, the unequal speeds at which these processes happen are determined by the flow of capital and decision-making ability of the people involved. In this way, *precariopolis* and *privatopolis* can be observed within the process of real estate restructuring,[33] which is a product of the exhaustion of growth of the periphery characterizing the metropolitan expansion of the industrial-developmentalist State. In contrast, real estate restructuring addresses the way in which the movement of national and international capital brings about the optimum conditions for recouping profits, which in the context of economic globalization is one of the symbols of change in large cities.

As we have seen, the spatial forms resulting from this restructuring are not all equal and different metropolitan areas or large cities do not respond in a homogenous way. Those who are involved at a global level may be the same agents but not at a local level: this is a result of not only the capital-production relationship but also of historical, social and cultural processes that transcend that question and provide a basic framework for understanding the characteristics of metropolitan expansion in Latin America.

*Precariopolis* and *privatopolis* are the Chilean experience of residential solutions in the metropolitan outskirts and express,[34] in part, a repetition of the socio-geographical patterns within the cities, including public housing directed at the poorest areas of self-built housing created by the working classes since the 1950s, and those middle and upper-class enclaves, built during the same period which are now being developed into condominiums leading to closed urbanization. By contrast, what is happening outside the SMA is associated with a phenomenon whose location and extension are at the root of what Pereira has called 'the end of the city, urbanization without limits'.[35]

**31**  See Mario Garcés, **Tomando su sitio: El movimiento de pobladores de Santiago, 1957-1970** (Santiago: LOM, 2003).
**32**  Hugo Zunino, 'Power Relations in Urban Decision-making: Neo-liberalism, "Techno-politicians" and Authoritarian Redevelopment in Santiago, Chile', **Urban Studies**, 43, 10 (2006), pp. 1825-1846.
**33**  Paulo Pereira (2006), pp. 43-63.
**34**  Ibid.
**35**  Paulo Pereira, 'São Paulo: a transição metropolitana e a dissolução do urbano', in **Resúmenes Coloquio Chile Metropolitano** (Santiago: Instituto de Geografía e Instituto de Estudios Urbanos y Territoriales, Pontificia Universidad Católica de Chile, 2007).

Therefore, public housing – that is associated with *precariopolis* – becomes important in that it conforms to state policies which tend to generate large areas of social marginalization with the bigger housing developments. These often materialize on main roads, which are part of the continual expansion of the city or of the exodus of the urban population towards smaller, or newer cities, as described by Semmoud[36] in the case of Paris. On the outskirts of this and other French cities, conflicts occurring in 2005 demonstrate that the accumulated immigrant population from the Magreb and other so-called Third World countries as well as others excluded from French society, demand opportunities for inclusion that are often denied them because of where they live. This must be highlighted because in Chile in recent decades, intense construction of housing for the poor has been carried out on the periphery of almost all the cities in the country, but to considerably lower standards than those built in France and other European countries, and in contrast to those, not targeting an immigrant population.

The closed communities that give rise to the *privatopolis* originate, as mentioned, in the flexibilization of the legal framework which allows the development of real estate projects on the outskirts of the SMA and are evidence of deliberate action by the Chilean State. Within this action are situations concerning the way in which the real estate market promotes its products and how these are received by purchasers. There is an increase in land availability and in completed construction that does not match growth in demand in terms of the demographic increase of the SMA. In other words, there are more units for construction/habitation than there are potential buyers. Availability increases, house prices tend to rise or remain static and demand levels off or grows slightly. At the same time, low-cost mortgages become easier to access, which in Europe and North America is known as the 'real estate bubble',[37] a concept meaning that house prices bear no relation to the basic principles of economic rationale and are determined solely by how much purchasers are willing to pay.

In the case of the *privatopolis*, other factors should be noted in addition, owing to the fact that these properties are often anchored by family investments which seek a secure income through leasing or use as second homes for those urbanites who aspire to have a place of recreation and relaxation outside the city. This adds an element of complexity to a purely economic analysis and is definitely a valuable point when considering the changes experienced in the metropolitan periphery, also highlighting the need for more research into the behaviour of agents involved in the shaping of the urban outskirts.

*Precariopolis* and *privatopolis* are factors of change within the socio-territorial complexes currently being created outside the perimeter of the SMA conurbation. They modify the socio-geographic pattern, which mainly consists of a migrant population from the consolidated urban nucleus of the SMA, and in the case of the gated communities constitutes a deliberate move away from the built-up areas of the SMA. For the inhabitants of the State-subsidized public housing developments, this is practically their only opportunity for home ownership, which solves many problems but at the same time has disadvantages, mainly concerning the location, these places being far away from where they traditionally go to work, school, etcetera.

Research into current territorial processes experienced by the urban areas of the country, and their respective theoretical implications, constitutes an area of knowledge to be explored further by those with a scientific interest in territorial transformation. Understanding and interpretation of the spatial dynamics should lead to an establishment of a framework of reference fitting with the country's reality and contributing to the study and solution of the difficulties facing the State and Chilean society in these matters.

It is therefore relevant to point out that the Chilean reality interpreted here may be useful in addressing the differences between metropolitan expansion in Western European and North American countries, and those of Latin America, and from there establish principles for correction regarding the views surrounding the countries of this region, above all of middle-income nations such as Chile and its neighbours, Argentina and Brazil. Dialogue must be established with both realities to ascertain similarities and asymmetries. Attention should be focused not only on this, but on local realities, if one can refer to these in a world of capitalist globalization, and on how, based on these, identifying elements can be established to recognize the contradictions which lead to *state precariopolis* and *real estate privatopolis*, both forming part of a new reality in Latin American cities.

**36** Bouziane Semmoud, **Introduction à la géographie des grandes villes** (Paris: Editions du temps, 2001).
**37** Robert Brenner, 'New Boom or New Bubble? The trajectory of the US economy', in **New Left Review**, No. 25 (2004), pp. 55-96.

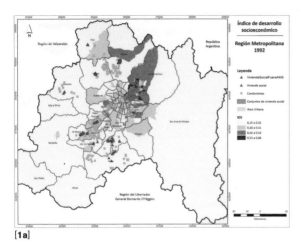

[1a]

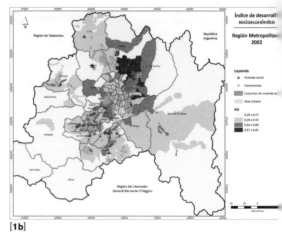

[1b]

[2a]

| Repulsion factors of the metropolis | Attraction factors of the periphery |
|---|---|
| Environmental factors: air pollution, noise, traffic jams. | Environmental factors: pure air, silence, open space immersed in 'nature' and 'rural life' (golf courses, lakes to enjoy nautical sports, etc.) |
| Lack of security, delinquency, and a perceived increase in crime. | Real estate supply: access to housing units located in large sites and constructed at lower costs in comparison to the metropolitan market. More vigilance and security. Possibilities of participating in the design of their 'own dwelling', in contrast to standardized units offered within the metropolitan area of Santiago. |
| Labour factors: changes in job opportunities or possibilities for retirement. | Opportunities to perform activities that do not involve daily commuting to work. |
| Personal factors: lack of attachment to urban lifestyle, migration to the countryside to live and work in it. Search for a different space, away from the 'evils' of the city, adequate to raise children. | Personal factors: more time for family. The physical wellbeing of the body. |

[3]

b]

# La Victoria, Santiago de Chile Project
# By the Santiago Study Group

Directed by **H. Sohn, G. Bruyns and M. Robles-Durán**

Participants **A. Distelbrink, T. Duinhoven, S. van den Heuvel, S. Jaffri, S. Kohut, A. Maessen, M. Marozas, N. Placella, D. Robers, V. Scheepers, E. Tijhuis, L. Verheul, K. Vervuurt, A. van Zweeden**

Building technology adviser **H. Plomp**

Urbanism adviser **D. Sepúlveda**

## La Victoria: resisting neoliberal urbanization
The role of Chile in the introduction, testing and spread of the neoliberal doctrine in the early 1970s is widely known today. What is less known, however, is the negative impact of this doctrine on the very particular urban situation of the country, and in particular on its capital city Santiago de Chile. Over the past three decades, but especially since the 1990s the advancement of neoliberalism has followed two related urban strategies that have generated important reconfigurations of the metropolitan area of Santiago. On the one hand, the insertion of several central business districts into the existing tissue of the inner city and the introduction of financial and economic service networks has effectively meant the imposition of a polycentric model into the existing centralized morphology. On the other hand, the transformations registered in residential preferences, and in the private and state-led approaches to dwelling and housing have deeply affected its urban morphology.

A marked 'exodus' of the wealthy towards the northeast of the metropolitan area has been paralleled by pervasive, massive displacements and dislocations of entire neighbourhoods, communities, and lower-income populations from the inner city into the far periphery of the Santiago Metropolitan Area. The effect has been the creation of a sea of low-density, uniform and anti-urban settlements (of spatial, architectural and urban poverty) in the areas in which the real estate prices and land-values are not of interest for private investment.

This landscape represents the growing socio-spatial and economic asymmetries that have resulted from continuous uneven development. It also evidences very specific practices of governance: urban policies for the construction and relocation of housing for the poor ('*los sin techo*') in Chile have been directly enforced by the state, according to free-market logics and private capital interests, and arguably with more authoritarian and strict rules than in less effective state politics found in other Latin American countries. Nevertheless, and although the results are less strident visually than say *favelas* or slum-urbanization in many of Santiago's regional counterparts, the outcomes of the neoliberal approach show that it has been as ineffective and unsatisfactory in Santiago as it has been in any other city across Latin America.

An outstanding exception to this model of neoliberal urbanization in Santiago de Chile is the inner-city neighbourhood of La Victoria. Occupied in 1957 as the first squatter settlement (*campamento*) – in fact, as the first organized massive land seizure in Latin America –, La Victoria has

**1** Pedro Aguirre Cerdá (PAC) Municipality, Santiago de Chile. Aerial view of Lo Vallador abattoir and wholesale market with the modernist neighbourhood of San Joaquín (centre) and former squatter settlement La Victoria in the background (right).

withstood not only the dictatorship of Pinochet during the 1970s and 1980s, but also has been able to ward itself and its community from the forces of neoliberalism throughout its existence. Resisting many eviction attempts, the inhabitants of La Victoria have also achieved what seemed impossible under the rule of Pinochet: to claim land ownership and legalize their occupation by attaining property rights on their plots. Today, this high-density neighbourhood remains as an island of exception in the morphology of Santiago, something which in spite of being a logical outcome of the socio-spatial history of La Victoria, also accounts for its contemporary problematic: as an enclave in a landscape under the stress of dynamics of spatial restructuring and gentrification it has had to cope with pressure at its borders, especially as these mark extreme cases of asymmetrical development.

Under this light, the main objectives of this project were to develop a series of analytical and design methodologies, as well as planning strategies, which may serve as the basis of a more coherent approach for the neighbourhood of La Victoria and its contemporary socio-spatial challenges. The outcome of this project is a series of urban and architectural intervention proposals which deal with issues of densification, auto-construction, infilling, redesign of urban blocks and the redefinition of functional and programmatic schemes that include integrated facilities for self-employment, workshops and other urban services. But primarily all projects give priority to the development of alternative housing modalities. In the following project section only the result of the analysis and the collective strategy are presented.

## Santiago de Chile: a history of socio-spatial segregation
The turn of the twentieth century marks the entry of Chile into the race towards industrial modernization. Fuelled by the investments of a strong rural elite, the country transitioned from a mostly agricultural economy into an urban and industrial one. This had deep consequences for its cities, in particular for its capital city, Santiago de Chile. The demographic explosion that accompanied rapid industrial urbanization during the first four decades of the twentieth century had important effects on the socio-spatial composition of the city. As the environmental conditions worsened in the metropolis the social gaps became evident. While the rural migrants were forced to squat in the southern fringes of the city, urban poor in the inner city struggled with deteriorating urban conditions. Brunner's plan of 1928 for the restructuring of the city heralded a modern urban era: building heights were increased, large investments were made in infrastructural works, and the traditional Spanish block was subdivided to accommodate to a more lucrative model of urbanization.

From the 1940s to 1973, Santiago de Chile continued to experience unabated demographic explosion and rural-urban migrations flows, which also explain the pervasiveness of so-called *campamentos*, or squatter settlements in the urban periphery. By the 1960s, Santiago had over 500,000 informal dwellers or *callampas*. The problem of housing the poor became an important incentive for the socialist governments of the period, who in addition to founding the Ministry of Housing and Urban Affairs also nationalized large and medium sized industries to cope with the politico-economic and social problems afflicting the country.

This situation obviously brought social unrest and a general crisis, which led to the infamous Pinochet military coup of 1973 and to the subsequent military neoliberal dictatorship. During this time Chile served as the laboratory for a series of neoliberal policies, which later informed the neoliberal doctrine around the world. The effects for the urban poor were dire: as the new government dealt with the problem of homelessness and squatting by simply deleting the concept altogether, it also displaced the poor sectors further out into the urban periphery. The city centre was reserved for new economic activities, the so-called Central Business Districts, while the periphery became a homogenous landscape of precariousness and blight. The resulting centralized urban model was not only dependent on long-distance commuting for the workers and the lower income groups; it also generated and sustained socio-spatial segregation and exclusion.

After the fall of the authoritarian state, Chile entered a period of aperture, and of profitable market climates to attract foreign investment. No differently than in other Latin American capitals the 1990s transformed Santiago into a postmodern neoliberal city, following a clear polycentric city model, which encouraged the creation of new centralities and the accumulation of wealth. The present is simply a re-intensification of the last two decades, with the rise and prevalence of gated communities, peripheral housing for the urban poor, and a focus on generating propitious economic climates for private and foreign capitals.

**2** For over half a century, the inhabitants of La Victoria have struggled to maintain their socio-spatial identity and autonomy. Their murals and graffiti art are a testimony to the historical consciousness and the social cohesion of the population.

Historical Center [CBD]

PAC

Site
Highway
Railway          Population  5,500,000
River            Area        641 km²

Santiago de Chile

km  1   2        5

## Neoliberal urban restructuring

In Santiago de Chile neoliberal urban restructuring has generated a myriad of interrelated problems at various scales, which ultimately form a vicious cycle of uneven development. While the investment in the redevelopment of the city centre and many inner city areas has created new central business districts thus increasing employment opportunities in select sectors, it has been accompanied by the forced displacement of lower-income populations, as well as by the voluntary migration of high-income groups into the peripheries. This has produced the division between the mono-functional suburbs and the city, and in turn, has raised important mobility issues as much of public transportation as of traffic infrastructure. Contemporary urban projects, such as the Transantiago public transport system, the ring railroad, as well as several other important projects realized under public-private partnerships in the past two decades are emblematic of neoliberal restructuring.

**3** Urban poor and working class neighbourhoods in the periphery of the city.

High

Low

Economic Flow

Centrality

Bicentenary Plan

Highway

Railway

Metro                    M

River

**Contemporary Socio-
Economic Stratification**

km  1  2          5

CBD II

CBD

PAC

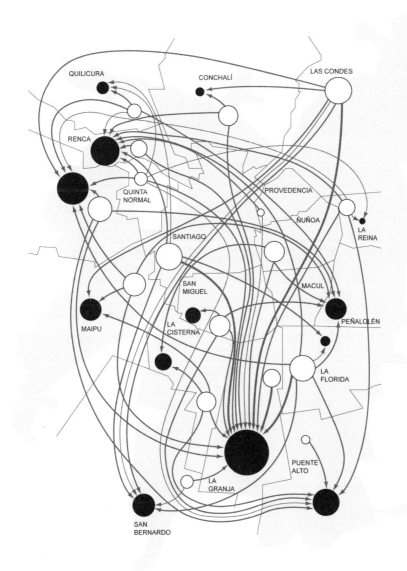

QUILICURA

CONCHALÍ

LAS CONDES

RENCA

QUINTA
NORMAL

PROVEDENCIA

ÑUÑOA

LA
REINA

SANTIAGO

SAN
MIGUEL

MACUL

MAIPU

LA
CISTERNA

PEÑALOLÉN

LA
FLORIDA

PUENTE
ALTO

LA
GRANJA

SAN
BERNARDO

Urban Extension

Area of Origin

Area of Relocation

Displacement
of Families

1001 - 2000
101 - 1000
1 - 100

Number of
Displaced and
Relocated
Families

9000
7000
5000
3000
1500
1000
500
100

* Map has been redrawn from Eduardo Morales and Sergio Rochas
*Relocalizatión socio-espacial de la pobreza,* Santiago 1985

**Displacement of the Poor
during Pinochet Regime**

km  1  2        5

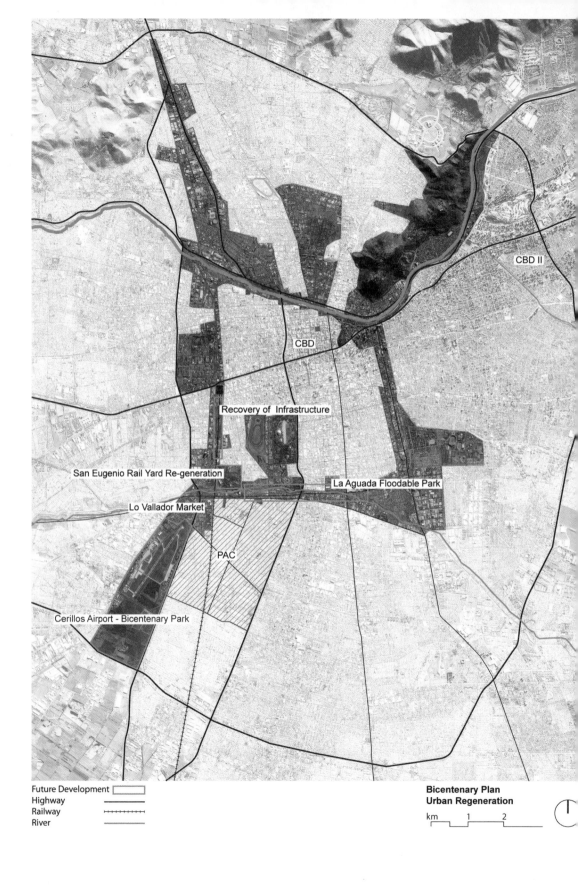

CBD II

CBD

Recovery of Infrastructure

San Eugenio Rail Yard Re-generation

La Aguada Floodable Park

Lo Vallador Market

PAC

Cerillos Airport - Bicentenary Park

Future Development
Highway
Railway
River

**Bicentenary Plan**
**Urban Regeneration**

km          1          2

## Forces and elements of gentrification
The justification of recent urban mega-projects in Santiago tends to be most effective at the regional and metropolitan scales because these deal with large-scaled infrastructural issues and problems such as mobility and connectivity. When looked at from the urban, but especially from the local and neighbourhood scales, however, the argumentation in favour of these projects begins to pale as the negative consequences and forces begin to manifest. One such force is gentrification.

The municipality of Pedro Aguirre Cerdá (PAC) is interesting in this respect because its particular character and urban situation make it prone to strong forces of gentrification and real estate speculation. PAC stands out for its semi-industrial character and the prevalence of working class residential areas that mix with older morphologies conventionally found in the fringes of the inner city. It houses the Lo Valledor – Santiago's largest meat and agricultural wholesale market – and a former slaughterhouse of the same name (now under redevelopment), as well as two low-income, but privately owned housing projects dating from the 1970s and 1980s – San Joaquín (to the north) and Nueva Lo Valledor (to the west). Similar to the areas to the east and south of the municipality, these low and medium-density neighbourhoods lack well-maintained and articulated open public spaces. But perhaps most importantly, the neighbourhood of La Victoria is located right in the middle of the municipality.

At present the municipality is flanked by two strategic urban megaprojects – to the north by 'La Aguada' park and to the west by the 'Bicentenario' park – and crossed longitudinally by an important regional railroad line and the Transantiago transit system. These elements are exerting significant pressure to redevelop the different areas of the municipality, in particular the outdated post-industrial sites, and the housing projects. This is especially detrimental for the community of La Victoria, whose survival depends on the struggle of the local population to resist the pressures of gentrification and to strengthen its position in the municipality.

Thus, the main objective of the Urban Asymmetries Santiago Study Group was to formulate integrated, relational strategies that could strengthen the community by providing it with better opportunities to face the challenges presented by the dynamics of gentrification and urban erosion occurring in its surroundings. The study group developed a collective strategy composed of four layers which tackle the questions of 'public space networks', 'connectivity', 'means of production', and 'density'.

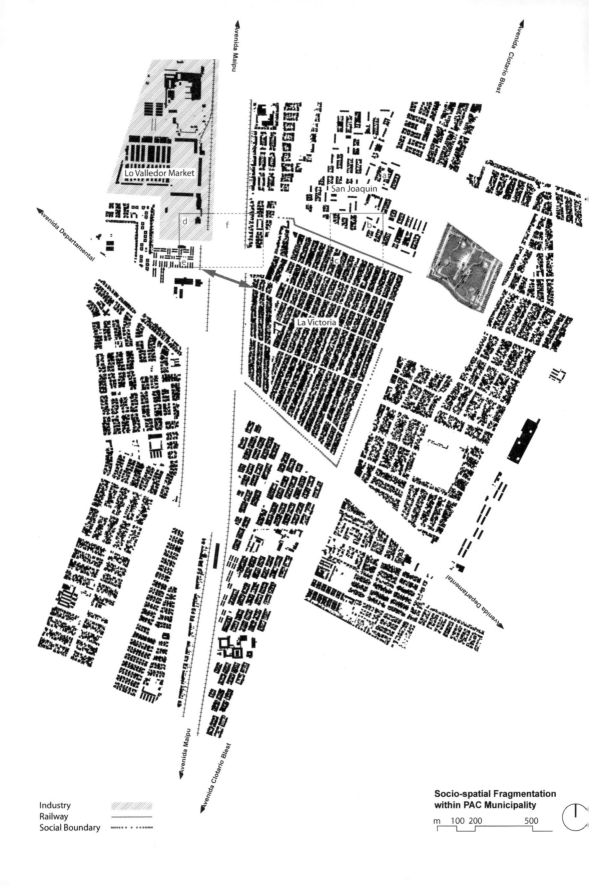

Avenida Maipu

Avenida Clotario Blest

Lo Valledor Market

Avenida Departamental

d    f

San Joaquin

a

b

c

e

La Victoria

Avenida Maipu

Avenida Clotario Blest

Avenida Departamental

Industry
Railway
Social Boundary

**Socio-spatial Fragmentation
within PAC Municipality**

m    100  200              500

(a)

(b)

(c)

[5]

(d)

(e)

The railroad creates a clear physical border
between La Victoria and Lo Vallador, which
are completely disconnected, except for one
dangerous crossing point.
The physical border between La Victoria
and San Joaquin marks a strident social
boundary.

(f)

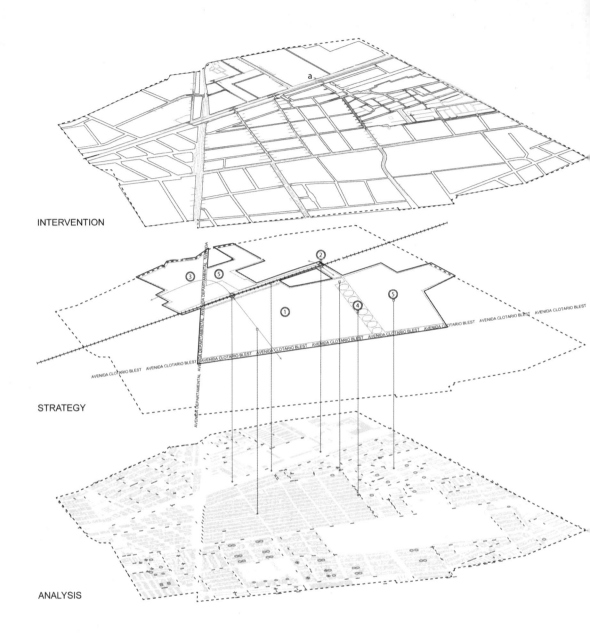

INTERVENTION

STRATEGY

ANALYSIS

Desired Connected Area ——
Masterplan Boundary - - - - - -
Existing Connected Area ——
Railway       +++++++++
Desired Connection ←------→
Neighbourhood Boundary ——
Strategy Reference     ①
Railway Crossing      -○-
Pedestrian Railway Crossing -□-
Urban Wall        —
Dead-end Street      ○
Junction          □
Intervention    ▬▬▬▬

Strategies
① Maintaining Good Internal Connectivity
② Railway Crossing
③ Road Crossing
④ Morphological Permeation
⑤ Internal Reconfiguration

**Urban Strategy: Connectivity**

m   100  200        500

**Connectivity**   La Victoria's morphological composition follows a simple grid of regular blocks and relatively homogenous plot sizes. This accounts for a regular street-pattern with few discontinuities and a fluid mobility to the interior of the neighbourhood. This pattern is the result of self-governance and autonomous planning practices of the community of La Victoria with very little intervention from municipal and city authorities. In more than one sense, La Victoria is an urban enclave that follows its own urban logic. Nevertheless, this also explains the discontinuities found at the edges and boundaries of La Victoria and the neighbouring areas, where morphological breaks and grid 'accidents' are the rule. The changes in the grid patterns also correspond to very different typological patterns between the modernistic social housing projects with their large empty spaces and massive uniformity, and the much more complex, intricate system of self-building or auto-construction found in La Victoria. All these morphological differences enhance the introverted, secluded character of La Victoria, thus contributing to its weakening position within the area.

The introduction of planned, strategic infrastructural and morphological connections to the surrounding areas will improve La Victoria's economic and social exchanges with the neighbouring areas, thus fostering a better spatial integration. In particular, the planned crossings of large-scaled urban transit and traffic infrastructure, such as the railroad, will ensure the physical permeation of barriers and this will allow a stronger connection among different neighbourhoods.

The strategies designed to improve connectivity deal with subtle interventions to the morphological structure of the neighbourhoods of San Joaquín and Nueva Lo Valledor, rather than to La Victoria itself. These interventions will function in a relational way to other strategic interventions of typology and density, for instance, as well as with the strengthening of public spaces. The infrastructural connectivity such as the railroad line that divides Lo Valledor from La Victoria, however, as well as other important connections to the north, south and east of the area, will be enforced and improved.

**6** Railway crossings facilitating better connectivity between neighbourhoods.

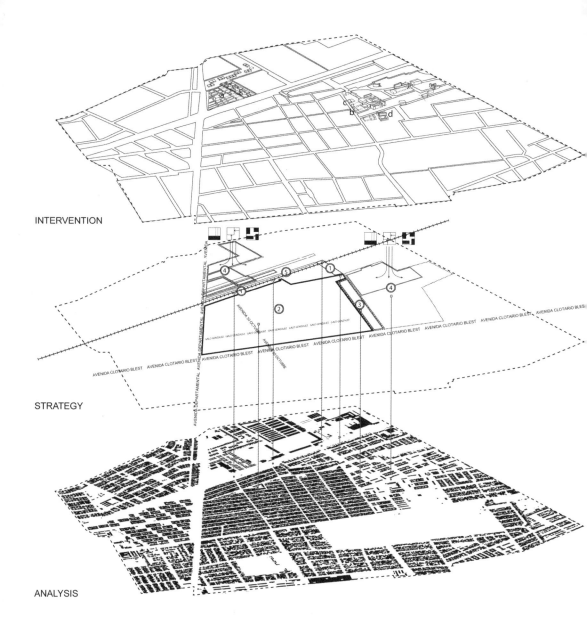

INTERVENTION

STRATEGY

ANALYSIS

Masterplan Boundary ----------
Existing Densification ————
Railway +++++++++++
Border Redevelopment
   for Commercial Use .............
Strategy Reference ①
Construction ————
Addition, Reconstruction ..........
Public Space Maintenance ———
Building Footprint ▉▉▉▉
Intervention ▢▢▢▢

Strategies
① Open Space, Low Density
② Renovation
③ Additions, Sectional Adjustments
④ Redistribution
⑤ New Construction

**Urban Strategy: Density**

m   100  200        500

**Density**   In spite of their own complex compositions and differences, La Victoria, San Joaquín and Nueva Lo Valledor register extremely high population densities, while the building densities are on average medium to low. This translates into overcrowding and its accompanying problems, poor use of open space, and other spatial constraints that decrease the quality of life of the inhabitants. But, while one of the problems in San Joaquín and Nueva Lo Valledor – the 'state-built' projects – is mono-functionality, in La Victoria – a 'self-built' neighbourhood – the problem seems to be overcrowding and insularity which is explained by a propensity of the inhabitants to stay in La Victoria despite the increasing lack of space.

A strategic introduction of mixed functions and changes in density aimed at improving household indexes, as well as a new approach to morphology that allows the redefinition of open space as *public* space, will serve as the basis for other, case-specific strategic interventions aimed at the implementation of new built structures, and/or the extensions, additions, and transformations of existing buildings and structures.

Thus, the proposed interventions run along two main fronts: morphological transformations and typological interventions, by the infill of open, empty or underused space, and by the intensification of programme and function. On the one hand, this will result in stronger and more coherent street profiles both physically and functionally, as well as a more complex mix of commercial, productive and residential functions in select areas. On the other, the problem of density will be tackled with a set of strategic interventions aimed at achieving a more balanced distribution of housing in all three neighbourhoods.

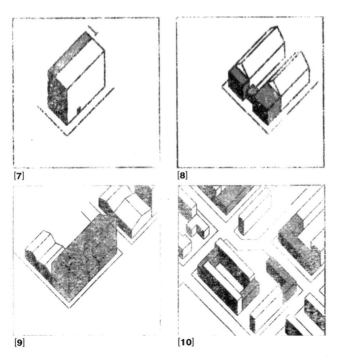

[7]

[8]

[9]

[10]

**7** Lateral additions to existing housing units in San Joaquin and Nueva Lo Valledor facilitate growth and flexibility.
**8** Densification by use of leftover spaces with small extensions to housing and local commercial activities.
**9** Infill projects on empty plots for a mix of productive and commercial spaces with higher-density residential use.
**10** Infill projects that close open morphologies will create functional and programmatic diversity and allow a better use of public space.

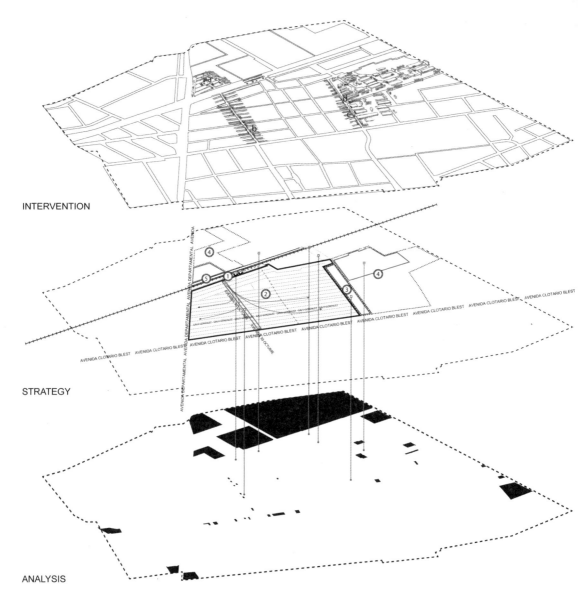

INTERVENTION

STRATEGY

ANALYSIS

Masterplan Boundary - - - - - - -
Border Redevelopment
   for Commercial Use - - - - - - - - -
Railway +++++++++
Redevelopment ·····················
Commercial Use ——————
Self-sufficiency ━━━━━
Strategy Reference ①
Organic Waste Collection ·····▶
Gas Supply ————▶
Light Commercialization ————
Gas Production ◉
Modes of Production ■■■■
Intervention ▭▭▭

Strategies
① Gas Production
② Self Sufficiency
③ Commercial Permeation
④ Site-specific Production Modes
⑤ Creation of new Modes of Production

**Urban Strategy: Modes of Production**

m  100 200       500

**Means of production**    In addition to the problems of connectivity and density the neighbourhoods in this municipality also suffer from mono-functionality and hence from the lack of sources of employment. Instead of depending solely on an inefficient public transport system to reach work opportunities, the overall strategy for this project considers the inclusion of alternative means of production and local employment in the intervention areas as crucial. Thus, small-scale interventions that strengthen existing programmes of social exchange and local production, as well as new, self-sustainable programmes, are proposed along the borders and the main arteries of La Victoria. Along the three main axes forming the U-shaped border of La Victoria and San Joaquín and Nueva Lo Valledor the interventions differ significantly from one another.

Av. Dos de Abril will offer a new typology of combined living and working units, which will be adapted to the morphological structure of the street, forming a continuous commercial strip on street level. On Av. Maipú, along the railroad, the interventions will consist of a dual strategy based on the introduction of a new street profile along the side of Nueva Lo Valledor of both housing and commercial functions, as well as an intense public programme along the west flank of La Victoria, which is an underused spatial barrier today. This intervention aims at integrating the functions of the market of Lo Valledor and the community of La Victoria by transforming this area into a lively urban zone. Along Av. 30 de Octubre the interventions will be specific projects, aimed at enhancing commercial activities on street corners.

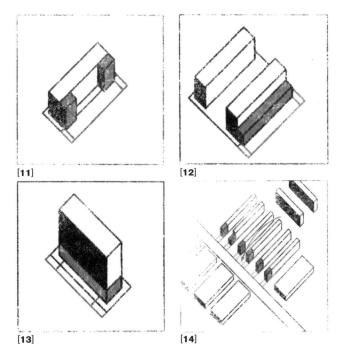

[11]

[12]

[13]

[14]

**11** Extensions to existing housing units with space for commercial and productive use on street fronts.
**12** Extensions and additions to existing structures with additional facilities will strengthen the self-sufficiency of the population.
**13** Introducing spaces for commercial and local productive activities such as small workshops on street level enforces alternative inhabitation modalities.
**14** The morphological transformations on the borders of La Victoria hinge on the insertion of commercial activities along important streets and avenues, such as Av. Dos de Abril.

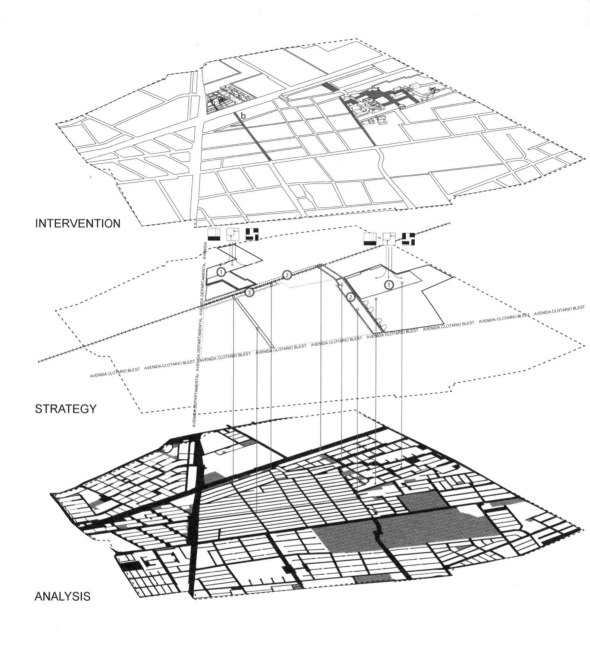

INTERVENTION

STRATEGY

ANALYSIS

Masterplan Boundary  --------
Maintenance of Existing  ..........
Border Redevelopment
   for Commercial Use  ----------
Railway  +++++++++++
Public Space
   Redevelopment  ————
Strategy Reference    ①
Public Space
Intervention    ▭

Strategies
① Addition, Concentration, Redistribution
② New Space for Production and Commerce
③ Green Space Maintenance

**Urban Strategy: Public Space**

m   100  200       500

**Public space**    The history of La Victoria has largely determined its spatial characteristics. While its grid-structure allows for efficient plot division and a relatively organized street pattern, it also has its disadvantages. One of them is the lack of planned public space. Due to the very strong social cohesion of the community, however, public space is understood more as an activity than as a designed, conceived physical space. Social exchange takes place on the streets. On the other hand, in the planned neighbourhoods of Nueva Lo Valledor and San Joaquín, 'public space' is physically available in the form of open space, usually in expanses of dirt and dust, which is not used at all. The social cohesion in these neighbourhoods is understandably much lower than in La Victoria.

A strategy that manages to replicate some of La Victoria's successful public spaces in the neighbouring areas – be it by the redevelopment and reorganization of existing open spaces or by the inclusion of social and public programmes – and which simultaneously is able to make resource of the few spatial opportunities in La Victoria itself and on its borders, will be essential.

The introduction of commercial and trade activities at the borders that intensify social exchange between the neighbourhoods and their communities, as is dealt with in the strategy of 'means of production'; and the integration of a public programme that considers social practices and reproduction at its core, as well as a more efficient definition of spaces, typologies and morphologies that take into account more complex and rich programmes and functions, will ensure that the integration of all four strategies and their concrete interventions result in a unitary, relational urbanism in which planning and design work with the social cohesion and community participation found in La Victoria to endow it with instruments to ward off some of the negative forces of neoliberal urbanization.

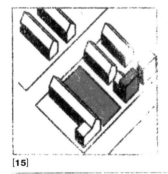

[15]

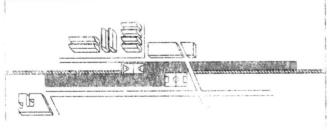

[16]

15 Redevelopment of square to enhance public facilities.
16 The introduction of public programmes and facilities along the railway track will improve the use of available open space and diminish spatial barriers.

# Newark

# An Introduction to Newark: The Continuous Crisis of the Obsolete City

**Tahl Kaminer**

**Crisis**   Crises are a recurring and fundamental phenomenon of the capitalist mode of production. They can affect a specific manufacturer, they can be limited to a single sector of the economy, or they can become a much larger crisis affecting economy and society at large. Crises are the result of the impossibility of reaching equilibrium of supply and demand: producers in a free market can never accurately predict the number of commodities which will be sold, despite diverse tools developed specifically to aid such predictions and calculations. As a result, there is always an abundance of some commodities and scarcity of others on the market, and correspondently a shortage of labour in one industry and abundance in another. Crises are thus a means of economic and social reorganization, of redistributing labour according to the needs of production. The reorganization serves to increase productivity and profitability, and is intended as a means of placing capitalism once again on a trajectory of growth. Crises are, therefore, a 'correcting' mechanism. A severe crisis often spreads because the constant reinvestment of capital interweaves industries and producers which are otherwise unrelated, inevitably spreading instability to highly profitable sectors of the economy. Jürgen Habermas has described a severe crisis as one which affects not only the economy, but also the steering of society, generating a dissolution of social institutions and a restructuring of society.[1]

Such severe crises affect cities as well. City administrations' tax-revenues shrink, development is brought to a halt, and real estate value drops, leaving some urban areas impoverished, derelict and desolate. Unemployment grows, and with it homelessness, crime and other social ailments. Businesses shrink or go bust, shops remain vacant and homes are repossessed by banks. Moreover, severe crises are often related to a transformation of the political economy – a general restructuring of society – and therefore can also mark a change in the type of urban development undertaken and in the urban morphologies which emerge, as both urban development and morphology are directly shaped by political economy. Before turning to the specific case of the ex-industrial American city, which is the interest of this section of *Urban Asymmetries*, it is necessary to concisely outline in general terms the relation of urban morphology to political economy.

Nineteenth-century laissez-faire and its specific characteristics, namely its domination by small and medium scale producers, developers and retailers, engendered precisely the type of urban development which is exemplified by the era's slums in cities such as New York, Paris or London – amalgams of self-built sheds, appropriated decaying structures and speculative development, as well as other piecemeal, unregulated development throughout the city. The urban development and the types of morphology introduced to the city gradually changed as the political economy began shifting from the extremes of early and mid-nineteenth century capitalism to a political economy based on larger corporations and an increased governmental involvement.

---

**1** Jürgen Habermas, **Legitimation Crisis** (Boston: Beacon Press, 2005), pp. 3-4 and 222-35.

The 1929 crisis and the Great Depression were the impetus for the wide implementation of the Keynesian plan throughout society, completing within a few decades a drive against laissez-faire capitalism. Keynes' anti-cyclical plan was designed to prevent the type of speculation which led to economic meltdown by subordinating economy to political will. By intervening in the economy via regulations and planning, by controlling the printing and investment of money, by managing the interest rates, and by taxation and specific social programmes, government could, Keynes and his supporters believed, 'fine tune' the economy and prevent crisis. The implementation of the Keynesian plan was not immediate, and took place gradually, beginning in the 1930s and culminating in the establishment of the welfare state in Europe in the post-war years. The Keynesian plan would encourage rationalized, planned urban development rather than the disorganized piecemeal city of nineteenth-century laissez-faire. The planned city would become emblematic of social democracy in Europe, whereas the United States would mostly shy away from the type of wide-reaching, all-encompassing and systematic planning carried out across the Atlantic, following, instead, a 'light' version of Keynesian economics with only limited planning at the level of the city. Instead, the United States focused on large scale development of the type carried out by Robert Moses in the New York.

The de-industrialization of cities and fast growth of suburbia in the West in the 1950s and 1960s brought about the decline of inner-cities which was manifested in a fall in population, in the flight of the middle class, in the decrease of real-estate values, in the growth of inner-city ghettos, in the rise in poverty and crime, and in the dilapidation of the physical environment. The malaise of Western cities, and particularly of the American cities, was expressed in social unrest and riots in the late 1960s and 1970s. By the end of the 1970s cities seemed doomed, populated primarily by the very poor and very rich, an amalgam of decay and poverty contrasted with bastions of power and wealth.

The malaise of cities in this era was related to the decline of industry. Cities had lost their position as the locus of production once industry was relocated to their outer areas. Peter Marcuse has written that 'decentralization came about because efficient production, particularly of heavy capital goods – steel, automobile, machinery – could, by the first decades of the twentieth century, be undertaken in large, single-story, space-consuming buildings, in which assembly lines and automatic movements of pieces of work and machinery were easier'.[2] Fordism was thus one of the major forces responsible for destroying the industrial city, causing not only white collar workers but also skilled labour to move to suburban areas in proximity to the relocated factories. The passage to a post-industrial society which began in the 1960s would only exacerbate the situation.

Whereas the 1929 crisis was caused by unregulated speculation, the crisis of the Keynesian plan in the 1970s was expressed by the term 'stagflation' – the combined effects of stagnation and inflation. Habermas claimed that the crisis was brought about by the internal contradiction of the Keynesian system – the conflation of the often opposing interests of capitalist economy and citizens.[3] The urban crisis of the 1970s reflected the loss of the city's role as industrial producer, but also enabled a restructuring of the city by drastically reducing real-estate values and weakening city administrations. The new role of cities in post-industrial society was directly defined by the new forms and organization of production. The rise of information industries and of the service sector, accompanied by the relocation of industrial production to ever more distant places and the need for specific types of concentrated office work, including sales, distribution, contracts, marketing and accounting, meant that the ex-industrial city could re-define its role as a global hub for these functions. The motivation for the white collar employees of this new order was found in 'lifestyle', which, in turn, was provided by gentrified urban districts. The post-industrial city thus needed to provide not only the high-end headquarters for international corporations, but also the playing field for the white collar employees of these companies: loft apartments in renovated industrial buildings, unique shops catering to subcultures and idiosyncratic interests, a wide selection of cafes, bars and restaurants, and cultural activities and programmes absent in suburbia.

The restructuring of cities was a process which required a number of steps, beginning with crisis as a means of starving the city for funds and credit and making it susceptible to investment, a process described as 'redlining', followed by gentrification.[4] Gentrification, meaning the replacement of a weak social group by a stronger social group within a defined territory, is usually understood as a negative phenomenon which delineates a process of expulsion of working class and immigrants from desirable neighbourhoods with a potential for high real-estate value. Since the early 1990s, gentrification has become a staple of urban renewal programmes and has been widely implemented as part of urban policies of local councils in European and American cities.[5] Gentrification was made possible by the crisis of cities and resulted in the new urban order demanded by post-industrial society. Unskilled labour, blue collar workers, less vital to the new economy and mostly unemployed by the late 1970s, were banished to peripheral areas, whereas the city's property market, which not long beforehand suffered from the urban decline, could enjoy unprecedented growth.

**Newark**   Not all Western cities which declined in the post-war years have been 'rescued' via the new economy and gentrification. In the era of globalization and neoliberalism the idea of a

**2** Peter Marcuse, 'Do Cities Have a Future?', in Robert Chery [ed.], **The Imperiled Economy: Through the Safety Net** (New York: Union of Radical Political Economists, 1988), p. 190.
**3** Jürgen Habermas, **Legitimation Crisis** (Boston: Beacon Press, 2005), pp. 222-35.
**4** 'Redlining' in the United States is a term with strong connotations of racial strife, as the process was typically carried out in black ghettos.
**5** 'Gentrification' existed before the 1990s, of course, but was not a standard feature of planned city renewal projects in the calculated, intentional manner in which it appears in the 1990s urban regeneration projects. See Neil Smith, 'The Evolution of Gentrification', in JaapJan Berg, Tahl Kaminer, Marc Schoonderbeek and Joost Zonneveld [eds], **Houses in Transformation: Interventions in European Gentrification** (Rotterdam: NAi Publishers, 2008), pp. 15-25.

centre infers an international rather than local hub, meaning that fewer centres are needed than in the industrial age, and consequently that not all ex-industrial cities could be remodelled as post-Fordist global centres. Located a mere twenty-two minutes' train ride from the most spectacular of 'urban reversals', Manhattan, is Newark, a city which has suffered a constant decline since the Great Depression. The case of Newark demonstrates some of the ambiguities and difficulties of finding alternatives to the urban remedies prescribed by neoliberalism, such as gentrification. Newark is New Jersey's largest city, and while New Jersey has in the last decades become the epitome of urban sprawl – the densest state of the United States, but with no cities of more than 300,000 inhabitants – Newark has suffered from a decline which has never been brought to a complete halt.

In the late nineteenth century, Newark, nicknamed 'Brick City', was a centre of industrial production which rivalled New York City, with a huge leather industry and one of the largest ports of the United States. However, the twentieth century brought about the gradual decline of industrial production in the city, and, in the post-war years, the exodus of skilled labour and the middle class to the new sub-urbs. Whereas New York, which experienced similar transformations, incorpor-ated some of the new suburbs in its administrative area – meaning that it could continue benefiting from the taxes of the middle class – Newark was unable to expand. Several attempts to annex neighbouring territories failed after they were met with strong resistance from locals. This meant that Newark – not only its centre, but the entire territory controlled by the city council – lost much of its industries and middle-class tax revenues. The city became a locus of tension between black migrants escaping segregation and poverty in the south and unionized white – and predominantly Italian – harbour workers who were pre-pared to defend the decreasing number of jobs by whatever means necessary. The downturn and tension led to the 1967 riots which left twenty-six people dead and were accompanied by looting and severe damage to property. The riots came to symbolize the city's decline, and while new community-based organizations and initiatives were created in response, the symbolic effect of the riots only made Newark even more unattractive to the white middle class. The crisis of Newark is thus a familiar phenomenon which could be dated back, excluding the war years, to the Great Depression, an ongoing crisis which persists as long as Newark remains obsolete from the perspective of capitalism, as long as Newark fails to finds itself a new role.[6]

There has been no absence of development in the city, though much of it is highly questionable from the perspective of the interests of the city and its residents. The development of infrastructure such as the 1932 Pulaski Skyway and especially the Interstate 78 and the Interstate 280 highways, constructed in the 1960s and 1970s, dissected the city, physically carving it into detached areas. The highway system offered suburbanites and arrivals at the Newark Airport easy access to New York, with the city of Newark serving, in effect, as the pedestal for the infrastructure. The passage from an industrial to a post-industrial society beginning in the 1960s and from a Keynesian to a neoliberal form of capitalism only increased the city's difficulties; as a result of the shrinkage of government in the 1980s the city was left with limited means of coping with its worsening conditions. In line with urban remedies prescribed at the time, the downtown area was designated in 1984 an enterprise zone of tax exemptions in order to attract investors. Educational institutions were given land and benefits to lure them to the city or, alternatively, to make sure they stayed. The landmark projects of the last decades perfectly express the shortcomings of the form of piecemeal development encouraged and supported by the city administration and neoliberal urban development.

The Gateway commerce and office buildings developed in four stages by the local Prudential Insurance Company in the 1970s and 1980s represent perhaps the major attempt to 'rescue' Newark by investment. Presented as a statement of confidence in the city's future following the riots, a majority of the employees at the Gateway remained commuters, with few white collar workers living in Newark itself. The towers, meant to create a corporate-friendly image for the city by emulating the architecture of mid-Western city centres, were brutally implanted in downtown according to the opportunities of real estate at the moment of their realization. Their detachment from the city fabric and city life was enhanced by skywalks connecting the towers to each other and directly to Newark's Penn Station, allowing commuters to avoid the city's streets altogether. Security and monitoring as a means of preventing unwarranted visitors completed the total detachment of the Gateway buildings from the city, rendering them a fortress rather than a participant in Newark's life.[7] More recently, the New Jersey Performing Arts Center (NJPAC) [fig. 1] and the hockey arena have been major projects which required a large investment of public funds, projects which express the desire to restore Newark to its position as regional centre, and called attention to the disparity between their public cost and their limited benefit to Newark itself. All these projects also represent the fragmented and partial solutions sought by city government in recent decades which did little to help the city and its residents.

Newark, in the early twentieth century, resembled other East Coast cities, with a strong urban fabric and vibrant downtown. In the decades which have elapsed since the Great Depression, this original urban fabric has eroded, destroyed by piecemeal development which directed the city's transformation towards a typical mid-sized American town, with a downtown central business district of high-rise glass office towers surrounded by residential neighbourhoods mostly comprising suburban villas and dotted with post-war public housing blocks. The physical erosion of the once strong urban fabric and the death of the once vibrant downtown, echoed in the many

---

**6** In a meeting in Newark on April 21st 2009, Richard Cammarieri, NCC's director for special projects, cited figures from a Rutgers University report which demonstrate Newark's malaise: one third of Newark households do not receive a regular wage or an hourly income; median income in Newark is 85% of the national median income; 40.7% of Newark households are just above the poverty line – twice the national norm and three times that for New Jersey.
**7** Thomas Dolan, 'Newark and Its Gateway Complex', **The Newark Metro**, available at http://www.newarkmetro.rutgers.edu/reports/display.php?id=17 [accessed 5.07.2009].

empty plots in both centre and periphery, are the physical embodiment of the city's decay.

The landmark development projects such as the Gateway buildings, the NJPAC or the hockey arena can all be understood as attempts to create a better image for the city by investing and encouraging investment in large-scale, attention-grabbing landmark projects which would demonstrate the city's vitality, relevance and potential. Such an image would, presumably, counter the lingering memory of the 1967 riots, a memory which, due to its strong presence in the collective conscious-ness, is mostly seen as a detriment to attracting investors and middle-class resi-dents despite marking an important moment in the development of black identity and power. In the 1980s, city administrators, emulating other regenerated cities, rushed to name Newark 'Renaissance City'.[8] However, the 'Renaissance City' label demonstrates the questionable belief that the city's difficulties are caused by the bad image of Newark rather than by real problems, and that the solution therefore is within the realm of the mind and could be addressed by city branding. In any case, the 2000 census showed that the number of inhabitants had stopped its decrease, and the election in 2006 of the Obama-clone Cory Booker as mayor further encouraged certain optimism. The rise of real-estate prices in Manhattan and the spillage of Manhattan into Jersey City and Hoboken raised hopes that Newark would finally benefit from the prowess of Manhattan's real-estate market. These hopes were scuttled by the recent crisis, with Newark hard-hit by subprime mortgages, resulting in foreclosures surpassing 10% of residential prop-erties in many of the city's neighbourhoods [fig. 2].[9]

A constant in the last decades has been Newark's desire to attract middle-class residents and private investment to the city. Whereas such goals are shared by the administrations of many cities, and are perfectly tuned to the demands of the post-industrial city, the need for both middle-class residents and private capital in Newark is very evident and acute. The decline of industry meant a lack of jobs for the unqualified labour available within Newark. With unemployment sur-passing national averages in many of the city's neighbourhoods, Newark is evi-dently starved for employment opportunities. In addition, attracting white collar business to the city could bring with it the desired middle class and their taxes – though, as the Gateway project demonstrated, a large majority of white collar workers prefer to commute from suburbia rather than live in the city, a choice based not only on lifestyle desires but on education opportunities for children and fear of crime.

**Predicament**   Considering the limited interest of corporate business in Newark, the city administration finds itself, quite literally, on its knees, begging for investment. The mayor and his administration have little more than negotiating power, with limited incentives to offer investors, mostly in the form of tax breaks which are already taken for granted. The cost-cutting measures introduced by cities in the 1980s, including the reduction of public services associated with the 'roll-back' neoliberalism of the period, resulted in the weakened city administrations of today. A multitude of community-based organizations have filled-in the void by accepting a role previously carried out by the cities' authorities themselves. Margit Mayer argues that while the 'empowerment' of community-based organizations in the 1980s via out-contracting and a transfer of responsibilities expressed, in a sense, an internalization and acceptance of the progressive demands of the 1960s for participation and self-governance, such policies were an instrument of neoliberal restructuring aimed at deregulation, shrinking the governmental role and abandoning social responsibilities. She also identified the manner in which the expanding participation of such community-based organizations ended up diminishing their original protest and advocacy features and subjugating their operation to the demands of neoliberalism:

> [T]he complex work of 'empowering' the groups disadvantaged by neoliberalism is embedded in a process of permanent production and reproduction of inequalities through competition. As local administrations resort to competitive contracting in order to meet their economic development and social policy tasks, this tendering along with its criteria gets passed down to the nonprofits they partner with. As a result, the nonprofits find it more and more difficult to use the (state) funding for progressive goals and for political struggles around the design of programs, or even to build empowerment and solidarity, which originally was the basis for their inclusion and valorization.[10]

The New Community Corporation (NCC), a non-profit, is the most visible of the organizations which were created in Newark after and in reaction to the 1967 riots. The corporation builds public housing, runs old age homes and day care centres, provides counselling services, offers homes for homeless families and professional training, and runs businesses which provide some of NCC's income. It has become a vast organization, stepping in to provide for locals where city and state are absent. In effect, Newark has splintered into fiefdoms, each of which functions as a city within a city; not only the NCC, but also the Gateway project acts as an independent entity, as do some of the neighbourhoods, or the harbour and airport run by the Port Authority. Therefore the physical erosion and the piecemeal development of Newark are echoed also in the institutional and administrative fragmentation of the city. The once bustling 'Brick City' can now only be described as a dismembered, fragmented city. Within such harsh conditions, the pressure on the city government to find investment, to offer jobs and to attract middle-class residents is clear enough. There seem to be no alternative solutions in the current conditions, and gentrification appears, in

---

**8** See the article by Mark Krasovic in this section.
**9** See a map of foreclosures in the New York region, including Newark, at 'Mapping Foreclosures in the New York Region', **New York Times**, 15 June 2009; available at http://www.nytimes.com/interactive/2009/05/15/nyregion/0515-foreclose.html [accessed 6.07.2009].
**10** Margit Mayer, 'Contesting the Neoliberalization of Urban Governance', in Helga Leitner, Jamie Peck and Eric S. Sheppard [eds], **Contesting Neoliberalism** (New York; London: Guilford Press, 2006), pp. 99.

Newark's case, a warranted rather than negative phenomenon. Presumably, the taxes of incoming middle-class residents could enable the city government to offer the needy more assistance, and the presence of middle-class residents would provide a solid base for the regeneration of the city.

However, the crisis of cities in the 1970s, especially in the United States, created very similar conditions to those of Newark today. Whereas some of the cities in crisis in those years – such as Baltimore or Detroit – have similarly continued their decline, others, most prominently Manhattan, have completely reversed their downward spiral, reaching unprecedented levels of affluence. Contemporary Manhattan, as a gentrified neoliberal city, was 'made' in the years of crisis, being reduced to such a pitiful existence that it yearned for any investment under any conditions, badly craving for the return of the middle class.[11] In other words, Newark's need for middle-class residents and for investment resembles the condition of Manhattan in the 1970s, a condition of crisis which later allowed the usurping of the city and its residents by forces of real estate and capitalist re-organization and development.

The chances of Newark bringing about a similar reversal of fortunes seem slim; the geographical distance from Manhattan, on the one hand, and the relative proximity to Manhattan, on the other hand, position it in the unfortunate place of neither being able to be completely autonomous of New York – and hence also a rival in terms of production – nor being able to benefit from the proximity – it is too distant to enjoy the effects of Manhattan's property market. 'Stuck' between New York and Philadelphia, the arguments for Newark's rebirth as a global centre are nil, meaning that its position as a city is under direct threat; New Jersey and the entire region would simply prefer Newark to disappear, to integrate into the urban sprawl between the two big cities. Moreover, the example of Manhattan's reversal is a special case of a city with powerful and committed financiers, a city which directly taps into people's imagination and desires. Manhattan was, in current political jargon, 'too big to fail'. In contrast, Newark's failure has had few consequences for New Jersey, let alone the rest of the United States. Whereas Newark's role in the current political economy is mostly extinct, it can still offer New Jersey and the region a limited service: the ghettoization of the socially excluded, keeping the socially deprived and the economically 'useless' – contemporary lepers of sorts – within a clearly defined and bounded territory, a 'black hole'.

**Alternatives**   Rather than attempt to apply to Newark the same remedies which reversed Manhattan's decline, it is necessary to question whether following Manhattan's footsteps is desirable, whether the crisis is not an opportunity to discover a different trajectory, whether there are alternatives to integrating Newark into the current political economy at the moment when the status quo is crumbling. After all, it is the globalized, corporate neoliberal status quo which rendered Newark obsolete and offers little hope of finding a new role for the city.

The discussion of the current international economic crisis has raised the possibility that society is experiencing a restructuring, both economically and socially, a possibility raised not only by ever-optimistic Marxists but also by politicians and economists who had previously embraced the neoliberal order.[12] Presuming that this assessment is correct, and in the context of a retreat into the safety of policies previously associated with Keynesian economics, a contemporary restructuring would mean a move in the opposite direction than the one taken in the 1970s. It is precisely this counter-trajectory which could mean that salvation to cities like Newark could avoid the prescriptions of the 1980s and 1990s, could avoid the cleansing of cities from their underclass: accompanying the so-called 'death of neoliberalism' is also the end of its particular remedy for urban malaise: gentrification.

The precise form the new prescription will take is no more lucid at the moment than the course economy and society are about to follow; it is merely reasonable to imagine that the involvement of the federal government, whether via superfunds, stimulus package capital or new mechanisms, may facilitate a solution to Newark's ills in the immediate future.[13] Whether via direct federal intervention or by empowering the city government, a comprehensive plan which will bring new unity and consistency to the city, both physically, administratively and socially, will, possibly, express a new Keynesian approach rather than the discredited neoliberal solutions sought in the last decades.

**11** The restructuring of New York included the loss of 750,000 manufacturing jobs and altering the ratio of manufacturing to office work from 2:1 to 1:2 by the 1990s. See Robert Fitch, **The Assassination of New York** (London: Verso, 1993), p. 40.

**12** Whether a restructuring is underway or imminent is a focus of current debate; as an economic meltdown at the scale of 1929 has so far been averted, opposition to change has mounted. For some of the ideas being discussed, see, for example, Barbara Ehrenreich and Bill Fletcher Jr., 'Rising to the Occasion', **The Nation**, 4 March 2009, available at http://www.thenation.com/doc/20090323/ehrenreich_fletcher [accessed 15.09.09], and, from very different perspectives, James Macdonald, 'Lessons from the Jazz Age for Creditor Nations', **Financial Times**, 24 June 2009; at http://www.ft.com/cms/s/0/8c1da3da-60f1-11de-aa12-00144feabdc0.html?nclick_check=1 [accessed 2.07.2009]; 'Out of Keynes's Shadow', **The Economist**, 12 February 2009; at http://www.economist.com/businessfinance/displayStory.cfm?story_id=13104022 [accessed 2.07.2009]; Paul Krugman, 'Hanging Tough with Keynes', **New York Times**, 18 June 2009; at http://krugman.blogs.nytimes.com/2009/06/18/hanging-tough-with-keynes/?scp=1&sq=keynes&st=cse [accessed 2.07.2009]; Gregory Mankiw, 'What Would Keynes Have done?', **New York Times**, 28 November 2008; at http://www.nytimes.com/2008/11/30/business/economy/30view.html?scp=2&sq=keynes&st=cse [accessed 2.07.2009]; Robert Skidelsky, 'The Remedist', **New York Times**, 12 December 2008; at http://www.nytimes.com/2008/12/14/magazine/14wwln-lede-t.html?scp=4&sq=keynes&st=cse [accessed 2.07.2009].

**13** In Detroit, which suffers from similar problems to those of Newark, proposals of a planned city-shrinkage, emulating precedents in East Germany, have been delineated by groups such as Community Development Advocates of Detroit; see <http://detroitcommunitydevelopment.org/> [accessed 20.06.2010].

However, it is necessary to keep in mind that any return to Keynesian policies will take a different form than in the past, just as the return to free-trade capitalism beginning in the 1970s did not emulate nineteenth-century laissez-faire: the more recent incarnation of free-trade was dominated by a global worldview and corporate capitalism, in contrast to the more local and dispersed small and medium scale producers, traders and retailers of the previous era. Furthermore, just as the implementation of Keynesian and later neoliberal economics were processes which took decades to complete, there is no reason to expect a swift change but rather a gradual change and a mixed condition in the forthcoming years.

From an urban perspective, the return of free-trade in the 1980s did not mean a return of the forms of urban development of the nineteenth-century laissez-faire. The neoliberal status quo is best represented in urban form by urban sprawl, by high-end business districts and by the new role found for obsolete industrial areas by the creative industries. New Jersey's urban sprawl, based on catalogue housing and catalogue planning, for instance; the London Docklands, in which the city surrendered planning to private corporations in order to regenerate the derelict docks; the Tate Modern, a cathedral for art in a disused power station. Such forms were, of course, absent in the era of nineteenth-century laissez-faire. Similarly, there is no reason to expect a repetition of the urban development typical of the Keynesian plan: the assembly-line architecture and spiritless cities built under late modernism. Antagonism to determinist plans, to 'top down' prescriptions, fear of authoritarianism, demands for spontaneity, freedom and creativity, all of which characterized the critique of industrial society and of the Keynesian plan, and which accompanied and aided the rise of neoliberalism, are still entrenched in society. Planners still prefer to speak of 'a framework' rather than 'a blueprint'.[14]

**Newark Study Group**   The retreat from the Keynesian plan which began in the 1970s marked an end to the new towns and tabula rasa solutions typical of modernist architecture and urbanism. Tafuri traced their utopian zeal and totality to Antolini's Foro Bonaparte in Milan in the early nineteenth century – the insertion into the city of a totality in the form of an urban morphology which manifested the new enclave's complete freedom from the existing urban environment. In contrast, Tafuri described the plan for Milan by the Napoleonic Commission, produced in the same era, as a pragmatic negotiation with the existing city, an attempt to fix rather than eradicate the compromised urban environment.[15] Such an approach could be described as inherently reformist, in contrast to the radicalism of Antolini's plan and its complete rejection of the existing city and society.

The Newark Study Group, which began its work in early 2009, sought solutions to Newark's hardship by focusing on this second, reformist paradigm. The group's ambition was to identify solutions to Newark's predicament by applying the tools and instruments at the disposal of architects and planners, yet without shying from addressing specific hurdles to such solutions – whether economic, political or social, fields which are traditionally considered outside the sphere of architecture. An extensive historical analysis carried out by the group was a means of comprehending urban transformation and identifying the relationship between diverse forces such as labour, class and politics and their impact on urban morphology and typology. The analysis addressed not only the administrative area of Newark, but the greater New York region in order to enable the delineation of forces which are not limited by administrative boundaries.

An important absence in the historical analysis performed by the Newark Study Group was culture. Culture has largely been circumvented not because it has not played a part in the formation of contemporary Newark – the contribution to this section by Mark Krasovic demonstrates the contrary – but because culture and identity issues have come to overshadow others to the extent that issues related to labour, class and production are usually completely disregarded. Due to the prominence of culture and identity since the late 1960s, disparities and conditions which are the result of class differences or the outcome of the organization of labour are typically understood as identity-related issues: class interests have been substituted by identity-group interests. This has brought about extensive fragmentation in areas in which unity would have aided in forwarding the common interests of diverse social groups. Nevertheless, the manner in which culture and identity issues have exacerbated and enhanced class differences, creating a volatile mix of class, ethnicity, race and culture in Newark, cannot be ignored.

Following the historical analysis and a series of meetings with diverse experts in Newark and Manhattan, the Newark Study Group focused on the city's North Ward. The work of the group coincided with a plan forwarded by the city's administration to revitalize the Passaic River waterfront, replacing the derelict industry along the river with leisure, recreation, business and housing. The plan capitalizes on a federally funded effort to clean the heavily polluted Passaic and the precedents of transforming derelict industrial areas into thriving new districts by leveraging the beauty of the waterfront and the romantic appeal of historic industrial structures.

Within Newark, the Ironbound neighbourhood with its brightly coloured detached houses and Portuguese heritage is one of the city's best preserved areas with relatively minor social problems. In contrast, the Central Ward and especially the Afro-American dominated neighbourhoods to the south of the downtown have some of the worst statistics for unemployment, crime, poverty and foreclosure in the entire United States. The North Ward was originally home to the city's Italian community – skilled, unionized labourers, many of whom were employed at the port. It is currently a fragmented area, with mostly derelict industry along the Passaic River, and inhabited

**14** At the International New Town Institute Conference in Almere, June 2009, at the heart of a planned city in a nation which is arguably more planned than any other, virtually all planners and academics presenting papers declined to support any notion of 'top-down' or 'blueprint'.
**15** Manfredo Tafuri, 'Towards a Critique of Architectural Ideology', K. Michael Hays [ed.], **Architecture Theory since 1968** (Cambridge, Mass.; London: MIT Press, 2000), p. 12.

by a mix of Latinos, blacks and whites, with pockets of high poverty such as the southern edge of the ward and an affluent area, Forest Hill, perched near the Branch Brook Park [fig. 3]. Forest Hill is a protected historic neighbourhood with access to a light railway connection to the downtown and Penn Station. The North Ward is thus neither a 'problem area' which manifests extreme deprivation, nor an area of high real-estate value or potential; its hardship is dwarfed by the malaise of the Central Ward and its 'potential' is overshadowed by Ironbound.

The study of the North Ward, which included interviews with local residents and community groups and extensive tours of the area, was followed by discussing the means of intervening in the city via urbanism and architecture, attempting to define a strategy which would be the basis for a masterplan and architectural interventions. The discussion revealed not only the typical discrepancies between the approach to the city of urbanists and architects, but the dependency of these disciplines on deeply flawed solutions typical of neoliberal policies. Among approaches discussed were Ungers' archipelago model, Rowe's collage city, gentrification, neo-urbanism and 'theme park' urbanism. The discussion demonstrated the fear of planning and of over-deterministic solutions. It also demonstrated the timidity of many architects and urbanists while attempting to address a condition which is extreme rather than timid in any sense. However, the most striking conclusion was the absence of existing, pragmatic, articulated and well-defined approaches to the city which are neither related to planning in the Keynesian era nor to more recent remedies prescribed by neoliberalism.

The Newark section of *Urban Asymmetries* includes excerpts from the work of the Newark Study Group, with special emphasis on the historical analysis; Mark Krasovic has contributed an article which extends the discussion of specific cases of development carried out in Newark in recent decades and offers an insight into local politics and sentiments which suggests that post-riots Newark has more to offer than merely a story of decline; an interview with Monsignor William J. Linder enables a better understanding of the positions of committed activists involved in Newark from the specific perspective of the New Community Corporation. Newark does not represent here the condition of the North American city; rather, it exemplifies the specific case of the ex-industrial American city which has not found a new role in post-Fordist society, a condition shared with some other cities but by no means universal. It expresses the hardship brought about to certain sectors of society and to the urban environment by the onset of neoliberalism, and it raises the hope that current changes affecting political economy will provide Newark with a new role and, consequently, a route to recovery in the near future – a recovery which will be manifested at all levels: social, economic and physical, and will directly benefit the embattled residents of the city.

**Acknowledgements**   This article is developed from research carried out in 2009 by the Newark Study Group (NSG) of the Delft School of Design, directed by T. Kaminer, M. Robles-Durán and H. Sohn. The group included S. van Berkel, M. Daane Bolier, E. Franken, J. Hilkhuijsen, S. Hoogerheide, C. Karelse, D. Meurs, H. Park and R. Thijs. The illustrations and photographs presented in this section are a selection of the group's work, unless attributed to others. This article is based on a paper delivered at The New Urban Question conference at TU Delft, 2009. The Newark Study Group wishes to thank the scholars, activists, administrators and urbanists who supported the project with their time and knowledge, and particularly Joel Blau, Christine Boyer, Richard Cammarieri, Mark Krasovic, Joseph Matara and Damon Rich.

[1]

[2]

1 The New Jersey Performing Arts Center.
2 Foreclosures in Newark.
3 The affluent Forest Hill neighbourhood in the North Ward.

# The Culture of Development in the Brick City

**Mark Krasovic**

If you walk through downtown Newark along Park Place, past the glass office tower of New Jersey's largest utility company, then the glass and brick of the New Jersey Performing Arts Center, and turn onto Rector Street, you will walk past an old brewery building, a red-brick behemoth. If you wander south from Pennsylvania Station, you might turn down Hamilton Street, one of the last streets in Newark whose red-brick paving has survived into the twenty-first century. At the corner of Hamilton and McWhorter Street, an old brick factory is now an apartment house. The splashes of red brick you see throughout Newark might seem an anachronism among the newer glass and metal office buildings, but much of the city's history – the stories Newarkers tell themselves and the stories others tell about Newark – has been built on a foundation of the industrial-age's preferred building material. Newark is known as The Brick City, a name that originated in the local hip-hop culture of the 1980s to refer to the city's now largely vanished high-rise housing projects, but that often hearkens back to a storied industrial past when Newark was the home of the Ballantine, Krueger, and Feigenspan breweries; Edward Weston's pioneering electrical lighting company; Tiffany & Company's sterling-silver manufacturing plant; and innumerable tanneries.

In American narratives that celebrate ingenuity, the pluck of immigrant ancestors, and the development of prosperity, the industrial age of the nineteenth and early twentieth centuries is often remembered with great nostalgia. It is the urban heyday from which our cities have since declined. Its glory is the cultural yardstick by which our cities are so often measured. It is the paradise lost of Philip Roth's ironically self-aware Pulitzer-Prize-winning *American Pastoral*, whose hero enjoys its fruits well into the post-World War II period only to feel betrayed by a wave of 1960s revolutionary violence.[1] More often, the story is told without any sense of irony. Newark's 1967 riots are too convenient a trope, a simple handle on a much longer, messier history of urban development. For many, the sirens and gunshots that rang out over five days that July were the city's death knell, the moment at which middle-class residence, capital investment, and retail development – perhaps the very fabric of urban life itself – became suddenly untenable. For others, urban rioting marked the nadir of cities already suffering from global shifts in industrial organization, misguided federal policy, and conflict-laden migrations into and out of the city. While it is hard to argue with the statistical evidence of disinvestment, unemployment, and poverty – to take perhaps the most popular fields of analysis concerning the urban crisis – we might question the plotting of events, the seeming insistence that the urban crisis is marked only by various forms of socioeconomic declension.[2]

Intertwined with these narratives of urban decline is always the story of race. Rioting, after all, is rarely taken as a multiracial phenomenon (even when, as in Newark, it has been), and American cities in the aftermath of such violence are so often cast solely as black, histories of more recent

1 Philip Roth, **American Pastoral** (New York: Random House, 1997).
2 For recent historiographical examples, see Thomas Sugrue, **The Origins of the Urban Crisis: Race and Inequality in Postwar Detroit** (Princeton: Princeton UP, 1996); and on Newark specifically, Kevin J. Mumford, **Newark: A History of Race, Rights, and Riots in America** (New York: New York University Press, 2007); and Brad R. Tuttle, **How Newark Became Newark: The Rise, Fall, and Rebirth of an American City** (New Brunswick: Rutgers UP, 2009).

immigrants remaining largely unwritten. But Newark is a special case for the ways in which its history of violence, the frequent direness of its socioeconomic status, and its black political development have combined synergistically to make it, as one journalist put it in 1981, 'a paradigm for the American urban crisis'.[3] After black rioting, Newark's decline was steep and overseen by successive black city administrations whose political roots lay in a surge of black political nationalism. The city had a long history of black activism, not a small part of which was tied to the civil rights and antipoverty campaigns of the 1950s and 1960s, but in the summer of 1968 the tide of black politics in Newark shifted decidedly and took aim at city hall.[4] The United Brothers, a politically minded coterie of local activists and politicians brought together by Amiri Baraka, organized a political convention at a junior high school in the Central Ward to push for the creation of a black united front. Attendees chose two black candidates for an upcoming special city council election. Phil Hutchings, the new chief spokesman for the Student Nonviolent Coordinating Committee, the pre-eminent student-based civil rights organization in America, declared Newark an 'urban Mississippi.' 'If we can't get black power here,' he told the crowd, 'we can't get it anywhere.'[5]

Despite the broad base of black politics represented at the convention – participants included moderate and militant black power advocates, businessmen and lawyers, teachers, antipoverty workers, and city officials – its candidates failed to win a seat on the city council that year. But the political logic proved irrepressible, and another large black political convention was convened in late 1969 to choose a ticket for the big prize: City Hall itself. The convention's platform called for a civilian review board to monitor the police department, a reorganization of the city's Central Planning Board (whose actions had been central to so many controversies in the city, most notably that surrounding the city's promise of 150 acres of mostly black, mostly residential land in the Central Ward to the state medical college), teacher pay raises based on student performance, a single state agency to oversee all welfare programmes, and greater racial inclusiveness in all agencies and boards that handled housing issues. On the last day of the convention, attendees chose an expanded slate of candidates for city council – including a local teacher and antipoverty worker from the South Ward named Sharpe James – and nominated an unassuming city engineer named Kenneth Gibson to be their 'community choice' candidate for the mayor's office.

The result was an object lesson in both the possibilities and limitations of black politics in late-twentieth-century America. Gibson won the election against an incumbent mayor weakened by the riots and their aftermath and by his indictment on charges of corruption. Black Newark – and not an insignificant slice of white and corporate Newark, embarrassed by the old machine politics – celebrated his inauguration in grand fashion on a sparkling summer day. But what exactly

Gibson and his supporters inherited is a matter with which the historiography has not yet much grappled.[6] Their campaign dreams had to contend with several aspects of reality. For one, federal policy under President Richard Nixon was retreating from large-scale urban programmes and outlays (such as Model Cities, which Nixon told his aides to 'flush'), removing a crucial source of financial and political support from cities. Many social programmes and their respective federal agencies were slashed or reorganized. In their place, Nixon offered his New Federalism, by which state and local governments would be recipients of federal block grants to distribute at their discretion and private developers would be the recipients of new public incentives, such as tax abatements.[7] For another, Gibson inherited a city on the verge of bankruptcy. As Newark's population – residential, commercial, and industrial – continued its postwar decline, city tax revenues plummeted. The increasing costs of running a city with an increasingly needy population, even with some of the new federal aid and the highest property tax rates in New Jersey, rendered annual budget-writing an excruciating process of ruthlessly distinguishing essentials from non-essentials.

Though Gibson brought some stability to city hall, helped reduce infant mortality (a special target of his), and won for Newark some of the new federal revenue-sharing programmes' largesse, much of the outside world remained unimpressed with Newark and bestowed on it a variety of dubious recognitions. Early in Gibson's second term, Arthur M. Louis, an editor at *Fortune* magazine, decided to rank the fifty most populous American cities according to twenty-four different indices. Newark ranked dead last in nine categories and in the bottom five in nineteen, earning for itself the title of 'worst of all' American cities.[8] In 1986, the year Gibson lost the mayoral election to Sharpe James, who promised a more energetic confrontation with the city's problems, the u.s. Census Bureau announced that Newark had the highest poverty rate of any major American city.

But perhaps no other image has stuck to Newark as stubbornly as that of black violence. Each new city administration since the riots has staked a significant chunk of its record on public safety. In the mid-1980s, immediate family members of both Gibson and James were mugged in Newark, in the case of James's son violently. In the early 1990s, Newark became known as the carjacking capital of the world, an identity twice captured on film, the first time somewhat ironically in *Jersey Drive* (1995) and the second time less so in the cable-television reality show, *Jacked: Auto Theft Task Force* (2008). In 1996, *Money* magazine dubbed Newark the nation's most dangerous city, where

3 **New York Times**, April 5, 1981, p. NJ1.
4 This history of black power in Newark is chronicled in most detail in Komozi Woodard,
**A Nation Within a Nation: Amiri Baraka (LeRoi Jones) and Black Power Politics**
(Chapel Hill: University of North Carolina Press, 1999). For a deeper history of black activism in Newark, see Clement Alexander Price, 'The Afro-American Community of Newark, 1917-1947: A Social History' (unpublished doctoral dissertation, Rutgers University, 1975).
5 **Newark Evening News**, June 24, 1968, p. 8.
6 An early, unpublished attempt to tell this history is Robert Curvin, 'The Persistent Minority: The Black Political Experience in Newark' (unpublished doctoral dissertation, Princeton University, 1975).
7 For a good overview, see Raymond A. Mohl, 'Shifting Patterns of American Urban Policy since 1900', in **Urban Policy in Twentieth-Century America**, ed. by Arnold R. Hirsch and Raymond A. Mohl (New Brunswick: Rutgers UP, 1993).
8 Arthur M. Louis, 'The Worst American City', **Harper's**, January 1975, pp. 67-71.

both the violent-crime and car-theft rates measured six times the national average.[9] The *New York Times* reporter who covered the thirtieth anniversary of the riots captured the continued salience of black violence in the moribund city when he wrote, in a front-page special report entitled 'The Fall of Newark', that 'all the millions of dollars in national and state aid that have flowed into the city since the riots in 1967, all the corporate assistance, both in dollars and sense, all the jobs and education and housing programmes, have failed to change this fundamental fact about Newark: It is a city in the clutches of poverty, a city sliding ever downward, one that many say is in worse shape now than it was on July 12, 1967, the night the riots began.'[10]

What with larger neoliberal shifts in American politics and the seemingly relentless bad press Newark's black neighbourhoods received in the post-riot decades, it is little wonder that city government looked as much as it did to private capital to help develop the downtown area. Public funds were limited and few private developers wanted to take a chance on any area not within walking distance of Penn Station. The Gateway Center, one of the first downtown development projects to be realized after the riots, rose directly across the street from the railway station. Though commuters had only about fifty yards to walk to the office complex's door, the designers included an elevated walkway that would assure none of them would have to set foot on city streets. In 1971, Gateway II opened just the other side of its predecessor, an elevated walkway once again connecting them. Since then, elevated walkways have extended from the first Gateway complex to several other office buildings and parking garages.

Various hospitals and universities expanded their campuses in the years after the riots and the airport and light industry spread out over the meadowlands southeast of downtown, but downtown office development came to eclipse so many other possible notions of progress. It was central to the notion of Newark's 'renaissance', a trope that gained currency in the 1980s. In the first year of that decade, Mayor Gibson, along with state and federal officials and corporate leaders, announced the formation of a new nonprofit corporation: Renaissance Newark. Ideas for development had come and gone, explained an official from Public Service Electric and Gas (PSE&G) who took a two-year leave of absence to serve as the group's president, but Renaissance Newark would emphasize actual implementation, concrete and steel and glass achievements. Fourteen companies and the federal government had put together the quarter of a million dollars needed to start the corporation, which they tasked with devising a comprehensive development plan and aggressively courting developers. The president, who enjoyed an office in a gleaming new downtown office tower, asserted a high demand for city-centre office space, but hoped such development would prove contagious, spreading to 'the manufacturing sector of the economy, which is crucial for improving the quality of life for people in Newark.' In its first five years of existence, Renaissance Newark attracted $2 billion in investment.[11]

The hallmarks of this idea of renaissance, then, were public-private partnership, an emphasis on downtown construction, and a faith that the benefits thereof would spread, somehow, to people in the city's neighbourhoods. But if those purportedly communicable benefits were not so easily discernible, the development of the city's business core could not be denied. Soon after the forma-tion of Renaissance Newark, the Prudential Insurance Company, perhaps Newark's most storied corporate citizen, announced plans for a third phase to its Gateway Center, whose growth had stalled since the initial spurt in the early 1970s. Gateway Center III opened in 1984, and the next year Prudential submitted plans for Gateway IV to the city's planning board. It opened in 1988. Another elevated walkway sprouted from the north side of the Gateway complex to deliver com-muters to the Newark Legal and Communications Center, a mirrored-glass colossus developed by the Port Authority of New York and New Jersey, with the help of a federal Urban Development Action Grant that helped pay for the walkway and a parking garage. In 1986, across the street from the latest phases of the Gateway Complex, residential condos went on sale in the old *Newark Evening News* building. The luxury units sold out in less than two days, sparking great optimism about the possibilities of residential development in downtown Newark. The building was dubbed Renaissance Towers.

Yet no one sparked as much excitement at the prospect of a downtown renaissance as an enigmatic Iraqi immigrant named Harry Grant who rode into Newark on a wave of extraordinary promises in 1986. Declaring that 'this is soon to be a great town,' Grant bought at public auction an abandoned railway station on Broad Street, just north of City Hall, paying the bargain price of $1.2 million for the prime real estate. He promised a 60,000 square foot, two-storey shopping mall, a quarter of whose jobs would be reserved for Newark residents. He called it, predictably, Renaissance Mall. Soon after this purchase, Grant announced to Mayor James and the city council that he intended to build a 121-storey office tower – the world's tallest building – in downtown Newark. At first, he called it the Grant USA Tower, but soon incorporated all his ideas (the mall, the tower, a hotel, and plenty of parking) into the ostentatious Newark Renaissance Center.[12] It never happened. Construction on Renaissance Mall hobbled along for years, but was never completed. Grant gilded the dome atop City Hall and laid Belgian brick along Broad Street as assurances of his good intentions (or, as some thought more likely, in return for tax abatements and blight declara-tions), but just over fifteen years later work crews tore down what little existed of the planned Renaissance Center to make way for the Prudential Center, where the New Jersey Devils hockey team now plays. Harry Grant had gone bankrupt.

**9** Carla Fried, 'America's Safest City: Amherst, NY; The Most Dangerous: Newark, NJ', **Money**, November 27, 1996.
**10 New York Times**, July 14, 1997, p. A1.
**11** ibid., November 16, 1980, p. NJ1; April 5, 1981, p. NJ1; and November 10, 1985, p. NJ1.
**12** For a rendering of the project, see **New York Times**, June 21, 1987, p. R12.

This was one failure, even if a spectacular one, in a largely successful season of building in Newark. But overshadowing all this development was always a grim sense of the city's history. For what does 'renaissance' imply but death? What is a rebirth without some demise? Hardly a *New York Times* article on Newark, for example, opened without some reminder of the 1967 riots as a way to measure how far the city had or had not come. The memory of violence haunted all of this development, and it promised political power for those willing to cynically wield it. If downtown development signalled Newark's rebirth, power accrued to those who could claim for themselves the midwife's role.

Ken Gibson announced his bid for re-election in 1986 by telling a crowd of cheering supporters that, though Newark had been 'a dying city' when he became mayor in the wake of the riots, it was 'no longer a terminal case'.[13] Not enough people, however, gave Gibson the credit for whatever improvements they saw, and Sharpe James unseated him in the ensuing election. It was James more than anyone else who capitalized on the notion of renaissance and its ties to what had happened in Newark in the late 1960s. Only days after taking office, James praised the condominium project planned for the old *Newark Evening News* building. 'Renaissance Towers is aptly named because it is further testimony to the rebirth, progress and accelerated development that is taking place in our city,' he said. 'But the towers are just the tip of the iceberg. I believe this renaissance will spread to our residential areas and neighbourhood commercial strips.' James loved to point to the development that *was* occurring beyond the city's downtown business core as evidence for Newark's comeback, even when he had little or nothing to do with it. When a private developer began building over one thousand units, fifteen per cent of which would be subsidized for low- and moderate-income families, in the Central Ward in 1987, James declared it the beginning of the 'housing renaissance, the true renaissance, the tip of the iceberg of the resurgence of new housing in the city of Newark'.[14] In 1991, citing this development and others – hundreds of townhouses, the city's first new movie theatre in fifty years, the first new grocery store in twenty – the u.s. Conference of Mayors, to whose board of trustees Mayor James was elected that year, formally commended Newark for its 'true renaissance'.[15]

Less impressed with the spread of the renaissance from downtown into the neighbourhoods was the *New York Times*, which published a series on this theme just months after the Conference of Mayors had lauded Newark. 'Newark presents two different images to visitors,' one entry declared. 'One of gleaming steel and glass towers, the other of 100-year-old railroad shacks and multifamily wood frame houses in neighbourhoods with few stores or amenities, not even a movie theatre.' The vibrant downtown area had witnessed astounding progress, but not much was happening in the neighbourhoods, according to the story, where crime, unemployment, welfare, and poor schools had not improved much since 1967.[16]

But in this case the *Times*, the Conference of Mayors, and Sharpe James shared at least one perspective: progress was to be measured by the development of the built environment. Though you would not know it from the language being deployed, there *were* people living out in the neighbourhoods and they were not stuck in 1967. What these popular narratives of decline and renaissance so often missed was the remarkable ingenuity and dedication of the communities that lay outside the central business district. The months and years immediately following the disorders of July 1967 witnessed an explosion of new organizations committed to and anchored in – and in many cases, *anchoring* – specific neighbourhoods. The development energy generated outside the downtown corporate-City Hall nexus created more inclusive development processes that were better attuned to the needs and desires of neighbourhood residents. These organizations and the fortitude with which they met Newark's socioeconomic challenges give the lie to simplistic narratives of decline and downtown-centred revival.[17]

Less immediately concerned with economic development – especially of the downtown variety – a young Catholic priest at Queen of Angels Church in the Central Ward began organizing meetings in the church's basement in 1968. Father Bill Linder, working with and learning from several veteran Newark organizers, challenged the parishioners, who came from the surrounding neighbourhood and from the suburbs, to think of ways to get the neighbourhood back on its feet after the losses of 1967. Emphasizing human dignity and ability, they decided to focus not on attracting businesses to the Central Ward or building office towers or manufacturing plants, but on the maintenance of a viable residential community. They decided to build housing at what many considered the epicentre of black violence in America, the area in which Newark's riots had begun and the area that since then had become a symbol for the nation's urban crisis. They steered clear of traditional urban renewal, Mary Smith, one of the early participants in these meetings, later explained. 'To many of us,' she said, 'urban renewal meant people removal and that meant removal of large segments of the black population.'[18] Progress, then, would be measured not by the attracting of wealthy corporations and their largely middle-class employees to Newark, but by the viability of a low- and moderate-income community in the Central Ward.

**13** Gibson quoted in **New York Times**, May 5, 1986, p. B5.
**14** **New York Times**, December 7, 1987, p. B2.
**15** **New York Times**, June 18, 1991, p. B1. Just the week before, the National Civic League had named Newark an All-America City.
**16** **New York Times**, August 13, 1991, p. A1.
**17** I am limiting myself here mostly to new community development organizations. These were joined, of course, by organizations with broader mandates, like the Greater Newark Urban Coalition, whose first director has worked tirelessly for decades to erase discriminatory hiring practices in multiple industries and job sites in Essex County, and the Committee of Concern, which gathered reports on Newark's post-riot situation and urged increased business involvement in the city. And many older groups that were founded before the riot provided much-needed services and advocacy in the city. These would include War on Poverty-based groups like the United Community Corporation, FOCUS, Essex-Newark Legal Services, and the Newark Pre-School Council, as well as even older groups like the Boys and Girls Clubs and the Urban League.
**18** **New York Times**, August 11, 1979, p. 22.

About sixty families met regularly over the next two years, visited several planned communities along the eastern seaboard, talked with planners and architects, and, essentially, learned how to be developers. They formed a corporation and sold symbolic $5 shares to residents of the wealthier surrounding suburbs, raising enough money to purchase a small piece of land, part of the property that had originally been slated to go to the state medical school. And they discussed what kind of housing they wanted to build there. Downtown interests held no sway. These were neighbourhood leaders – some of whom were among the first to move into the new housing – and concerned suburbanites deciding what should be built in Newark. They did not want high-rise housing projects, for instance, and decided against interior hallways, opting instead for exterior balconies and private entrances. They spent years developing their plans and putting into place the necessary funding. In 1976, a full decade before Sharpe James's declaration of a 'housing renaissance' in Newark, the New Community Corporation (NCC) opened 120 units of low- and moderate-income housing – New Community Homes – at the corner of South Orange and Morris Avenues, in the heart of the worst city in America.

This start was modest only in comparison with what the NCC has accomplished since. It has added to the housing stock in the Central Ward co-ops, and has surrounded that with the trappings of a sustainable neighbourhood: healthcare clinics, a shopping mall anchored by a grocery store, a chain of childcare centres, job-training facilities, community meeting spaces, and even a restaurant *cum* jazz club. Its history of community-building success is tempered by often-strained relationships with City Hall and the inevitable problems that arise between land-lord and tenant (the latest occurring at the now problem-plagued original devel-opment over maintenance issues and plans to demolish the complex and relocate its residents).[19] But the energy and attention the NCC has brought to a much-derided neighbourhood has to be recognized in any serious account of Newark's post-riot history.

So, too, must it acknowledge that the NCC has no monopoly on community-based efforts to sustain Newark's neighbourhoods at a time when so many people pre-ferred to view the city from the distance afforded by elevated walkways or by journalists from *Harper's* magazine. Pick a neighbourhood, and there's a community development and service organization working there. Even before the riots struck the Central Ward, the Tri-City Citizens Union for Progress (1966) had drawn up community-development plans centred on housing. The Citizens Union rehabili-tated homes further west in the Central Ward and called their development Amity Village. Over the decades, they have branched out into health, family, and educa-tional services. The Ironbound Community Corporation (1969) has tackled housing, education, and environmental issues in the East Ward through social services and community organizing. The Unified Vailsburg Services Organization (1972) has performed similar work with residents in the West Ward. As Richard Cammarieri, lifelong Newarker and community organizer, put it when he was the director of the Newark Coalition for Neighbourhoods in the early 1990s, these groups – and others like them – 'deserve as much credit as anyone' for any sort of renaissance Newark has experienced. 'There is still some equity here because of them.'[20]

As some community-based groups focused on development and social services, meeting needs left unattended by downtown development, others confronted that development head-on. Though there was little to stop downtown development once city government and corporate leaders had joined hands, several groups succeeded in slowing it down and making it more equitable. As many of the public housing projects managed by the Newark Housing Authority (NHA) fell into disrepair, tenants at the Scudder Homes in the Central Ward, among others, launched a rent strike in April 1969 to protest the state of their apartment buildings. A year and a housing-authority director later, the tenants' association at the nearby Stella Wright Homes began their own strike, which soon spread to other projects and eventually became the nation's longest-running public housing rent strike. A federal suit filed on behalf of the tenants against the Newark Housing Authority and the federal Department of Housing and Urban Development (HUD) alleged that the city's housing programme had constructed a black ghetto that was nearly impossible for residents to escape. At first, the tenants demanded renovations, but later drew up plans for the depopulation of the projects altogether. Between April 1970 and July 1971, when a judge ordered them to stop, tenants paid their rents into an escrow account. When strike organizers defied a court order to maintain the account and instead returned the money to the tenants, two of them were thrown in jail. In April 1973, after several failed attempts to reach a settlement, the NHA signed an agreement with the Stella Wright tenants in which both sides declared 'that high-rise housing had failed miserably in the City of Newark' and that included a petition to the federal government to assist Newark in finding new housing for the poor and to begin phasing out the projects. 'Tear them down,' the head of the tenants' association said. 'Now that's my only goal.'[21]

19  Bob Braun, 'Newark Residents Decry Living Conditions at Homes Court', **Newark Star-Ledger**, March 29, 2009. On some of the tensions between NCC and City Hall, see Julia Rabig, 'What's the Matter With Newark?' **Shelterforce** (fall 2008), <http://www.shelterforce. org/article/1108/whats_the_matter_with_newark/> [accessed October 5, 2009]; and **New York Times**, February 18, 1996, pp. NJ1 and NJ8.
20  **New York Times**, August 13, 1991, p. B4.
21  **New York Times**, April 4, 1973, p. 91. The story does not quite end there, of course. Soon, when few repairs were forthcoming, the tenants struck again. In 1974, the NHA, after relocating the families that had continued to pay rent, threatened to shut off all utilities to the Wright Homes and abandon them. In July, the two sides finally reached an agreement, whereby rent payments would resume, repairs would be made, and a new tenants' organization would be formed to manage the Wright Homes. In 1978, the Regional Plan Association, a group that advises the federal government on metropolitan planning policy, praised the rent strikers for a seeming renaissance at Stella Wright. The buildings are now well-maintained and its apartments have tenants. 'A project that had been called unmanageable is being managed by tenants once thought unable to manage anything.' **New York Times**, November 26, 1978, p. NJ21. Stella Wright proved to be Newark's last high-rise public housing project. After several further suits against the city for not maintaining it, it was demolished in the spring of 2002. But it does suggest what good management can do, if only one has good partners and good resources.

In the 1980s, the Newark Housing Authority began demolishing high-rise housing projects in order to replace them with townhouse-style homes. They began with the eight towers of the Scudder Homes, each of which contained 200 apartments. But when two towers were razed in May 1987, only a little over 100 units of new housing had been planned to replace them. The photographer, writer, and housing advocate Camilo José Vergara called the demolition 'an orgy of waste'. Others, including a Newark city councilman and a local clergyman, deemed it absurd in a city with an estimated 5,000 homeless residents.[22] Now it seemed that, rather than concentrating poor African Americans in a public housing ghetto, the housing authority was trying to throw them out of Newark altogether.

When demolition plans were announced for other housing projects, fears over the amount and availability of replacement housing reached a critical point. A group of area activists and tenants formed the Newark Coalition for Low-Income Housing and filed suit against the housing authority and the federal Department of Housing and Urban Development in 1989. Later that year, when the judge (who, in the 1960s, had been president of Newark Legal Services) ordered the disputants to work with a state mediator, the sides reached an agreement. The Housing Authority agreed to slow some of its demolition plans and curtail others. All eight towers at Columbus Homes would come down, but in stages, each dependent on the NHA beginning construction on enough town-houses to replace all of the units lost. In return for making substantial repairs to over 1,600 subsidized apartments and to two buildings at the Kretchmer Homes in the South Ward, the Authority was allowed to demolish three other high-rises at Kretchmer. In any future destruction, the city would have to demonstrate that the buildings were beyond rehabilitation and would have to begin building replacement homes.

In 1991, the Coalition was still waiting for the NHA to fulfil its part of the deal, and demanded that the Authority be placed under receivership. The Authority *had* constructed town homes on the old Scudder site, but a windstorm blew some of them down, so shoddy was the construction. Those that survived the storm were razed. Many public housing residents whose homes were renovated under the agreement complained that the renovations were mostly cosmetic and not near what they had been promised. Victor DeLuca, chair of the Coalition, said that the city's housing programme suffered from 'institutional paralysis' and that Newarkers could not wait any longer for new affordable housing.[23] After HUD, citing a turnover in leadership at the housing authority, refused the Coalition's request to place it in federal receivership, the Coalition filed suit again in 1992. Though that, too, was unsuccessful in creating a receivership, the Coalition's pressure finally produced results. In 1994, after the NHA began construction on almost 1,800 new townhouses, the federal government removed it from its list of troubled housing authorities and allowed it to demolish four more towers at the Columbus Homes. Though the housing authority still had plenty of problems to deal with, the executive director of the Coalition for Low-Income Housing called the delay in blowing up the Columbus Homes and the construction of so many new townhouses 'a victory'.[24]

While so many of the battles over development centred on the creation and maintenance of decent, affordable housing out in the neighbourhoods, the struggle did reach into downtown development plans at different times and for varying reasons. In the early 1980s, at a time when Newark had no historic preservation laws (Mayor Gibson once argued they would discourage private investment), the Newark Preservation and Landmarks Committee fought to save the Cass-Gilbert-designed American Life Insurance Company Building when PSE&G moved out of it and into their new glass high-rise. Though the committee brought suit against the utility company and succeeded in delaying the destruction, PSE&G was too valuable a downtown patron for them to succeed in halting demolition altogether. The executive director of the quasi-public Newark Economic Development Corporation noted that Newark could not be 'overbearing' with a developer, especially one who had sunk so much money into its new downtown office tower. (It had, of course, been wooed with a tax abatement.)[25]

A stretch of Broad Street further south, surrounding City Hall and extending two blocks east to Mulberry Street, has been massively redeveloped in the last couple of decades. Few residents remain, but that is not because residents simply fled before the downtown development jugger- naut. In the early eighties, the inhabitants of the apartment building at 30 Walnut Street had been all but abandoned by their landlord. In the dead of winter, they had no heating or hot water. In May 1980, with the help of Essex-Newark Legal Services, the tenants succeeded in having the building placed in receivership. When the city assumed ownership the following year because taxes on it had not been paid, it sent out eviction notices. The tenants explained that they had sunk all their money into repairs, had succeeded in stabilizing the building, and would resume tax payments very soon. They negotiated an agreement with the city whereby the building remained in receivership, but would be managed by the tenants. But early in 1983, the city asked the courts to take the building out of receivership and quickly moved to evict the tenants who had struggled to maintain it. The land it stood on was too valuable. By the end of the decade, the entire block had been cleared for the Martin Luther King, Jr. Federal Courthouse. Mayor James, the hallway to whose office was said to be lined with dozens of ceremonial shovels, predicted the courthouse would be 'a magnet for other developments in the city' and declared that 'the name selected for it is so right, so appropriate at this time.'[26]

**22** John T. Cunningham, **Newark** (Newark: New Jersey Historical Society, 200), p. 366; and Vergara in **New York Times**, June 14, 1987, p. NJ28.

**23** **New York Times**, September 14, 1990, pp. B1 and B2; and December 27, 1991, p. B5.

**24** **New York Times**, March 7, 1994, p. B1.

**25** **New York Times**, April 19, 1981, pp. NJ1 and NJ13.

**26** James quoted in **New York Times**, November 1, 1987, p. 64. On the shovels, Cunningham, **Newark**, pp. 371-73.

Less than ten years later, Ray Chambers – a Newark native son and first chairman of the New Jersey Performing Arts Center, who had made his fortune in leveraged buy-outs and quit the business world to invest his money in Newark's cultural and educational infrastructure – took the next step in developing the Mulberry Street corridor by forming a consortium to buy the New Jersey Nets and Devils professional sports teams and to build for them an arena in Newark. The James administration was enthusiastic and, when the time was right, commissioned a redevelopment plan for the Mulberry Street corridor.

When the plan for an urban village of condos, stores, and restaurants was unveiled in 2003, local residents and business owners accused the city of wanting to take over their neighbourhood not because it was blighted, but because it had become so valuable. They formed the Mulberry Street Coalition and, rather than be run over by the city's planning process, demanded that they be a part of it. 'Our roots are here, and we stuck it out when no one else cared about the neighbourhood,' one Coalition member who owned a laundromat in the redevelopment area explained.[27] At first, the city council voted against the redevelopment plan, but later in 2003, after some members received donations from the developers, reversed itself. The city condemned the property, claiming it was blighted. Still, the members of the Coalition held out, and in 2007 a state Superior Court judge ruled that the city had acted improperly in hiring developers and approving plans before seeking the blight declaration. The large financial contributions to city councilmen and to James himself from the developers rendered the city's blight finding a political *fait accompli*, rather than a reasoned decision. The judge reversed it, and the Mulberry Street Coalition was vindicated.

When a young upstart city councilman named Cory Booker announced his intention to run against Sharpe James in 2002, his focus on Newark's most intractable problems – the crime rate, poverty, unemployment – contrasted sharply with Sharpe James's boosterish proclamations of a renaissance. 'If there is a renaissance in Newark,' Booker intoned, 'then it is time for a renaissance for the rest of us.'[28] Though Booker lost that election, he was back at it four years later, accusing James of 'giving away our land' to politically connected developers.[29] Booker was making use of the considerable media attention he garners to communicate to a larger audience what so many Newarkers had come to believe: city government was beholden to outside development interests often at the expense of its own citizens.

Ironically, it was exactly the same trope of the mutually constitutive Newark insider and outsider that Mayor James deployed against Booker. James could draw on a much longer history in the city than his rival, who had moved to Newark in 1996 during his final year at the Yale Law School. James had moved to Newark from Florida with his mother and brother in the 1940s, when he was still a child.

He made his way to college, became a teacher in the Newark public schools and later the athletic director at Essex County College. When the War on Poverty set up a neighbourhood office in the South Ward, James worked there as an organizer, and he had been chosen in 1969 as one of the black political convention's 'community choice' candidates for city council. He served there for sixteen years before being elected mayor.

James could have run against Booker on this personal history alone, and he made good use of it in the 2002 campaign. In a city that so much of the world had written off, a stubborn local pride was politically powerful. When announcing his bid for re-election, James told a cheering crowd of supporters that he wished 'to continue to give something back to the City of Newark that took a poor boy, living on Howard Street and South Orange Ave, in one room with a pot-bellied stove, with an outhouse in the backyard, one pair of sneakers, one pair of pants, one t-shirt, and today the poor boy from Howard Street is your mayor and seeking re-election.'[30] James attacked Booker as the consummate outsider who had no claim on Newark history. His assault had a geographical logic (Booker grew up in suburban Harrington Park), a generational logic (he was a child of the civil rights struggle rather than a participant in it), and a socioeconomic logic (his family was relatively affluent and he had attended Stanford, Yale, and Oxford Universities). But most damningly – and most cynically – James gave his attack a racial logic: his campaign consistently claimed that Booker was not really black. James was quoted calling Booker a 'white Republican,' a 'faggot white boy' who took money from the Ku Klux Klan, and a Jew. 'You have to learn to be an African-American,' he famously mocked Booker, 'and we don't have time to train you all night.'

A further irony of James's campaign is that any honest history of Newark since 1967 can no longer be told solely in terms of black and white. It has to include stories of the new waves of immigrants that have made Newark home since then. One might begin with the fact that the coalition formed to challenge the proposed massive land-grab in the Central Ward for the state medical school was called the Committee Against Negro and Puerto Rican Removal, or with the fact that the political convention that nominated Ken Gibson for mayor and Sharpe James for councilman in 1969 was called the Black and Puerto Rican Political Convention and that the pledge of unity conferees made was delivered by Hilda Hidalgo, local Puerto Rican activist, sometime political candidate, and secretary of the city's antipoverty agency. One of that agency's subdivisions was the Field Orientation Center for Underprivileged Spanish (FOCUS), whose Puerto Rican chairman was nominated for the city council with James. FOCUS has since broadened its mission to economic and community development; youth, senior, and education services; job training; and cultural events. In 1972, ten families founded La Casa de Don Pedro in the North Ward to address the specific needs of Latinos and recent immigrants. La Casa has since developed a planning initiative in the Lower

27  **New York Times**, September 5, 2004, p. NJ6.
28  Quoted in Cunningham, **Newark**, p. 395.
29  **New York Times**, April 19, 2006, p. B7.
30  This rally is shown in the film **Street Fight**, DVD, directed by Marshall Curry
(2005; Red Envelope Entertainment, 2007).

Broadway area, in addition to its multiple social services. Any honest history must also deal with the city's Asian population, like the Korean immigrant merchants who helped sustain the commercial district along Halsey Street for much of the 1980s, as well as, of course, the Portuguese and Brazilian communities in the Ironbound neighbourhood.

The final irony of James's campaign is that it may have been the last election cycle in which the old narratives of 1967 and the ensuing renaissance would wield much power. Four years after that campaign, on the eve of the fortieth anniversary of the 1967 disorders, local academics, members of the city's arts and cultural establishment, community organizers and activists, members of the clergy, journalists, and assorted other interested parties formed what they called The Big Bad Committee and launched an ambitious commemorative project. In a series of public events and displays – two conferences, a reconvening of the state commission that studied the riots, a public conversation with the former county prosecutor who oversaw the riot trials, an exhibition at the New Jersey Historical Society based on over one hundred oral history interviews – Newarkers, past and present, very publicly confronted 1967 and its implications. The city, for so long at the mercy of the memory of the riots, was taking control of that memory and approaching it with some degree of irony and even, at times, humour. People who participated in the commemorative effort were forced to confront other people's stories, to grapple with the realization that theirs was not the only perspective on history and, by extension, that no individual enjoyed exclusive rights to that history.

Sharpe James decided not to run for mayor in 2006, and Cory Booker swept into office almost effortlessly. Newark's longstanding problems with poverty, entrenched bureaucracy, and crime (to name but three) have not disappeared during Booker's first term, but his administration has signalled that it takes planning very seriously as a process in which a larger public should be engaged. After almost ten years of delay and pressure from an ad hoc Master Plan Working Group created by several Newark community development organizations, the Booker administration took an important first step toward realizing a fully updated and comprehensive master plan by issuing a planning re-examination report in February 2009. Included in the reports goals is 'a new culture of planning and design', which 'continually places the community at the table with city government and with developers in a partnership for progress'.[31]

Newark's community-based organizations – especially those organized into the Newark Community Development Network, the parent of the Master Plan Working Group – have been more than willing to take up the invitation. They are the ones who kept the momentum going for so long, and the prospect of having a true partner in City Hall, they seem to feel, is worth pursuing. For his part,

Mayor Booker seems to appreciate the need for new narrative tropes that move beyond notions of civic death and rebirth, tropes that honour the undying commitment of so many Newarkers to their city. In a letter that opens the re-examination report, he writes, in typically eloquent fashion, 'We are a city of pride and accomplishment, fierce faith and flawless fortitude. We are New Jersey's oldest city, her largest city and her greatest city. We are Newark – Brick City, tough, resilient, strong, enduring and when we come together, there is nothing we can not create or overcome.'[32]

Talk of a renaissance has fallen out of fashion in Newark. Newark never died. More and more, the city seems to be reclaiming a different identity – the Brick City – and retooling it so that it no longer hearkens back to some long-lost industrial Golden Age, but to the perseverance, the hard work, and the toughness of the people in a city once known as the worst in the United States.

---

**31** The re-examination report can be downloaded from <http://www.ci.newark.nj.us/govern-ment/city_departments/economic__housing_development/newarks_master_plan.php> [accessed October 5, 2009].
**32** Unfortunately, Booker has also opened up the 'Brick City' label to a potential hijacking. His welcoming of a documentary film crew to Newark during the summer of 2008 resulted in a five-hour documentary series that premiered on the U.S. cable-television network, the Sundance Channel, in September 2009. The film intertwines two stories: Booker and his administration trying to get crime statistics under control and the personal lives of two former members of rival street gangs who are now a couple. It is titled, simply, **Brick City**.

**1** Derelict industrial buildings on Newark's
waterfront.
**2** Newark's downtown area.
**3** Mostly abandoned industrial infrastructure
in Newark's North Ward.

2]

3]

# Newark and Community Development.
# An Interview with
# Monsignor William J. Linder,
# Founder of Newark's
# New Community
# Corporation (NCC)

**Stephanie Choi**[I]

**Stephanie Choi**  To start, I would like to ask you to introduce to our readers the NCC, its mission in Newark, and how it operates.

**Msgr. Linder**  Well, we were founded as a result of the summer disorders of '67. The movement for community development was beginning in the 60s, and was very much tied to the civil rights movement. I think the majority of the board came from the civil rights movement. [We] began to realize that we were achieving victories – legal victories and regulations, but we were not really bringing on the number one, the young male African-American, particularly in the urban areas. And that was really King's thinking too, Dr. King. And in fact I was scheduled to take a leave for a year and go to Detroit and organize; Saul Alinsky in Chicago had a great influence on a lot of us, and many of us actually worked in civil rights and had a background in organizing, and so that really led to what we call the community development movement. The other thing we had going was the Johnson Great Society programme,[2] because it actually organized communities. So in the '60s up to the summer disorders here that movement was growing with the Great Society programme and at the same time the civil rights movement came together on the same thing. You know – you go to demonstrate and then eventually you want to see something permanent.

**SC**  So it was gestating since 1964 or even earlier.

**ML**  Yeah. In my case I came to Newark in 1963, and that really was the height of the civil rights movement anyway. I was sent to an African-American parish, and the parish was definitely in the middle of the civil rights movement, both nationally and locally, and also with the church, we did a number of direct actions, but we were very aggressive at the time, the civil rights part of it.

**SC**  So the 1967 riots were the impetus for the formation of the NCC?

**ML**  Yes, they were. We were having discussions about the problems of the Great Society programme here in Newark, the discussions were here. Basically the political was corrupt, and the political, the last thing they wanted to do was to have a local power base, and then the summer disorders came and, for example, a housing authority had given out a hundred acres of land for development for some for-profit venture that had no roots in the city, the roots were campaign contributions and things. Those were the things that everybody said that we have to do something about. In the beginning we didn't even have access to urban renewal so we could get land, a dollar for a square foot, so instead what we did is negotiate privately for land just for our first project, and to receive the subsidies necessary we went out to the suburbs to work with churches, and we created a new

---

**1**  The interview took place in January 2010, in Newark. This is an edited version, condensing the complete interview into about a quarter of its full length. Editing and notes by T. Kaminer, transcripts by H. Sohn.
**2**  The Great Society was a series of programmes initiated by President Lyndon B. Johnson as a fight for racial equality and a war on poverty. It included programmes such as Medicaid and Medicare.

community foundation which ran parallel. You didn't own anything, but you had a certificate. You had a square foot of land in Newark.

**SC** So the NCC began with a housing project.

**ML** It was housing right from the beginning. We knew the whole community – if you told everybody we need to change everything it would have been a little too much, so we started with housing, and housing was the number one thing here in Newark. Newark at the time had more than 50,000 people in public housing in the city, it was the highest percentage per capita for public housing in the nation, and half of it was in the Central Ward and was in three high-rise projects and one low-rise project, and that represented half of it, and it was all centralized, and in fact the summer disorders were exactly centralized, while in Detroit and Los Angeles it was spread out, here it was very intense, it was all in the public housing.

**SC** Was there a specific phrase at the beginning which described the organization's position?

**ML** Well, I think we had a few things, not so much a phrase – the people had to participate, it had to be bottom-up planning. The other is that the civil rights movement was religious but it was ecumenical, so it was kind of an inclusive thing – everybody of good will who believed things should be better, was welcome. It was built upon economic development in which the people had to participate; too many of the projects that we did benefited people outside, so we did the university hospital. The university hospital didn't create many jobs for local people. The amount of people who worked and lived in Newark and were coming from average Newark residences was very low, so we really looked at an economic model that would create more jobs here, and became interested in early childhood: there was no infant care. [Children of] one to four we got into nursing home, and these were all services that didn't exist in the Central Ward, but we really created economic opportunities for people who were here. So we saw the whole thing tying together: we needed to control the jobs, and solve the housing first. We didn't hire a management firm, we got our own manager, our own security force, our own maintenance – in other words, the model is to keep everything here and create the opportunity for people here, and that led us to training and adult education which we're still running.

**SC** It seems that the ambition of NCC is so huge that as your scope grew more and more, its prominence in the Central Ward in Newark meant that the NCC began functioning as a city within a city. What do you think about the growth and development and its relationship to the rest of Newark?

**ML** Well, we are a city within a city, we intended to be. We actually take in part of the West Ward too. So we saw ourselves as that, but remember we had a very corrupt government until Booker was elected,[3] and the former mayor would say in the meetings that now it's our turn and he was vocal in the previous election when he beat Booker, and in his victory party he spoke about how he was going to get even… everything was on the table, it's not a matter of any secrets.

**SC** I think this leads to my next question, which is in regard to the NCC's relationship with local government. How much does NCC depend on the good will of the city administration?

**ML** Well, we never depended… We might in the future go into a transition politically, but we haven't so far. We were always friends with state government and it didn't matter whether or not it was Republican or Democrat – they all feared the politics of Newark, the corruption part.

**SC** So you circumvented local government through state intervention?

**ML** Right. And then under the Clinton years we did federal, and we never did federal before. We were very much into community banking issues, housing issues and employment issues, so we really got into a whole new relationship with the federal government, and did very well. I mean, we got the largest HOPE grant[4] for housing in the United States actually, and we got 25 million and it was great because we were allowed to work on home ownership and we were able to do the underwriting of individual applicants and then plug-in a grant to them.

**SC** And this was during the Clinton years. Because originally you started out doing low income housing, mainly rental units, and this is a kind of move into actually subsidizing home ownership.

**ML** Right. And that we couldn't have done without it…. We could, for example, take thirty families which were foster parents, and if they put in three years in foster care, the state could propose them to us as candidates for home ownership, and some of them got grants of 50-60,000, so it was both an award for them for the years they've put in – and not too many years – but they couldn't sell it for seven years so they had to keep the equity and it did great things. We could tie it to other things – we were concerned that foster families were moving quite frequently, more frequently than is good for the family, so how do we stabilize home ownership? Well, we started a pilot project.

**SC** So the seven years also encourage the home owner to stay in the area, stabilizing the area?

**3** Cory Booker, mayor of Newark.
**4** 'The HOPE VI Program was developed as a result of recommendations by National Commission on Severely Distressed Public Housing, which was charged with proposing a National Action Plan to eradicate severely distressed public housing. The Commission recommended revitalization in three general areas: physical improvements, management improvements, and social and community services to address resident needs'; <http://209.85.229.132/ search?q=cache:nlbFypGYyrwJ:www.hud.gov/offices/pih/programs/ph/hope6/+hope+grant+us &cd=1&hl=en&ct=clnk&gl=nl&client=firefox-a> (accessed 13.03.2010).

**ML** Sure. Our goal was to keep families stabilized in the area. We were concentrating on those who have raised their families here because we felt there was a greater stake in staying in the community and developing a good community.

**SC** How much of NCC's funding is coming from local, state or federal government grants? I'm curious to know, ultimately, how much is private funding?

**ML** We built upon what we call third party contracts – the Section 8 for the housing is federal money,[5] the vast majority of our money. What we try to do is make those contracts work: in housing it's great because the contract is for thirty years, so that gives you a chance to work on community development. But the federal government is really paying on behalf of the resident and we make sure we set up the mechanism that we can use to leverage economic development – housing, and so on. Then what we do is we got zero mortgages, it was totally paid for by this cash flow, plus our operating expenses. By federal law we were allowed to sell the excess, so in other words keep 3% of the ownership and sell 97% of the ownership, although we would be the managing general partner and raise money that way – we raised probably about 18 million at that time, thirty years ago. And that money we reinvested, so we began to have equity to do a shopping centre, a nursing home, the first newly-built-from-scratch day care centre, to do St. Joseph plaza, the headquarters, so then we had cash, and we had a good bit of cash, and we were able to invest it and leverage more with mortgages from that. Most of all – what we call third party contracts, the money is meant for the residents but we are the recipients because we are the contracting agency. The same with medical. Medical overnight grew to the size of housing because we got into Medicaid, which is the low income insurance money for health. Now, those contracts are large. And you can create careers in health. Someone can be on welfare and can go to a programme for 90 hours and become a nursing assistant, and then for example they get maybe about 11 dollars an hour, and then you can run – which we did – a licensed practical nurse programme and that goes on for about 15 to 18 months, and you can do that while you are working. And if you go from 11 dollars to 25 dollars an hour as a licensed practical nurse plus all your benefits, and then you go to 32 or 34 dollars an hour as an RN [resident nurse / registered nurse] in community college, from there you really have economic growth. And what you are really doing is that you are using contracts for which you are competing with for-profit companies, except you have another model of the workforce.

**SC** The corporation has assumed so many different roles – there's the day care, health care, creating local for-profit developments like the Pathmark, for instance, in addition to the housing and the home ownership. How does the NCC acquire or research the kind of expertise to run and manage all these different areas?

**ML** No, just the opposite, we wanted people who didn't, as it were. We wanted people whose real interest was in this community and not necessarily in their own economic growth. I think that if you are doing the right thing you can get people to volunteer. We then create a model. We do two things: we have the operating corporation and we have the real estate corporation. The rent paid by the operating corporation builds equity, and traditionally what we do is that we keep it for a while and then we refinance it and take that money and put it back into the operational so we have our own subsidies going. That's why we are struggling right now – because the refinance market is nothing right now. But hopefully we'll get out of that… Now, we have people obviously paying rents, but senior citizens are paying 50 dollars for a 1000 dollar house / apartment. Fifty dollars are a lot when you add them all together but it's nothing compared to the 950 of subsidy.

**SC** To go back to this question about the relationship with local government: you brought up the history of corruption in Newark city politics; has the recent election of Cory Booker changed the operations of NCC in any way?

**ML** First of all, you begin to be proud that a mayor isn't dishonest, and I haven't had that for 47 years in Newark. I think he's smart. He's an intelligent person. It's nice working with him. I think he has his problems, and that is that he's probably too national for what is good for Newark. It's nice to be a celebrity and raise money with celebrities, but it's not necessarily in itself good community development. Newark has now gone with developers looking for people with national names in entertainment and so on to sponsor housing. I don't know if that does much. If you ask him what their projects are he will give you about three or four celebrity housing they're doing. First of all they do not know anything about community development – you'll see that there's quite a bit of the housing projected for downtown and it's not family housing, and it doesn't address really the lower income levels, so we're getting into a kind of a fame and fortune model for development. I don't think that's good for this city, to tell you the truth.

**SC** Have there been since the election of Booker changes for the NCC in terms of availability of funding, access to permits, or land, or doing joint projects?

**ML** The project across the street which we are doing is a joint venture. We had the land and they've been cooperative. The money is so limited that you really have to put some kind of priority list. Low income housing as such in the state is not number one anymore. We also have changed the terminology nicely to 'affordable housing'. It is no longer housing for lower and moderate income. Affordable to whom? The affordable line has gone up.

---

5 Section 8: a programme created in 1937 to supply federal financial assistance for subsidized, low-income housing.

**SC** Speaking of housing, in terms of the recession, has the recent wave of fore-closures in Newark affected the priorities of NCC?

**ML** No, because all the mortgages we did, we negotiated with the bank to get blocks on them. We still have to do our own underwriting, so we'll know if we are playing it right. We didn't use any flexible interest rates, all fixed interest rates for thirty-year periods. And we also gave them enough equity so that if there was a depressed market they had plenty of room. So ours were pretty conservative, but negotiated in blocks. And we didn't allow the people to really do their own mortgages, because, you know, there were people all over the place selling mortgages. They'd go in the kitchen, have coffee and tell everybody everything was possible. They didn't care; it got passed on and on and on.

**SC** Has the subprime mortgage market given an opportunity to NCC to acquire new units of housing?

**ML** No, no we haven't. And one of the reasons is that unfortunately during the James administration[6] they allowed that housing to be investment housing and not owner-occupied investment housing. So we frankly stayed away from any foreclosures.

**SC** To what extent was the birth of the NCC more than an attempt to rebuild Newark after the riots – to challenge the planning and urban renewal policies of the 1960s?

**ML** On that physical planning side, as I mentioned, we were much better off in the beginning than we are now. But we really tried to involve everybody. In the first housing project, for example, we bought the land privately, and we then got a group together; eventually, it turned out to be about 120 units of a co-op. The co-op didn't work by the way. We had to dissolve it. The incomes we had were too low for a co-op, frankly. We were able to get a grant from the state to educate about 60 people involved... who eventually moved in, and they were part of the design team, but they also had to go through an education process. In the '60s everybody would get their own little lot with a white picket fence, with their own independent Cape Cod house; what people were dreaming of was not very real to what you could do. We really then started a programme where they would have to give us one Saturday a month for two years, and we brought in people to talk to them about design concepts, so we had architects and planners, and so on. And then we took them on field trips, for example, to get a sense of a planned city. We then took them up to New Haven. We also brought in the staff for design: one was Oscar Newman who had published some books on defensible space and housing.[7] So they were able to interact like that. Interestingly we abandoned this project, tore it down.

All of the defensible space concepts really are not working today. They worked well then, when we built them, but not today. Too open. Now we are going into more fortified building, you know, one entrance.

**SC** Could you describe defensible space in terms of what that means for the building or the plan?

**ML** Five-storey buildings because you had to have a certain amount of density if it was going to be something that you continue producing. It had a courtyard in the centre that was extremely attractive. You could see from every kitchen in every apartment down into the courtyard. One of the main concepts was that the mother at home would have sight of the children. The problem is that that might have worked in a society that didn't have so many single parents, 70% of them were female-headed homes, they were working, or at least they were trying to work. And the co-op part, the economic part, impacted because they really didn't have the type of money that was necessary for housing co-ops. And so the participation, really, while it was good in the pre-programme and the first couple of years, it would gradually start dying. Because people were really not involved as they were before.

**SC** Did the NCC see the political dimensions of the crisis in those years as intertwined with spatial issues, planning, and housing, the organization of space?

**ML** Oh, yeah, definitely. We had no planning department in the city; frankly, we had no master plan for about thirty years. In fact, what drove everything in the city were the payoffs to City Hall – you could build whatever you want. Well, we didn't, but we always had the state with us. New Jersey has the toughest constitution in the country in favour of an executive branch of government. The governor is very, very powerful in this state. More than any other state, and the governors all had integrity. While we did well with Republicans, we did well with Democrats; you would have to change the vocabulary, emphasize one thing over another, but still, it worked. We always got the help.

**SC** So in a sense, the NCC really upset local politics.

**ML** Yeah, very much. But we never ran candidates, or we weren't a threat to them. We stayed out of local politics for the most part.

**SC** Do you see organizations such as NCC taking on the responsibilities that the government should be doing in terms of providing affordable housing, or providing health care? Do you see

**6** Sharpe James, mayor of Newark 1986-2006. Convicted for fraud in 2008.
**7** See <www.defensiblespace.com> (accessed 20.03.2010).

that kind of capitulation of the government's responsibilities to private organizations as something of a move from public to private?

**ML** I think the need is different today. Elitist groups tend to be favoured. I think they don't tend to think of the bottom end of the community. And I haven't seen any of them willing to put in serious dollars of their own into this as donations. It's more like investment. We have such a strong push in this country that everybody needs to be a socially minded person. They need to be Newman's salad dressing, you know what I mean… Community development groups in the country are much weaker right now.

**SC** So on one hand you have a local government that is not fulfilling its responsibilities to local community, which is where NCC and other non-profit organizations have come in to fill in that void. On the other hand you're just talking about instances where private foundations don't have the best interests at heart.

**ML** I wouldn't say they don't have the best interests. I would say, I think that there are other interests that are weighing heavier. I don't think they are disinterested… I think you should try to get as many of the community development groups as possible. Cause they'll be out there, and they'll tend to use a measuring stick that's other than just profitability. It's closer to constituents. Even if we're big, we don't want to be the only ones.

**SC** Do you see a loss of autonomy for the organization in terms of becoming more embedded in local government?

**ML** We went through a period of taking entities in NCC and they're off on their own; for example, in our shopping centre we owned two thirds of the store itself. We sold it to them, back to Pathmark. We don't really have any control in the stores, we own the real estate. It was tough to get the real estate, and it's in the best place. But we're not the store anymore. We used to sit in there and have board meetings at the store. It's good and bad, but the ethics of our partners have changed. Really, we weren't going to work well together. The day-care, which was huge, about 850 children, wanted to go off on their own, we helped them to go on their own. So that's out. We just recently sold our license for Essex and half of Hudson for visiting nurse service, and we actually became partner, they gave us back for nothing 20% of it. They had about 150 employees, and that spun off, that's now separate.

We trimmed down quite a bit: we went down from 1300 employees to 750 right now. We're ready to start some new things. The housing across the street is a partnership. That's the first time we've ever been in partnership… We're going to do another one with the same developer. I would say he's probably got the reputation of the best one in the state. So at least we can negotiate and talk to the best. We're going to do a teenage mother residence. So we are starting to do different things. And it probably would have been a bit difficult to do because of our size. Now we're a little more a fighting weight as it were.

**SC** How do you see the position of NCC to still criticize or be able to comment on the local situation as NCC has become more embedded in the area?

**ML** Well, that for me is a big issue. You need conflict. Conflict is good for an organization. Obviously, the internal conflict isn't good. But when you have an outside entity that you're constantly battling, it's good for yourself, it really unites you; it keeps you focused on a mission and so on. I think we have too many people that think conflict is a bad word.

I don't think we have anyone new in years that comes out of the civil rights movement; that's a big problem. To tell you the truth, all they know is a Martin Luther King dinner; or they name a street after him. What do we do? We've got all these young men out there on the streets with no jobs... We've got to carry this further. So that was the idea of building up a kind of structure to deal with it. I don't think we have any of that. They drive me up the wall with traditional social work. We're trying to enable people to be self-supporting, independent; we're not trying to keep them under an umbrella or protection forever. That's very difficult to deal with. We're dealing with this every day, and I am not sure we're winning. We really do not have the thinking that we need right now.

Right now, we've got to get back to the first days, with a real sense of mission. A real sense that, OK, we're a large institution, but we need to be advocates and sometimes you have to sacrifice the institutional part of the thing when you want to be an advocate. That's very important. We don't just represent ourselves in building housing but we represent that something's wrong in this city. Newark Housing Authority, for example, has got out of housing below income. That blows my mind. If you're going to the city to get their support for something and at the same time you're criticizing them. It is not the easiest.

**SC** That gets to the autonomy question when you're dependent on local government for state grants or state government funding. How do you still maintain your critical position?

**ML** That's a difficult issue and I think so far that's why they don't totally embrace us. As you move out to the state or the federal government it's easier – they don't have any personal attachments here. It's really different, and it's particularly helpful in dealing with them. During

James's administration[8] it was particularly helpful in dealing with the state. He was the best thing we ever had in dealing with the state.

Some of the things were so outrageous, that the ordinary citizens working in state government were afraid that they would get caught in something by connecting Newark to some grant, and then the US attorney would be in. They made friends with us; and then we also as a philosophy always included them in the planning process. We never went in with an application for something which they hadn't seen; they were part of the process.

**SC** Does NCC work mostly with local architects?

**ML** We have used more regional, I think. Lately we've been using some local. We didn't use to have very good ones at the early stages if we had any. What we had were the political architects, they got the city jobs. They built our ugly public housing. That's where that came from – very little imagination. Very little need for imagination, in other words, you're going to get the contract… and the people you're working for don't care. In public housing here, there were three high-rises in the Central Ward that had been torn down. The oldest one was the nice one, the one you could have converted. Then you had the next two, and the disadvantage is that they could break code, so the corridors weren't even that wide. It's less than code because they're in public housing. The city let it go because it was federal jurisdiction. You don't have doors on the closet, slop sinks must have been in some warehouse, and they'd put those in the kitchen. And of course, you had the racism at the time. Public housing at the time was just about 100% African-American. And the leadership was all white. You certainly had racism playing a big role.

**SC** Well I think this has been really good. Thanks so much for taking the time.

**8** See note 6.

[1]

[2]

[3]

**1** Monsignor William J. Linder, left.
**2** The Newark Study Group visiting a home
run by the NCC.
**3** A day care centre run by the NCC.

# Newark Project
# By the Newark Study Group

Directed by **T. Kaminer, M. Robles-Durán and H. Sohn**

Participants **S. van Berkel, M. Daane Bolier, E. Franken, J. Hilkhuijsen, S. Hoogerheide, C. Karelse, D. Meurs, H. Park, R. Thijs**

Building technology adviser  **H. Plomp**

Urbanism adviser  **V. Nadin**

# Industrialization and labour in the New York region, 1870s

In the nineteenth century Newark rivalled New York as an industrial powerhouse, with its harbour playing a central role. Relics of this industrial past are still scattered throughout the city and occupy much of the Passaic River's waterfront.

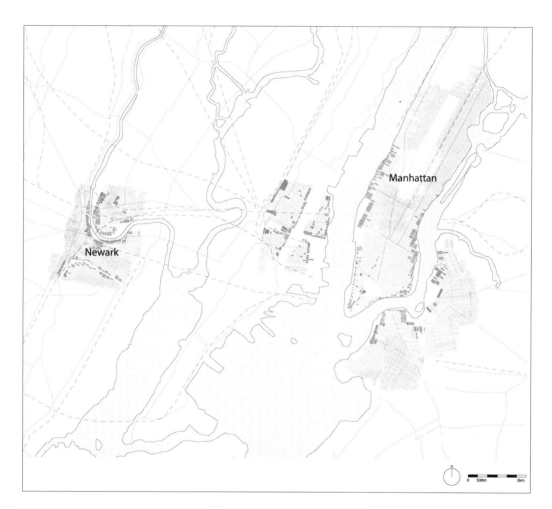

[1]

[2]

[3]

[4]

1 Newark, 1780s.
2 Newark, 1820s.
3 Newark, 1840s.
4 Newark, 1870s.

500m

Newark developed like many other East Coast cities, with a tight urban fabric, later organized in iron grid layouts, and dominated by brick buildings.

The train route connecting Manhattan via Newark with Philadelphia and the waterways were the main means of transport on the nineteenth-century East Coast. Industries along these infrastructural axes were quickly developed and shaped the growth of cities. Significant developments in the region were the construction of the Erie Canal in order to open up the vast agricultural inland markets, and the effects of the invention of the steamboat on long-distance trade.

Industrialization in the nineteenth century meant a shift from self-sufficiency based on land property to organized factory work. Rural and foreign migrant workers were organized as large teams of unskilled labour mass-producing lower quality goods at lower prices. At the same time, the relations of production shifted, due to technological advances, from a horizontal to a vertical relationship. The employee was merely seen as a 'worker' rather than a 'person'.

The nineteenth century thus evinced a constant struggle between the different classes. The social stratification was changing due to the rapid development of industries. The replacement of artisans and craftsmen by factories and related developments resulted in a huge polarization within society, the birth of the bourgeoisie and the proletariat. These divisions were reflected geographically and spatially, with notorious slums such as New York's Five Points developing in areas which the middle class avoided.

Dwellings in the New York region in the early nineteenth century consisted mainly of row houses that were based on European precedents. They housed both the rich and the poor. The rich were living on the light, spacious street level, while the poor were 'stored' together with the excrements of their upper neighbours in the dark cellars of the buildings or in the slums that consisted of cramped wind-prone sheds, where conditions were often worse.

Large tenement buildings started to replace the row housing developments in the nineteenth century, responding to the need for housing the newly emerging working class. Higher building densities allowed for lower building costs and higher profits. Living conditions for the poor deteriorated dramatically. Many dwellings in the New York region were marked as unfit for human occupation. The dirt and congestion brought rats that carried diseases; they and the bedbugs and the lice that spread typhus were just some of the burdens that needed to be addressed. The absence of proper plumbing and municipal sanitation removed the very possibility of domestic cleanliness or personal hygiene. The actions and policies undertaken in order to improve these conditions were the result of the influence of the hygiene movement and the belief that a better living environment would improve productivity. Some efforts were made also to improve or to invent new typologies to better these harsh living conditions, but the impact was minimal.

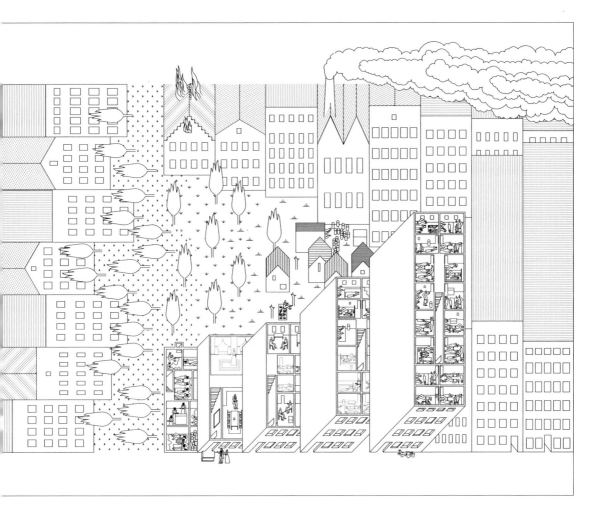

The development of housing types and
living conditions in the nineteenth century
in the New York region.

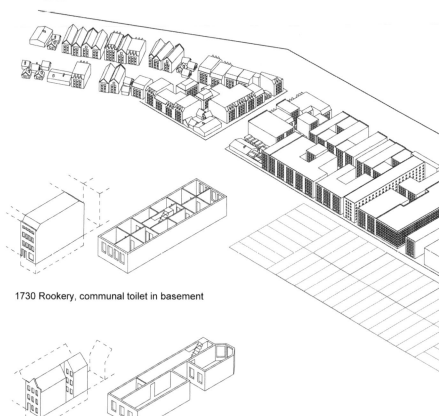

1730 Rookery, communal toilet in basement

1760 Brownstone, toilet and bathroom per apartment

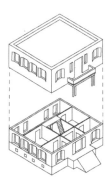

1801 Colonial mansion,
bathroom and kitchen in basement

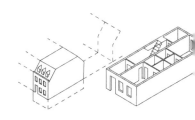

1830 Tenement,
communal toilet in basement

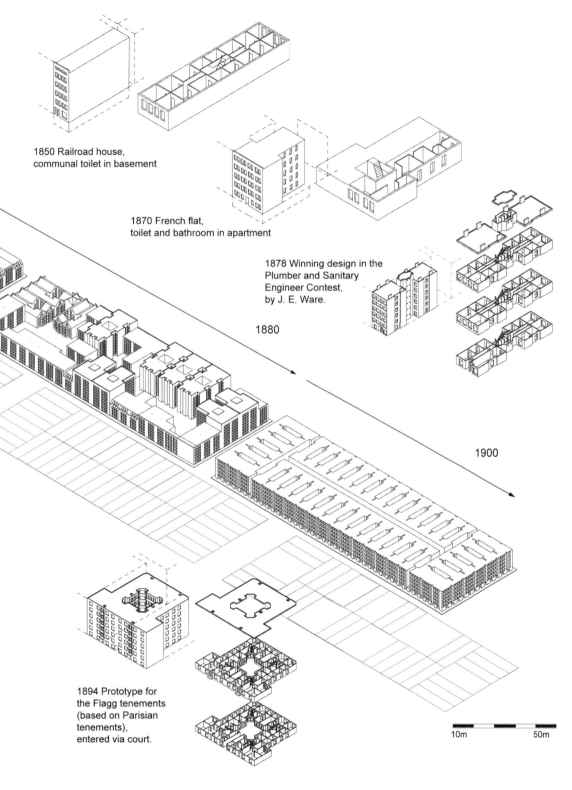

1850 Railroad house,
communal toilet in basement

1870 French flat,
toilet and bathroom in apartment

1878 Winning design in the
Plumber and Sanitary
Engineer Contest,
by J. E. Ware.

1880

1900

1894 Prototype for
the Flagg tenements
(based on Parisian
tenements),
entered via court.

10m          50m

The development of housing and
block typology in the New York region,
1700-1900.

The chaotic and uncoordinated growth of inner cities resulted in a potentially explosive situation with its mixture of ethnicities and classes. Exacerbated by an increasing congestion caused by inadequate infrastructure, the condition of cities such as Manhattan and Newark was threatening speculative investment and profits. In order to secure economic growth and the continued accumulation of capital, the city needed to be reorganized; planning on the regional scale was believed to be the answer. An important step was Manhattan's administrative growth by establishing in 1898 the Greater City of New York, a metropolitan area formed by what would become the five boroughs of contemporary New York.

On the other side of the Hudson Newark was expanding too. The accumulation of capital was clearly expressed in the numerous new theatres and in the wealth and splendour of Newark's nightlife. In addition to the development of infra- structure, Newark's Common Council policy of keeping taxes low and avoiding public debt was an important means of luring business to the city. While this policy did have the desired effect of promoting industrial growth, it proved a hurdle to initiating public projects directed at improving the city for its citizens.

In the 1920s New York City attempted to gain complete ownership of the means of transport. Despite the construction of the Holland Tunnel in 1927 by New York-New Jersey partnership, the level of connectivity in New Jersey and Greater New York differed significantly, whereas Newark's political class believed their city would become the largest industrial centre of the United States.

Trade unions were formed in the late nineteenth and early twentieth centuries in order to represent the workers and to act to improve wages, working conditions, workers' rights and job stability. This period is marked by violent riots and police brutality, by strikes and demonstrations. Crusades against the urban political bosses and corrupt industry moguls increased the segregation between the bour- geoisie and the working class. The election of Theodore Roosevelt as president and the signing of 'the square deal', a collection of laws which benefited the work- ers, marked a significant shift in governmental policy.

The New York region, including Newark, became a finance and insurance hub in the early twentieth century. Newark was lucrative for insurance businesses because of its importance as a train route and transportation hub. This develop- ment brought about an increase in the number of clerks and white collar workers in the region. The 'roaring twenties' saw the great expansion of the financial sector, while, in parallel, Taylorism was increasingly implemented in industrial produc- tion.

bourgeoisie (owners)
lower middle class
proletariat (workers)
poor & classless
— movement of bourgeoisie
......... arriving southern
ex-slaves

0        5km

Class in the New York region, 1928.

The New York Stock Exchange crashed on October 24, 1929, heralding the Great Depression which would dissipate only during the Second World War. It set in motion the deflation of assets and commodity prices, dramatic drops in demand and credit, and a disruption of trade, ultimately resulting in widespread poverty and unemployment. The shock of the depression and the subsequent near-collapse of capitalism invigorated the demand for new modes of state intervention. These interventions included managerial strategies applied by state authorities and programmes that set out to stabilize and regulate capitalism.

In the first term of Roosevelt's presidency, a set of domestic policies were introduced to reorganize and revive the ailing economy, aiming to prevent the complete disintegration of the financial system and prevent the situation deteriorating into social unrest. These governmental policies were the New Deal, which set out to restore confidence in the banking system, to stabilize prices to encourage business and farmers to resume production. The New Deal also set out several federal financial funding programmes to encourage federal, state and city infrastructural developments as a means of reducing mass unemployment and promoting home ownership. It was, basically, a federal stimulation programme. On an urban level it meant that the federal government took over from cities much of their responsibilities; it ushered in an era of economic and urban restructuring.

Thus, beginning in the 1930s, major urban projects and infrastructure such as the construction of roads and subway systems were federally funded in order to provide temporary work for the unemployed; federally secured mortgages were made available to the white middle class in order to stimulate the construction of suburban housing and the expansion of home ownership. The construction of affordable housing for low-income groups was stimulated by the creation, funding and sponsoring of local housing agencies and several rental subsidy programmes such as the 1937 Section 8 programme. In Newark this resulted in the Newark Housing Authority.

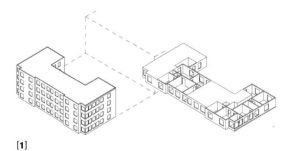

[1]

[2]

[3]

50% - 70%
40% - 50%
40% - 30%
20% - 30%
10% - 20%

n

0  500m          3km

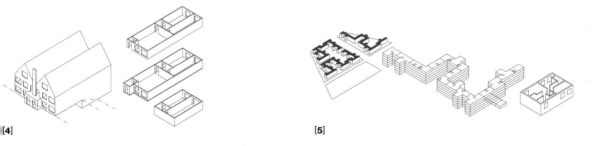

[4]                                              [5]

1  Garden apartments by A. Thomas, one of        3  New York region unemployment, 1930.         5  Harlem River houses (PWA), four NYC
the first block-filling garden apartments, 1920.  4  Row houses; urban housing for the bour-      blocks, 574 aps., Afro-American residents,
2  Typical developer-housing in the suburbs,     geoisie, a shift from block to street design,   1937.
1920.                                            1927.

**[1]**

**[2]**

**[3]**

bourgeoisie (owners)
white-collar workers
blue-collar workers
poor & classless

0m        500m

**1** Class in the New York region, 1940.
**2** Red Hook Houses (PWA / USHA),
15 Queens blocks, 3,149 aps., 1939.

**3** Stuyvesant Town (Met Life Insurance),
18 NYC blocks, 8,755 aps., white lower
middle class residents, 1949.

**4** Newark's slums, in percentage of residential
structures, 1959.

The federal funds that were made available by the New Deal policies radically reorganized the socio-economic and political spheres. New alliances between public and corporate actors were created, aimed at providing the conditions for the development of a mass-consumption culture enabling the stable growth of the u.s. economy.

Newark politics from the 1940s onwards were dominated by patronage. Newark's 'powerbroker' in this era, a Robert Moses of sorts, was Louis Danzig. During Danzig's twenty years as head of the Newark Housing Authority (NHA), Newark initiated a clearance and redevelopment programme that surpassed most American cities in terms of federal money spent and acres cleared per capita. Between 1953 and 1962, Mayor Leo Carlin, supported by business interests, reformers and the middle-class Jewish and Irish populations, backed the ideals of redevelopment and efficient administration.

75 - 99%
50 - 74%
40 - 49%
30 - 39%
10 - 29%
0 - 10%
Public Housing

n

0                    2km

[4]

The decline of the blue collar industry which began already during the Great Depression led to the dissipation of Newark's riverside industry, moving away towards low-cost areas and countries outside the administrative territory of the city. The Second World War temporarily alleviated some of Newark's industries' troubles, whereas the Port Authority of New York and New Jersey, established in 1921, consolidated in those years and ran the Newark harbour.

Danzig was a vigorous proponent of Federal assistance for affordable housing in cities and of expanded slum-clearance programmes. In the city's first urban renewal programme carried out under the Federal Housing Act of 1949, the NHA demolished Newark's Little Italy, the nation's fourth largest such enclave, and replaced it with high-rise public and private housing. It was precisely this type of urban renewal, exacerbated by the building of highways that dissected the city, which would become notorious by the 1960s for the damage done to communities, to the urban fabric and to social networks and vibrancy.

Danzig ignored the thousands of African Americans he was displacing and the overcrowding in other areas of the city caused by the central-city clearances he initiated, rapidly transforming large areas of the formerly healthy South Ward into slums.

Despite the efforts made to make the city more inhabitable, Newark's middle class, including lower middle class skilled labour, was increasingly relocating to the suburbs, lured by the possibility of owning a freestanding house, equipped with state-of-the-art technology and household commodities. The downtown slum clearances and the support of Section 8 subsidy programmes had the effect of transforming Newark's Central Ward in the 1940s and 50s to an area dominated by massive public apartment buildings for the lower income groups.

Around 1955, a migration of African Americans from the South to Newark and New York in search of industrial jobs and an alternative to poverty and segregation began increasing its pace. The migrants settled in the Central Ward, where the city provided cheap social housing as a means of maintaining a basic segregation, yet precisely in this period, industrial jobs for unskilled labour were decreasing at alarming rates. Zoning carried out by the city only worsened the situation: by allowing industry and commerce into the Central Ward and limiting other wards to residential use, the Central Ward inevitably developed into a slum.

[1]

bourgeoisie (owners)
white-collar workers
blue-collar workers

100m     500m

[2]

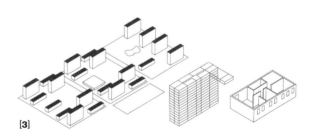

[3]

1 Class in Newark, 1960.
2 Bradley Courts, two Newark blocks, 1950s.
3 Van Dyck Houses (NYCHA), 9 Brooklyn
Blocks, 1,500 aps., 1955.

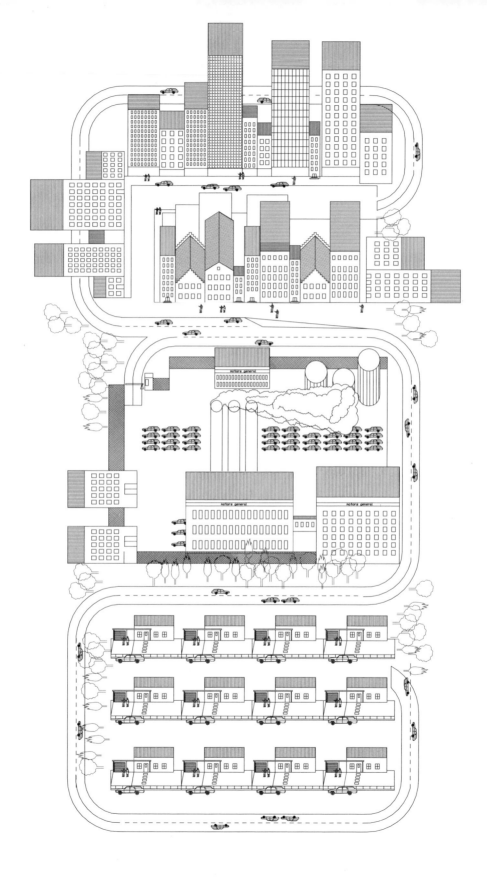

[1]

2]

3]

Diagram of spatial relations in the late
950s.
Unemployment in the New York region,
960.
Twin Parks complex, a breakthrough in
igh-rise housing, offering diverse types of
partments, 1973.

[1]

[2]

[3]

**1** Unemployment in the New York Region, 1980.
**2** Loft development in SoHo, renovation of industrial building, 1974.

**3** Trump Tower luxury housing, 1983.
**4** The transformation of Newark's Little Italy: changing solutions to urban challenges.

Legend:
50% - 70%
40% - 50%
40% - 30%
20% - 30%
10% - 20%

n
0 500m    3km

The tension between un- and under-employed African American newcomers, experiencing disempowerment and alienation, and a white city administration which did not satisfy the needs or the demands of the migrants exploded in the 1967 riots. The urban riots of these years, not only in Newark but also in cities such as Detroit and Chicago, coincided with the end of policies such as Johnson's 'war on poverty', which was brought to a halt by the Nixon administration shortly after the election of the Republican administration in 1968. Beginning with Nixon's presidency, and in a clearer, more determined and all-encompassing manner under Reagan, the policies which began with the New Deal were gradually abandoned. A period of retrenchment and deregulation began, with the 1980s dominated by 'roll-back neoliberalism', which included cuts in federal spending and a closure of federal programmes. City administrations were left with few options, and courted investment.

An immediate effect of the change in policy was the abandonment of the lower income groups as the market focused more on the middle and upper income groups which provided higher tax revenues. The ongoing polarization of society and continuation of the white flight brought about a decline of inner city population, leading to a condition of limited financial resources. The NHA was forced to operate within the logic of the market, thereby becoming more and more dependant on private capital flow and focusing less and less on the urban poor and lower middle class. The 1985 Fair Housing Act by the New Jersey legislature, a follow-up to the Mount Laurel NJ Supreme Court decisions, guaranteed a modicum of housing development for the poor and prevented a total abandonment of the under-privileged.

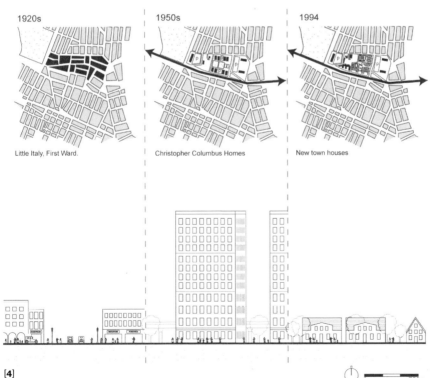

| 1920s | 1950s | 1994 |
|---|---|---|
| Little Italy, First Ward. | Christopher Columbus Homes | New town houses |

[4]

0   750m

257

[1]

**1** New Jersey enterprise zones, 2008.
**2** Diagrams of the relation of Newark to its
periphery (above), and the relegation of
Newark to the status of a gateway to the
New York region (below).

The 1980s were a period in which free enterprise zones were established as a means of encouraging business and investment via tax breaks and other policies. Newark's Free Enterprise Zone was established in 1984.

The post-Fordist era meant an end to high-rise public housing and a preference for housing which satisfied demands for personalization and individualism. Funding for the development of townhouses was often provided by state government. The idea behind the wide implementation of townhouses was to integrate lower income groups into middle class, capitalist society by emphasizing home ownership and plot-based housing instead of the renting units of the big high-rise projects of the Keynesian era. The 'Bayonne box' became a major typology for developing low and moderate income housing by the private sector, as such typologies could be easily inserted into the piecemeal development strategies of the private market. Consequently, the USA home ownership rate increased from 64% in 1994 (about where it had been since 1980) to an all-time high of 69.2% in 2004. Subprime lending was a major contributor to this increase in home ownership rates and in the overall demand for housing.

Considering what seem to be insurmountable hurdles to a regeneration of Newark as a global hub, coupled with the evident bankruptcy of neoliberal urban regeneration policies, the Newark Study Group developed a strategy to approach the city's North Ward that focuses on the needs of the current residents and departs from accepted formulae which are typically tailored to remake the city for the middle class. This led to a proposal of a series of strategic architectural interventions in Newark's North Ward as well as a masterplan for the area.

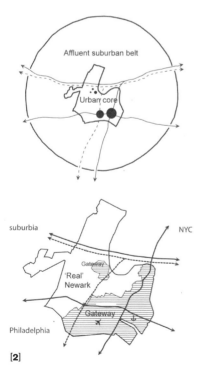

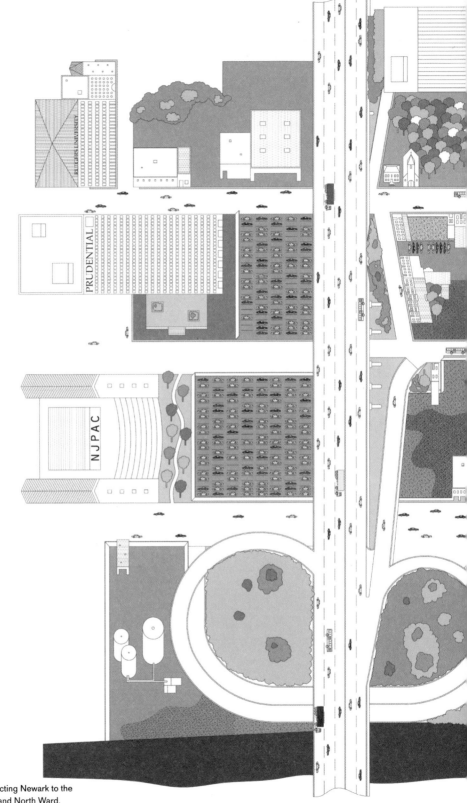

The interstate highway dissecting Newark to the
downtown area (south, left) and North Ward.

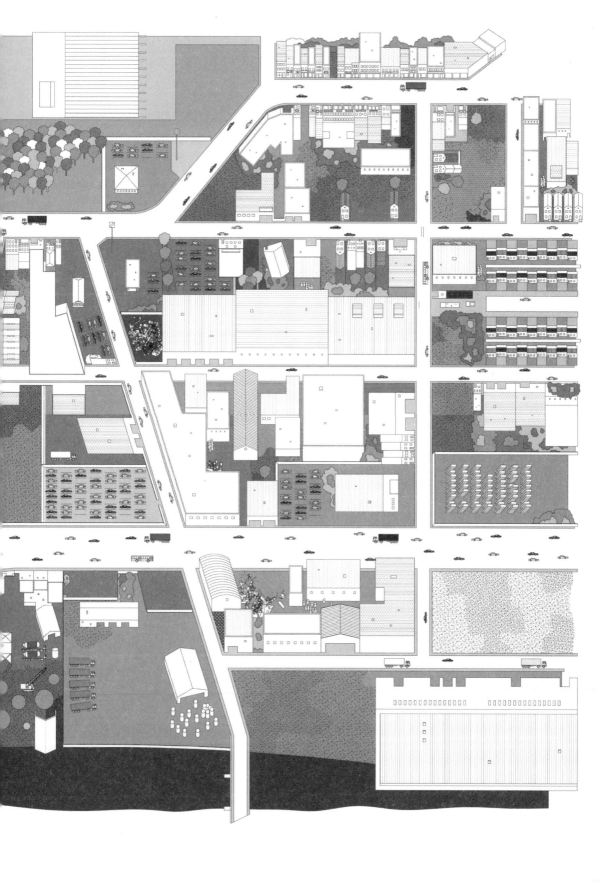

# Stakeholder map

1. BOSTON METROPOLITAN REGION
2. PHILADELPHIA METROPOLITAN REGION
3. WASHINGTON METROPOLITAN REGION
4. NEW YORK METROPOLITAN REGION
5. BOSWASH MEGALOPOLITAN REGION
6. OTHER MEGALOPOLITAN REGIONS
7. OTHER METROPOLITAN
   REGIONS
8. GATEWAY REGION

LIBERTY AIRPORT      PORT AUTHORIT

NEV

EPA

SUPERFUND

NJHS      EDC      EDA      BIN

ESSEX CO
DEVELOPI
CORPORA

## PUBLIC

9. 7TH AVENTUE NEIGHBOURHOOD
10. LOWER BROADWAY NEIGHBOURHOOD
11. FOREST HILL NEIGHBOURHOOD
12. NORTH BROADWAY NEIGHBOURHOOD

13. FEDERAL GOVERNMENT
14. NEW JERSEY STATE GOVERNMENT
15. ESSEX COUNTY GOVERNMENT
16. NEWARK MUNICIPAL GOVERNMENT

17. ECONOMIC & HOUSING DEVELOPMENT
18. CITY PLANNING DEPARTMENT
19. HOUSING DEPARTMENT

20. NORTH WARD

21. HISTORICAL DISTRICT

22. NEWARK LEGAL AND COMMUNICATIONS CENTRE, URBAN RENEWAL CORPORATION
23. EDISON INNOVATION ZONE
24. NEWARK ECONOMIC DEVELOPMENT CORPORATION
25. GREATER NEWARK BUSINESS DEVELOPMENT CONSORTIUM, GNBDC

26. THE SOCIAL CORRIDOR (S. v. BERKEL)
27. **WATERFRONT PROJECT** (H. PARK)

28. NEWARK REGIONAL BUSINESS PARTNERSHIP NRBP
29. SUPER NEIGHBOURHOOD

MATRIX
DEVELOPI

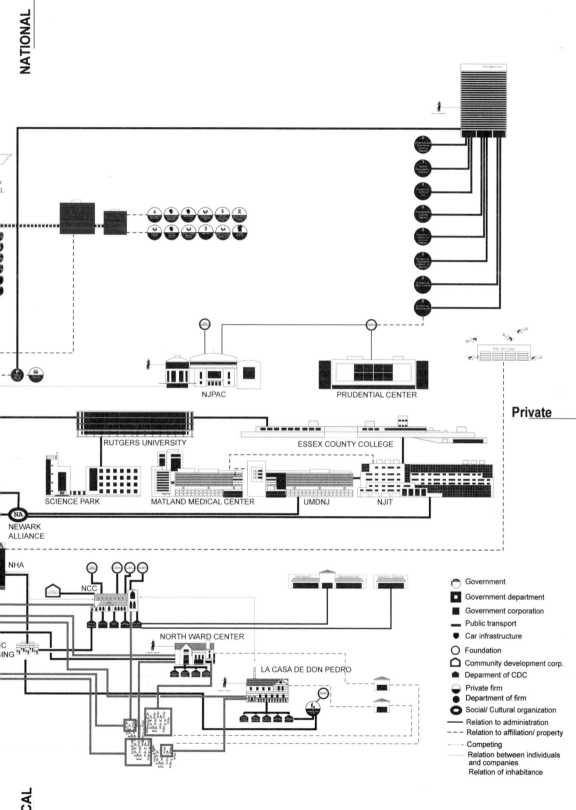

**Private**

NJPAC

PRUDENTIAL CENTER

RUTGERS UNIVERSITY

ESSEX COUNTY COLLEGE

SCIENCE PARK

MATLAND MEDICAL CENTER

UMDNJ

NJIT

NA
NEWARK
ALLIANCE

NHA

NCC

NORTH WARD CENTER

LA CASA DE DON PEDRO

Government
Government department
Government corporation
Public transport
Car infrastructure
Foundation
Community development corp.
Deparment of CDC
Private firm
Department of firm
Social/ Cultural organization
Relation to administration
Relation to affiliation/ property
Competing
Relation between individuals and companies
Relation of inhabitance

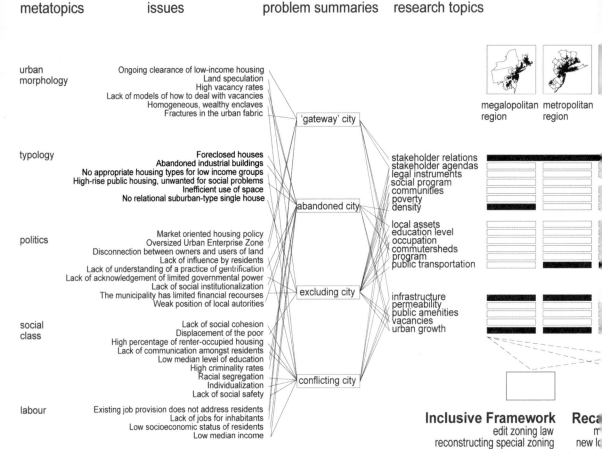

metatopics · issues · problem summaries · research topics

**metatopics**

urban
morphology

typology

politics

social
class

labour

**issues**

Ongoing clearance of low-income housing
Land speculation
High vacancy rates
Lack of models of how to deal with vacancies
Homogeneous, wealthy enclaves
Fractures in the urban fabric

Foreclosed houses
Abandoned industrial buildings
No appropriate housing types for low income groups
High-rise public housing, unwanted for social problems
Inefficient use of space
No relational suburban-type single house

Market oriented housing policy
Oversized Urban Enterprise Zone
Disconnection between owners and users of land
Lack of influence by residents
Lack of understanding of a practice of gentrification
Lack of acknowledgement of limited governmental power
Lack of social institutionalization
The municipality has limited financial recourses
Weak position of local autorities

Lack of social cohesion
Displacement of the poor
High percentage of renter-occupied housing
Lack of communication amongst residents
Low median level of education
High criminality rates
Racial segregation
Individualization
Lack of social safety

Existing job provision does not address residents
Lack of jobs for inhabitants
Low socioeconomic status of residents
Low median income

**problem summaries**

'gateway' city

abandoned city

excluding city

conflicting city

**research topics**

megalopolitan metropolitan
region          region

stakeholder relations
stakeholder agendas
legal instruments
social program
communities
poverty
density

local assets
education level
occupation
commutersheds
program
public transportation

infrastructure
permeability
public amenities
vacancies
urban growth

**Inclusive Framework**
edit zoning law
reconstructing special zoning
promoting participation process
foreclosure treatment

**Reca**
m
new lo
local c
sustaina

**Embed**

A diagram of the process of developing an
urban strategy and masterplan for Newark and
its North Ward (H. Park and S. van Berkel).

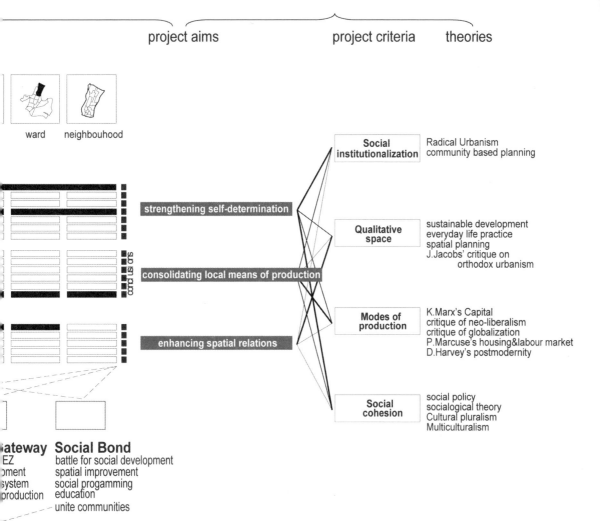

project aims          project criteria     theories

ward    neighbouhood

strengthening self-determination

consolidating local means of production

enhancing spatial relations

Social
institutionalization

Radical Urbanism
community based planning

Qualitative
space

sustainable development
everyday life practice
spatial planning
J.Jacobs' critique on
        orthodox urbanism

Modes of
production

K.Marx's Capital
critique of neo-liberalism
critique of globalization
P.Marcuse's housing&labour market
D.Harvey's postmodernity

Social
cohesion

social policy
sociological theory
Cultural pluralism
Multiculturalism

ateway    Social Bond
EZ              battle for social development
oment       spatial improvement
system      social progamming
production   education
                   unite communities

banization

G

F

E

C

D

A

B

## Architectural Interventions in the North Ward

Seven proposed interventions in the southern section of the North Ward by M. Daane Bolier (A), D. Meurs (B), S. Hoogerheide (C), R. Thijs (D), J. Hilkhuijsen (E), E. Franken (F) and C. Karelse (G).

**A Interventions along the Interstate**   The interstate highway which is the southern border of the North Ward severs the neighbourhood from downtown. The area is characterized by prostitution, drug dealing and homelessness, activities which take advantage of the protection offered by the elevated highway and the scant population in the area. The inclusion of this area of the North Ward in the Urban Enterprise Zone of Newark and the plans to extend Rutgers University to the highway suggest the city identifies a potential for development in the area. Consequently, interventions A and B are, among other things, an attempt to transgress the policies of exclusion-expansion affecting Newark.

Intervention A addresses an eroded block in proximity to the highway. The re-structuring of the block includes re-use of existing buildings and filling-in the empty spaces caused by dilapidation; it takes advantage of the existence of several organizations such as Aspira within the block, including them in a plan to turn the entire block into a social integration machine, addressing the needs of prostitutes and other current inhabitants of the area.

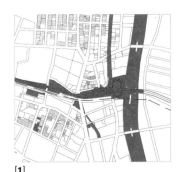
[1]

[2]

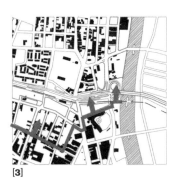
[3]

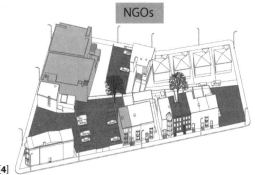

NGOs

**1** The interstate, McCarter Highway, the Passaic River and the light railway station.
**2** Vacant blocks, semi-occupied and empty warehouses and plots.
**3** The forces of exclusion-expansion directed to North Ward.
**4** The current condition of the block.

[4]

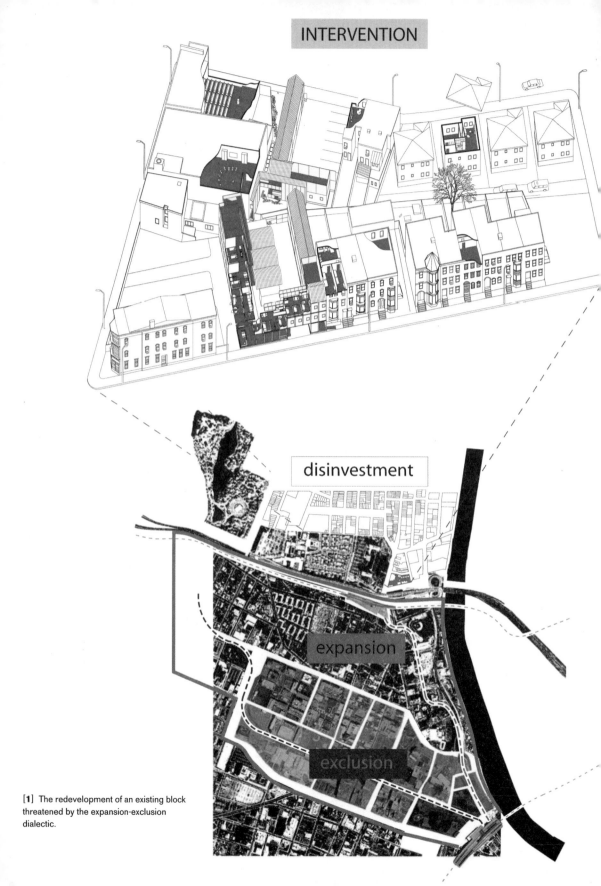

# INTERVENTION

disinvestment

expansion

exclusion

[1] The redevelopment of an existing block
threatened by the expansion-exclusion
dialectic.

**B Emergency Dwellings and Homeless Encampment** In this intervention the *terrain vague* beneath and adjacent to the highway becomes the locus of a temporary homeless encampment. The encampment addressed the immediate needs of growing numbers of homeless in Newark following recent foreclosures. The intervention proposes the distribution of basic mobile dwelling units to those in need, and the preparation of basic infrastructure by the city for setting up an encampment which could later be moved to other areas once the area is claimed for redevelopment.

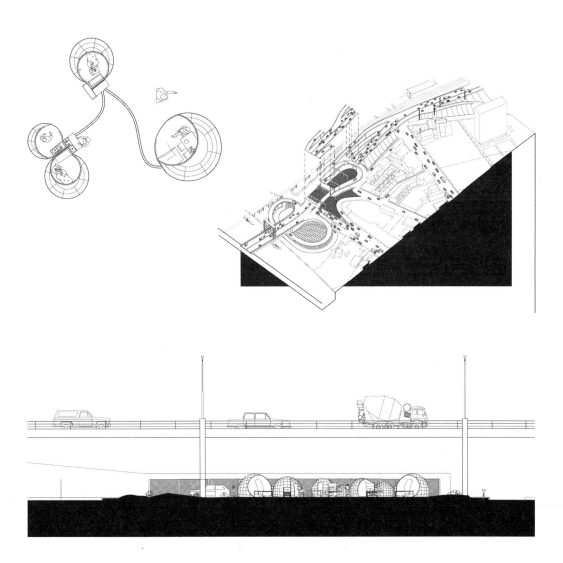

[1]

Unit type one

Unit type two

## C Waterfront Warehouse Redevelopment

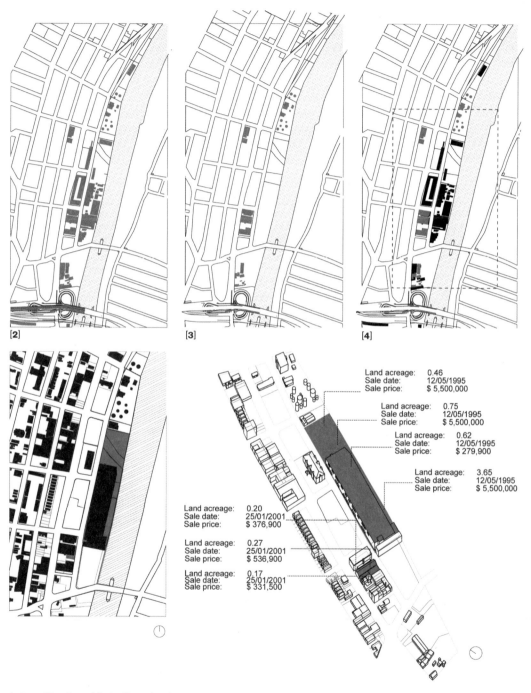

[2]

[3]

[4]

Land acreage: 0.46
Sale date: 12/05/1995
Sale price: $ 5,500,000

Land acreage: 0.75
Sale date: 12/05/1995
Sale price: $ 5,500,000

Land acreage: 0.62
Sale date: 12/05/1995
Sale price: $ 279,900

Land acreage: 3.65
Sale date: 12/05/1995
Sale price: $ 5,500,000

Land acreage: 0.20
Sale date: 25/01/2001
Sale price: $ 376,900

Land acreage: 0.27
Sale date: 25/01/2001
Sale price: $ 536,900

Land acreage: 0.17
Sale date: 25/01/2001
Sale price: $ 331,500

1 Assembling the mobile dwelling unit and an
encampment layout.
2 Industrial areas, 1960.
3 Industrial areas, 2009.
4 Area of intervention.

The waterfront area of the North Ward is dominated by industrial structures, many of which are vacant or partially vacant. The area is part of the city's enterprise zone and is included in the development plans of the city council. The focus of the proposed intervention is a 250m-long warehouse on the waterfront, a building with no architectural quality but well-situated in relation to the river and the North Ward.

The intervention will provide 150-200 low-income housing units developed by the City of Newark, facilities for social services and public space developed in cooperation with La Casa de Don Pedro, the community development corporation active in the North Ward, and in the base – the old warehouse – small-scale businesses and entrepreneurship employing locals, developed together with La Casa de Don Pedro and primarily in the form of a market.

**D Intervention in the Bloomfield Avenue Corridor**   Currently, Bloomfield Avenue is characterized by commerce and retail directed at both locals and suburbanites using Bloomfield as a route. In the last few years many of the shops have been bought by LLCs (Limited Liability Company), indicating the intention to develop chain-retail on a larger scale, excluding locals and small owner-run shops. The intervention proposed here is meant to preserve local, small-scale retail via the establishment of a co-op and to develop the areas at the back of Bloomfield with emphasis on pedestrian and local interests.

**E An Ideal Settlement on the Passaic Waterfront**   Intervention E proposes founding a new neighbourhood as an ideal alternative to the eroded grid and suburban housing of the North Ward, offering a tight urban fabric and quality of life to the urban poor, delineating a model to emulate.

**F Back Yard Building**   A long linear building which includes mostly dwellings and social facilities exhibits a monolithic facade to the highway to the east of it and an articulated, fractured facade to its west, facing a linear public inner courtyard which includes the back yards of the Bayonne boxes opposite – offering a very different type of public space than can be found in the North Ward.

**G Collective Housing**   This proposition intends to demonstrate the advantages of collective housing over suburban housing by developing the internal corridor and communal balconies into areas of communal interaction, spontaneity, and appropriation.

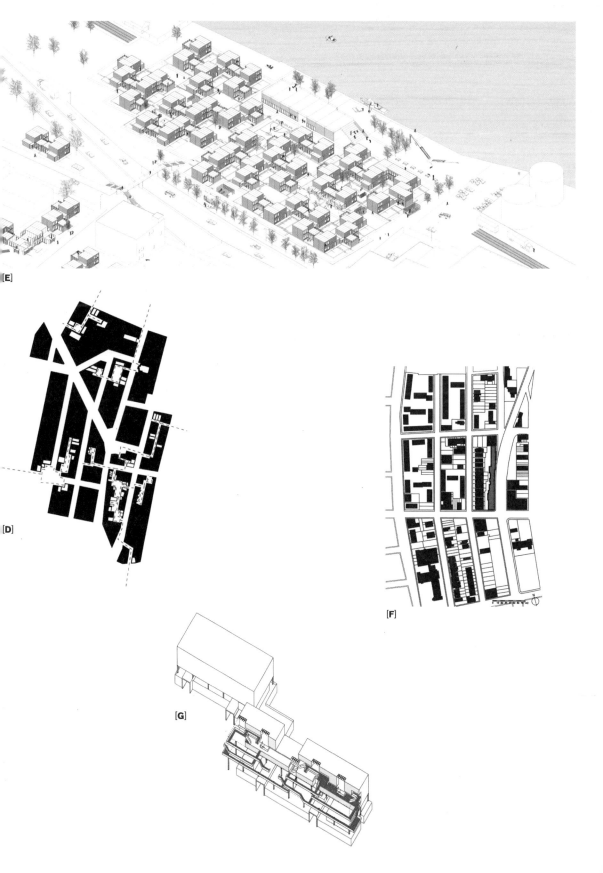

[E]

[D]

[F]

[G]

# An Afterthought on Urban Design

**Arie Graafland**

And to conclude this book, it would be beneficial to briefly pause at the critical intentions of the Urban Asymmetries (UA) study group, and especially the results of the urban design work it produced. The Delft School of Design (DSD), after all, is a design unit in the Delft faculty. Although our primary interests are critical theories, design is the ultimate goal of an architectural education institute. The urban analyses and plans in this book are not a mere illustration of the critical texts. They have their own relative autonomy. To be able to say anything relevant about the drawings, we need a frame to situate the design work. This frame, again, is conceptual. Nothing speaks 'from itself'. The mediation will go through what I provisionally call *ground*, a concept both abstract and concrete. 'Grounding' as an active, design-related activity, picks up, partially, on the more recent American debates on 'Everyday Urbanism' as initiated by Margaret Crawford and John Kaliski in the 1990s. Crawford's reference to Henri Lefebvre is of course understandable,[1] but the problem is that Crawford does not really relate to Lefebvre's Marxism. In the Michigan Debates (2004) Michael Speaks might be right: Everyday Urbanism as a theoretical position primarily draws on meaning and interpretation, and not so much on design issues.[2] It is mainly a form of 'bottom-up' (Speaks) planning, of course potentially valuable, but in reality it is 'entirely bottom' he argues. It never develops any kinds of comprehensive proposals that might be activated by small-scale interventions. He even qualifies it as a fetishization of the everyday – to him it is 'anti-design' and begs the question 'how do you design with *the banal* [my italics] and to what end?'[3] Speaks might be right here, aesthetic quality has been one of the recurring questions for the UA study group, and we certainly need to shed light on it.[4] Douglas Kelbaugh adequately describes Everyday Urbanism as building 'on the richness and vitality of daily life and ordinary reality. It has little pretence about the perfectibility of the built environment. Nor is it about utopian form. But it is idealistic about equity and citizen participation, especially for disadvantaged populations. It is grass-roots and populist'.[5] He underlines that in this view the city is shaped more by the forces of everyday life than by formal design and official plans. We see the same impulse in the DSD UA study group plans presented in this book. They share the same cooperative attitude towards the organizations Everyday Urbanism is interested in. '(O)ur work with residents, city governments, and local organizations on real projects has pointed to another important dimension of everyday urban practice: the many aspects of urban life that are deeply embedded in the daily workings of city government and its regulation and enforcement functions,' Margaret Crawford writes.[6] But at the same time as the UA study group is addressing Speaks' comments on Everyday Urbanism, the UA study group is interested in what Speaks calls 'post-modern philosophers' like David Harvey, who

1 Douglas Kelbaugh, **Everyday Urbanism: Margaret Crawford vs. Michael Speaks**, Michigan Debates on Urbanism (University of Michigan, 2005), vol. 1, p. 18.
2 Michael Speaks, 'Everyday Is Not Enough', in **Everyday Urbanism**, p. 34.
3 Michael Speaks, 'Everyday Is Not Enough', in **Everyday Urbanism**, p. 36.
4 This issue needs a more elaborated discussion on politics and aesthetics. I have done that in my discussion with Speaks 'On Criticality' in **Crossover: Architecture Urbanism Technology** (Rotterdam: 010 Publishers, 2006), p. 688, republished in Krista Sykes (ed.), **Constructing a New Agenda: Architectural Theory 1993-2009** (Princeton Architectural Press, 2010), p. 394.
5 Douglas Kelbaugh, **Everyday Urbanism**, Vol. 1, p. 8.
6 Margaret Crawford, 'The Current State of Everyday Urbanism', in John Leighton Chase, Margaret Crawford and John Kaliski (eds), **Everyday Urbanism** (The Monacelli Press, 2008), p. 13.

is most certainly working on a more comprehensive critical understanding of neoliberal capitalism.[7] This makes the studio quite unique. It is one of the few places where post-graduate students find a context for politically motivated urban analyses. Lefebvre's 'right to the city' is present in its contemporary form; 'while developers accumulate enormous monetary wealth and power, the city dwellers have been gradually confined into far-away, serialized dormitory quarters, excluded from the production of their own environment and ultimately pushed into urban poverty,' the opening lines of the UA Mexico City project read. The major difference between Everyday Urbanism and Urban Asymmetries lies in the extensive research curve of the latter. More than anything else, Urban Asymmetries deals with comprehensive political and economic theories in relation to urban design. Few architecture schools at the moment seem to be interested in these socio-political issues; the growth of neoliberal policies over the last decades has as its flipside a mostly light form of postmodern design education. It is at least remarkable that with the signing of the Bologna Accords for Higher Education in 1999 to streamline academic degrees and build quality standards, the increase in the student population was never met with the necessary funding. Ever since the preceding *Magna Charta Universitatum* drawn up in 1988 by the rectors of the European universities, the same universities in Europe have suffered from ongoing budget cuts. Although budgets have expanded during the last decades, they have never met the steep increase in students. The administrative vocabulary in the universities has changed into 'efficiency'; the older Humboldt categories are finally gone. Moreover, the recent interest in 'digital technologies' in Parametric Urbanism, increasingly popular in contemporary education, at, for instance, the Architectural Association in London, is blocking critical issues. Digital urban design is not only quite often a form of beautification, but has become 'footloose', much like the current international real estate market. The question remains: is there another way of dealing with urban design, more 'grounded', more related to this issue of 'the banal' as an aesthetic category, and to social political issues like 'the everyday'? And what does that mean for the 'ideology of the aesthetic' (Terry Eagleton) in urban design as it relates to these political issues?

I will try to explain this position by briefly 'reframing' theory for a European and (Latin) American context of understanding and practice. The Urban Asymmetries projects were operative in the context of Mexico City, Newark and Santiago de Chile. I will try to explain some of their workings through a plan we drew up some ten years ago for a site in Amsterdam, the Westerdok. Although the Urban Asymmetries projects in many aspects relate to Everyday Urbanism, they are also very different, first of all in scale, but more importantly in their analysis. The Amsterdam plan relates to what we call today Post Urbanism, be it only at first sight. I will try to explain where it differs and develop an alternative position to the current American and British discourse. I will relate that to the UA study group philosophy, not by 'choosing' Urban Asymmetries, Everyday Urbanism or Post Urbanism – I do not believe the containers really differ in the end – but in trying to develop 'the everyday' into a more theoretically based form of urbanism. 'Grounding', the critical term in this context, is at the same time critical about what in the current American debate is called 'Post Urbanism', the most heterotopian and least idealistic of what Kelbaugh calls the 'three urban paradigms'; Everyday Urbanism, New Urbanism, and Post Urbanism. Rem Koolhaas is most certainly the most outspoken representative of the last of the three. 'It attempts to wow an increasingly sophisticated clientele and public with provocative and audacious architecture and urbanism'.[8] Koolhaas's 'junk space' being the 'cynical' paradigm (Kelbaugh) of Post Urbanism. In Koolhaas there seems to be no alternative, 'junk space' is all around us. Crawford takes the opposite position; Everyday Urbanism tries to refamiliarize the urban environment, it seeks the opposite sensation to the one Koolhaas is describing. Refamiliarizing would be too naive for him, too much hope for the good, in a world where 'all that is solid melts into air'. It would not fit the form of his writing; the essay.[9] Koolhaas as the essayist does not take up 'a position', for many a recurring irritation, criticizing the world but building for the powers that be in China. I will leave that aside and instead recall another, lesser known idea of Koolhaas's, what he once called the instinctive *recoil from the void*, a fear of *nothingness*, a quality I believe is resented and kept at bay in most urban practices but can be used critically. This concept that will fit the urban plan for the Westerdok in Amsterdam and in certain aspects comes close to Urban Asymmetries' aesthetics will in the end distance itself from Koolhaas's ideas of junk space. I believe it can be used in a critical way as I tried to show in a previous work.[10]

Reframing here does not mean a final picture that incorporates all others, it is neither the final word nor the final solution to adjust the urban lens. Both terms, 'grounding' and 'reframing', get their meaning in relation to our 'means' of communication, an important aspect of our contemporary societies which only seems to play a certain modest role in Post Urbanism, and is fully embraced in Parametric Design. I believe urbanism needs to deal with the acceleration of communication systems in our network cities. Graham Shane, for instance, addresses what he calls the 'reforms'

7  David Harvey, **A Brief History of Neoliberalism** (Oxford University Press, 2005).
8  Douglas Kelbaugh, **Everyday Urbanism**, p. 9.
9  Adam Gopnik, 'Introduction', **The Best American Essays 2008** (Boston; New York: Houghton Mifflin Company, 2008). Peter Eisenman sees Koolhaas as a 'realist'. In a way, he writes, 'his ideas are not cynical but nihilistic'. Junk space 'is not a project because it is not critical, it is what Massimo Cacciari calls nihilism fulfilled'. ('Thoughts on the World Trade Center', in **Post Urbanism & ReUrbanism: Peter Eisenman vs. Barbara Littenberg and Steven Peterson**, Michigan Debates on Urbanism, Vol. III (University of Michigan, 2004, p. 12)). I believe that projects should be 'critical', I see that as a normative issue, but concepts are no different, they should develop critical thought. But 'critical' is used almost in any situation in architectural schools, what is meant is mostly unclear. It might be that Koolhaas has heard it too often. Eisenman believes that a critical project challenges the status quo, criticality has to enfold negativity, an interesting thought. The modern project still relied on it. I agree with Eisenman that Koolhaas's books on the Pearl River Delta and Lagos trivialize the problem of diversity. Cornell West charged Koolhaas with trivializing the problem of ethnicity by the kind of research that he was doing; as Eisenman says in the discussion with Peterson and Littenberg, it is both not serious and cynical (see the Discussion in **Post Urbanism & ReUrbanism**, p. 85).
10  Arie Graafland, **The Socius of Architecture: Amsterdam, Tokyo, New York** (Rotterdam: 010 Publishers, 2000).

of the 1980s and 1990s, the introduction of premium pay-per-use services run by private companies to replace the decaying public infrastructure. Free-market ideology has dictated the provision of differential levels of service to urban actors on a pay-per-use basis. The 'unbundling' of services (Shane) in the informational city goes hand in hand with the self-built barrios and favelas that are often the close neighbours of the informational city; the great majority of new houses are unplugged from public utilities (i.e. electricity, water, sewage). The people in Everyday Urbanism are quite often transposed to locations where they never choose to live, as a result of urban growth and investment policies driven by our network society. We cannot leave these developments untouched; if we do not pay attention to these developments, everyday life for many will mean being pushed around the globe without much understanding of its causes. We do need to understand what digital communication means in daily life. I think Deleuze and Guattari were right in saying that thinking takes place in the relationship of territory and earth. If we lose this notion, we lose the very notions of gender, sexuality, ethnic diversity and uneven distribution of wealth and class. Too easily the shift from harsh reality into the seemingly endless possibilities of the computer programmes is made, made without any interest in these categories. Cultural theory over the last decades has tended to think in terms of binary oppositions. Oppositions between closed and open, subject and infinity; between cognitive and aesthetic individualism, it has appeared as nature and culture, capitalism and schizophrenia, identity and difference. Scott Lash argues that there is a third party or a *third space* involved. It is not a fold, it is not, after all, some kind of sublation or reconciliation of totality and infinity, or of the beautiful and the sublime. The third space for him is a ground, an underneath, a base in the sense of basis.[11] We are reflexively judging animals, thus ground is in *perception* and *community*. Both notions are under a lot of pressure with our new digital technologies. So what could this mean for a contemporary urban practice?

Ten years ago we drew up a plan for one of Amsterdam's islands in the IJ river, an upscale place of waterfront development bordering on the heart of the old medieval city. This plan, the Westerdok plan, was, much like the UA study group, inspired by theoretical and social notions. The urban plan was involved in a specific point of view on what is important in the 'site' from both a theoretical and a social perspective. In an overview of what he calls 'the seven "ages"' of postmodernism, Shane describes the strong influence of Rowe and Koetter in the USA, and Aldo Rossi's Analogical City in Europe. One of the characteristics is the role assigned to memory and a residual sense of the whole Gestalt as an active agent in design. These notions are present in 'Decoupage', 'Collage City' and 'Bricolage'. 'Assemblage' differs from collage and bricolage since it discounts the redemptive quality of memory and the overall Gestalt: the piece or fragment should speak for itself. There is no point from an overall view putting everything in place. In

Graham Shane's description a rhizomatic assemblage differs from other assemblages in that it reintroduces the narrative path as an important element in the design. There is no emphasis on a single centre of command, no place of total control.[12] According to Deleuze and Guattari, one consequence resulting from this is the end of Freudian psychoanalysis with its Oedipal theatre; but it also signifies the end of state Marxism, where the state plants a rigid 'tree structure' in both our soul and body, and also in space, where it uses grids and axes to create these divisions, a notion very much present in Lefebvre.[13]

In Amsterdam's Westerdok, the dynamics of the past and present situation were also captured with the notion of a 'rhizome'. The plan itself has no architectural connotation other than its land use. It explores the possibilities of a pedestrian archipelago where the strips have no other meaning than a dimensional limit to the streets and the water. It formulates the design rules for the architectural practices that are to develop different parts of the overall plan. Where for instance Parametric Design is out for 'Elegance', the Westerdok plan and Urban Asymmetries plans set out for social and aesthetic 'Experimentalism'.[14] Amsterdam Westerdok explores a theoretical 'non-representability' in the urban scale. The 'experiment' in architecture here consists of taking apart and putting together; Tafuri sees it as a launching pad towards the unknown. The launching pad is, however, solidly anchored to the ground, he writes.[15] This design process is a form of 'tight rope walking' – the wire might break, but there is a strong net below. It is different from the avant-gardes who by definition perform without a net: 'they look in the face of disaster and accept it from the start', Tafuri writes. 'Experimentalism' here in this context is somewhat comparable with what Ackbar Abbas writes about Hong Kong cinema and colonial space. What he underlines is

**11** Scott Lash, **Another Modernity: A Different Rationality** (Blackwell, 1999), p. 232. I agree with Lash who writes that 'sociological and cultural theory – theories of "reflexivity" and of "difference" – have focused far too much on the subjective, anti-foundational moment of the other modernity. Both social and cultural theory have paid insufficient attention to the moment of ground'. This is even more so in contemporary architectural avant-gardes as in the work of Eisenman, FOA and Tschumi, and most certainly in Parametric Urbanism as in Patrick Schumacher and Neil Leach.

**12** David Grahame Shane, **Recombinant Urbanism: Conceptual Modelling in Architecture, Urban Design, and City Theory** (John Wiley & Sons, 2005), p. 147.

**13** Misunderstandings are commonplace when a philosophical figure such as the rhizome or the fold is introduced into thinking about architecture and urban planning. 'Tree structure', 'tissue' and 'urban body' found their way into this field long ago. For Deleuze, 'tree' had a different meaning. The metaphor 'tree structure' is misleading, as it does not embody the remotest analogy with space. Deleuze sees the tree as a **logical** tree, as revered by the philosophy of the Enlightenment. But this does not imply an abstract negation of this philosophy. Although, in his opinion, the philosophers of the Enlightenment always expressed their thoughts in the shadow of a despot and legitimized a given form of the state, he still considers them to be philosophical friends who should be criticized. In his ideas, the tree constitutes the shadow of the state; we also find the latter in the systematics of Kant's and Hegel's philosophy, a criticism which we have already seen in Benjamin and Adorno. The terms 'tissue' and 'urban body' suggest associations with healthy and unhealthy, so they easily result in normative thinking; a body in equilibrium should not be disturbed. That is certainly a risk with these terms, and a degree of caution should be exercised in their use.

**14** For 'Elegance', see Patrick Schumacher, 'Arguing for Elegance', in Ali Rahim and Hina Jamelle, **Architectural Design**, Elegance, vol. 77, no. 1, Jan/Feb 2007.

**15** Manfredo Tafuri, **Theories and History of Architecture** (Granada Publishing, 1980), p. 105.

that there is an urgent need to develop a critical discourse on Hong Kong architecture and urban space, where the dominance of visuality is put into question, as in the case of the Hong Kong new cinema which he analysed so beautifully.[16] Abbas claims that we need a notion of 'disappearance' that does not connote a vanishing without a trace. Architects and urbanists are not particularly fond of absence, or non-representability. Or, to put it differently; they like to do design, not withdraw from it. Rem Koolhaas describes it as the response to the horror of architecture's opposite, the instinctive *recoil from the void*, a fear of *nothingness*.[17] It is necessary to imagine ways in which density can be maintained, in Koolhaas's words, without recourse to substance, intensity without the encumbrance of architecture. Of course, this is ambiguous – to be 'critical' means we have to go back to substance, we have to *'climb back into real architectural structures'*, [my italics] as Tafuri writes. And this is exactly what is happening in the UA study group plans. The Mexico Study Group analyses the growth of Mexico City, its disastrous patterns of development, and, more importantly, develops a new urban strategy from within. The Newark Study Group analyses industrialization and labour developments in the New York Region from the 1870s until 2008. It analyses the development of industrial blocks, housing tenements and residential patterns. The Santiago de Chile Study Group takes La Victoria as its starting point; this centrally located community functions as an urban enclave characterized by its strong sense of identity; the site was after all seized by the inhabitants. The main objective of the project was to strengthen the position of the site within the urban context by applying a set of integrated, relational strategies that emphasize connectivity, density, public space and local modes of production. The kind of coherence the three metropolises can achieve is not that of a homogeneous, planned composition. At the most, it can be a system of fragments as the work of the Urban Asymmetries study group shows. In 'Learning from Ecatepec', the Mexico project shows how the process of urbanization together with the foreseen temporalities of interventions is fundamentally time-bound and piecemeal. The study group proposes a building system which will enable replacing existing buildings to provide households with more habitable conditions. Increasing the city's density is understood not only in the sense of increasing the density of built objects, but rather in the density of social relations. Maybe I can explain these procedures better by referring more concretely to the Westerdok plan in Amsterdam.

In the case of our Westerdok plan we are dealing with a 'connection' to the historic core, the late medieval fabric, densely packed and transacted by water. Water here was no blank space. Amsterdam centre is characterized by a lot of water, related to the notion of Deleuze and Guattari's rhizome, a figure of thought they relate to this part of the city. The way I relate to it here is this abstract construction they used in their book *Mille Plateaux*.[18] At the beginning of their book they call

Amsterdam a 'rhizome city'. Do the book and the city resemble each other? Is it actually possible to write a thousand plateaus about Amsterdam too? It would not surprise me if it were possible, and in fact it has already been done. Anyone who enters the library of the Amsterdams Historisch Museum will find it difficult to leave again. The building seems to imprison you, and the permanent exhibition keeps drawing you back to the diamond cutters, the hydraulic engineering works, and the rebellious citizens of the Wallen and the Jordaan. Today's commercial machinery had a forerunner in the trading and shipping of hundreds of years ago. If there is anywhere where the word 'tissue' is applicable, then it has to be here. Every major spatial intervention or intensification, be it the office blocks on the Rokin or the never-ending traffic congestion, is perceived as 'alien'. The 'body' of the city does not permit the traffic to function as the circulatory system for its blood. Deleuze and Guattari compare the rhizome to a map with an infinite number of entrances. In this map, power bases, centres of art, science, social struggle, politics and commerce are linked to each other. In so far as the rhizome is applicable to the old Amsterdam, to Bickerseiland, the Westerdok or the Eastern docks area, it always involves varying connections in our perceptions, or more accurately different 'plateaux' in our perceptions, which cannot be compressed into a tour of the city using a city guidebook. It is comparable to Michel de Certeau's walk; we are immersed in the context, we do not form overviews as we do in maps. The experience here might also be related to what Bruno Latour describes as the *oligopticon*, sites that he sees as the opposite of Michel Foucault's 'panopticon', the ideal prison allowing total surveillance. The oligopticons do the opposite of panoptica; they see far too little to feed the megalomania of the inspector or the paranoia of the inspected, Latour writes.[19] From these places, extremely narrow views of the (connected) social whole are possible, as the UA study group plans show. The question remains: Who is going to live in these new urban plans and for whom are they designed? And more importantly, why are they conceptualized the way they are? How are we going to deal with the social and aesthetic qualities in urbanism? Let's take a closer look at the Westerdok plan.

The Westerdok plan (*The Nieuwe Reael*) is characterized by the famous modernist strip, but it is a reinterpretation of it. The 'organic neighbourhood' is cast aside for density, one of the main issues in the municipality's plans for this island. *The Nieuwe Reael* is not fundamentally different from the modernist strips; it should be seen instead as being merely slightly out of focus in relation to what already exists in our memory. 'Memory', since it is a tabula rasa plan – the existing strip of lower warehouses, heavily contested by squatters who had to move out. Office buildings, smaller shops and housing were the new ingredients. Different from the work of the UA study group, in Amsterdam there is not much to go on in the sense of participation from the people who are

**16** Ackbar Abbas, **Hong Kong: Culture and the Politics of Disappearance** (University of Minnesota Press, 1997), p. 65.
**17** Rem Koolhaas, 'Imagining Nothingness', in **S,M,L,XL** (Rotterdam: 010 Publishers, 1996), p. 199.
**18** Gilles Deleuze and Felix Guattari, **A Thousand Plateaus**: **Capitalism and Schizophrenia** (University of Minnesota Press), p. 21; Arie Graafland, **The Socius of Architecture**, pp. 105 ff.
**19** Bruno Latour, **Reassembling the Social: An Introduction to Actor-Network Theory** (Oxford University Press, 2005), p. 181.

going to live here. 'Lived space' here is a complex and mostly 'projected', or hoped for, issue in a tabula rasa plan. The site might be empty, but the moment you look at it, it no longer is. Space is always 'full'. That, we can most certainly learn from Lefebvre. From the 'oligopticon' we could see the old layout of the Jordaan, an extremely dense area close to the site that was once built for the new labourers in Amsterdam. We emulated the Jordaan density in our new plan, quite contrary to the ideas of the modernists, as they considered high density 'unhealthy'. Children from the Jordaan used to swim in the public bath on the Westerdok. But there is more: the housing blocks were no longer the modernist ones; although four floors high, the 'strips' are in fact 'maisonettes', two houses on top of each other. Each house has an interior staircase, the top ones leading to flat roofs with terraces. Again an image from *de 8 en Opbouw* of a roof terrace made the connection. A substantial percentage of the houses had to be built for lower income groups, owned by the Amsterdam housing corporations – they actually own the greater part of the city. But also higher income groups had to be accommodated; a change in Amsterdam's housing policy that we followed. Higher income groups were already leaving the city since they could not find proper housing. We did not build high in the housing blocks, we stayed with the modern ideas, four floors, but made them into 'houses', another issue at the time. Communal entrances to flats are hard to keep in shape, we hoped for communication in the streets. The struggle was with density, and to reach that in low-rise is difficult. But we managed to get 145 units into a hectare, the average dwelling space being 120 m² (the realized plan has double the number of units per hectare). From the outside you cannot distinguish social housing and higher income housing, a common principle in Amsterdam's housing market. Units could be connected, vertically or horizontally, but the outside image is *bleak*. Compared to the realized project which is spectacular and mainly consists of higher income housing blocks, *The Nieuwe Reael* is hardly visible. It is, like the UA study group plans in this book, still paying tribute to Archizoom's *No-Stop City* (1969-1972). *No-Stop City* was a rigorous plan where the city is understood as an assembly line of the social. Despite their abstraction in the drawings, and their sublime surfaces, Archizoom formulate an explicit critique of the urban condition. It is also a critique on 'reformism' in Italian politics at the time, a 'negative Utopia' where modern architecture was a quintessential instrument of these policies. Unlike, say, Archigram, they deliver not 'a project' but an architectural image-based critique grounded in the abstraction of capitalist accumulation. There are many similarities with the designs in this book; the Newark study group in particular has delivered this kind of work. The drawings represent a language of grounded analytical work, far away from contemporary beautification. The work to me seems to be in line with both Archizoom and Gerd Arntz pictograms, but in a contemporary form that has climbed back into Tafuri's architectural and urban structures. But most drawings still show traces of their abstraction, the participants are not afraid of Koolhaas's 'void'. No beautification is present.

I do not believe that there exists a direct relation between physical form and social behaviour; moreover, in the Amsterdam plan, as mentioned above, we also needed urban density. All houses have indoor parking lots; streets are for pedestrians, an exception in Amsterdam. That also frees up the possibilities for the streets, you will not be able to park in the streets; Jane Jacobs would have loved it. We also designed a substantial number of anchoring places for house boats. Considering all the great urban design schemes, the many 'isms' and 'ages' of Graham Shane, I believe that urbanism at the moment has to do with what you do *not* do: '*the recoil from the void*', you cannot arrange life directly by built form. The main thing you do is try to create possibilities; you work on performative issues, 'lived space' if you like. And even that is questionable; here, in this urban void, the effects of the design are unpredictable. 'At its best, urban design creates a physical framework for the present city's myriad activities,' John Kaliski writes.[20] The urban designer must find 'new means of incorporating the elements that remain elusive: ephemerality, cacophony, multiplicity, and simultaneity'.[21] We cannot let go of 'meaning' or 'aesthetics' in urbanism. There is always 'meaning', we live in Lash's 'third space'; we are reflexively judging animals, 'ground' is in perception and community. But for the people living in our plans this is quite different from the discourses we use in urban theories. 'Meaning' in design is for the specialist, we load our designs with 'meaning', all 'isms' and 'ages' do so, the '*fear of nothingness*' is always present. I believe it was the Florentine Archizoom's implicit agenda to show this.[22] All this does not mean we should stop theorizing about space, on the contrary, what we should do is leave formalism aside and stop overestimating the forces of design *and* theory. Urban theory is relevant, but its range in daily design practice is limited. This goes for all 'isms' and 'ages'. This is not a plea to get 'political' again and withdraw from design, nor to abstain from image as Debord would have it. We need image, 'polluted' as it may be.

The question that remains is why this *bleak* image of the Westerdok? Why not a strong and *loaded* image full of references? The answer is in my *Socius of Architecture* book. It took a longer theoretical text to explain these issues on different levels. The levels relate to the notion of the *banal* in architecture (and art as in Arte Povera); the critical 'paragon or the aesthetics of the banal' as in Klaus Jürgen Bauer; the non-decorative as in Koolhaas's Kunsthal; and finally the relation to the philosophical notions of a contemporary 'sublime'. In the Kantian notion of the sublime, the schemata of the imagination are overwhelmed by the objects or events it encounters. Art and architecture as

**20** John Kaliski, 'The Present City and the Practice of City Design', in John Leighton Chase, Margaret Crawford and John Kaliski (eds), **Everyday Urbanism**, p. 103.
**21** John Kaliski, 'The Present City and the Practice of City Design', in John Leighton Chase, Margaret Crawford and John Kaliski (eds), **Everyday Urbanism**, p. 102.
**22** Archizoom connected Socialist Realism and Pop Art, working-classism and consumerism, Mario Tronti and Andy Warhol: opposite worlds but not so remote from one another, as Andrea Branzi writes. Both obeyed the materialist logic of 'more money and less work'. 'The critique of modernity thus became the critique of architecture as a disciplinary institution, and a qualitative category in a pagan world devoid of quality. Its role was not to offer a mediation between the extreme forms of logic of the system, but to represent them as clearly as possible'. But No-Stop City did away with every trace of Pop representation, it is catatonic architecture, both centreless and imageless. It is different from Superstudio's Continuous Monument which still relates to monumentality. Andrea Branzi, 'Postface', in Archizoom Associati, **No-Stop City** (Paris: Librairie de l'Architecture et de la Ville, 2006), pp. 145-47.

artefacts open out onto the emptiness, the void, or lack.[23] In the three designs closing the last three chapters on Amsterdam, Tokyo and New York in *The Socius of Architecture*, we tried to stay away from Architecture. Writing about the homeless shelter in Manhattan I wrote then, 'it is thoroughly "banal" architecture. Its day-to-day use may evoke on occasion an emotion that I have previously described as sublime, and this may yet transform the building into architecture'.[24] There is still that relation to architecture and the urban, but of another kind: a testing ground for the banal, the everyday, an interest in Everyday Urbanism but of a 'sublime' kind. An effort to slow down an object-based design strategy, an effort to establish a more relation-based strategy in urban design. I believe it is very much the case in all three projects of the Urban Asymmetries study group included here.

**23** Scott Lash, **Another Modernity**, p. 210.
**24** Arie Graafland, **The Socius of Architecture**, p. 236. I am following Lash here, judgements of the sublime presume a much more radical experience of finitude than those of beauty. We are dealing with an 'existential meaning', 'the path to these meanings is through the particular, through the eminently **trivial**, through **everyday cultural artefacts**', he writes (pp. 235 ff.). Lash's interest in judgements of the sublime is not an interest in the infinity to which it opens up, 'but because of the **means, the material**, the order of "sensation" we must go through as ground in order to get there' [my italics].

[1]

[2]

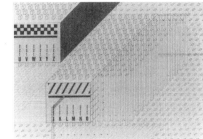

[3a]

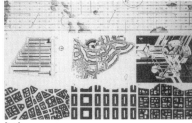

[3b]

[3c]

[3d]

**1** Urban Plan Kerssen Graafland Amsterdam
(2000)
**2** Urban Plan Westerdokseiland, OD 2005
(Defesche, 1999), Westerdok South, Meyer
en Van Schooten Architecten Amsterdam
**3a-d** Archizoom Associati, No Stop City
(1968)
**4** Archizoom Associati: Andrea Branzi, Lucia
Bartolini, Gilberto Corretti, (Natalino), Massimo Morozzi, Dario Bartolini, Paolo Degan-
rello (1968)

[4]

# Contributors' Biographies

**M. Christine Boyer** Professor at the University of Princeton, is an urban historian whose interests include the history of the American city, city planning, preservation planning, and computer science. She has written extensively about American urbanism. Her publications include **Dreaming the Rational City: The Myth of American City Planning 1890-1945** (Cambridge: The MIT Press, 1983), **Manhattan Manners: Architecture and Style 1850-1900** (New York: Rizzoli, 1985), **The City of Collective Memory** (Cambridge: The MIT Press, 1994), and **CyberCities** (New York: Princeton Architectural Press, 1996).

**Laura O. Carrillo** holds a Bachelor Degree in Territorial Planning from the Universidad Autónoma Metropolitana (UAM). Presently she is carrying out doctoral research in Urbanism at the Universidad Nacional Autónoma de México (UNAM). She is academic assistant of the undergraduate programme of Territorial Planning at the UAM-Xochimilco, and junior researcher in the University Programme in Metropolitan Studies.

**Stephanie Choi** received her M.Arch. from Princeton University and her B.A. in Comparative Literature at Stanford University. She has worked for Eisenman Architects, the Getty Foundation and the Los Angeles County Museum of Art. She currently works as an architect for Front in New York City.

**Roberto Eibenschutz** was trained as an architect, he holds a Masters in Urbanism from the Universidad Nacional Autónoma de México (UNAM), and a specialization awarded in the Netherlands. He is Senior Researcher at the Universidad Autónoma Metropolitana (UAM), where he has been Director of the Design Department; Secretary; Dean of the Xochimilco Unit, and Coordinator of the University Programme in Metropolitan Studies. He is former sub-secretary of Urban Development, Director of the National Fund for Popular Housing and Secretary of Urban Development and Housing of the Federal District, Mexico.

**Beatriz García Peralta** has a B.A. in Architecture, M.A. in urban development, and a Ph.D. in economics. Researcher at the UNAM Institute for Social Studies. Research areas: housing markets, housing policy and its link with the private business sector.

**Arie Graafland** Professor of Architecture, holds since 1999 the Antoni van Leeuwenhoek chair at the Faculty of Architecture, TU Delft. He was the founder and director of the Delft School of Design 2002-10, and is the editor of the DSD Series on Architecture and Urbanism with 010. His publications include **The Socius of Architecture**, **Versailles and the Mechanics of Power,** and **Architectural Bodies**. He is co-principal with Harry Kerssen of Kerssen Graafland Architects, Amsterdam.

**David Harvey** is Distinguished Professor of Anthropology at the Graduate Center of the City University of New York, and is an internationally acclaimed social theorist and urban geographer who specializes in the critique of political economy. His recent publications include **The Enigma of Capital and the Crises of Capitalism**, **A Companion to Marx's Capital**, and **A Brief History of Neoliberalism**.

**Rodrigo Hidalgo** born 1968 in Santiago, Chile. Studies in geography and regional planning at the Catholic University of Chile (PUC), Santiago. PhD 2000 at the University of Barcelona, Spain. Associate Professor at the Department of Geography, PUC, Santiago de Chile, from 2002-2005 head of the Human Geography Department.

Visiting Professor at the Universidade de São Paulo, Brazil. Editor of **Revista de Geografía Norte Grande** (index Thompson Reuters). He has participated in over 100 national and international scientific events. He is author and editor of ten books and about 100 articles.

**Tahl Kaminer** is an assistant professor at the Delft School of Design, TU Delft. His doctoral thesis, completed in 2008, has been recently published by Routledge as **Architecture, Crisis and Resuscitation: The Reproduction of Post-Fordism in Late-Twentieth-Century Architecture**. He co-founded the academic journal **Footprint** and co-edited the volumes **Critical Tools** (2011) and **Houses in Transformation** (2008), and is a member of the Urban Asymmetries research group.

**Mark Krasovic** is the Geraldine R. Dodge Postdoctoral Fellow at Rutgers University in Newark. He is writing a cultural history of Newark's urban crisis titled **The Struggle for Newark: Plotting Urban Crisis in the Great Society**.

**Margit Mayer** teaches comparative and North American politics at the Freie Universität in Berlin. Her research currently focuses on urban and social politics and social movements. She has been editor of the **International Journal of Urban and Regional Research** and has published on various aspects of contemporary urban politics and social and employment policy. Margit is co-editing with Neil Brenner and Peter Marcuse **Cities for People, Not for Profit** (2011) and working on the monograph **Urban Social Movements and the State**.

**Miguel Robles-Durán** is assistant professor at Parsons, New York, and a partner at the studio Cohabitation Strategies. He is currently involved in the Right to the City organization in the Netherlands. Miguel studied at the ITESM, Monterrey, Sci-Arc and the Berlage Institute. In 2001 he received the Honor Award of the American Institute of Architects, and his work has been widely and internationally exhibited. Miguel has taught at KU Leuven, at the Berlage Institute, in Zurich and at the Delft School of Design.

**Heidi Sohn** is assistant professor of architecture theory at the Delft School of Design, Faculty of Architecture, TU Delft. She is founder and programme director of the Urban Asymmetries research and design project, and academic coordinator of the Future Cities graduate programme of the DSD. She is a trained architect and holds an MSc degree in urban planning. She received her PhD in architecture theory from the Faculty of Architecture of the TU Delft in 2006. She has lectured and published extensively.

**Erik Swyngedouw** is Professor of Geography at the University of Manchester in its School of Environment and Development. He has previously worked at St. Peter's College, Oxford University, University of Leuven, the University of Washington (Marshall-Monet Fellow in European Studies), and the Universities of Seville and Thessaloniki. He has a background in Engineering, Urban and Regional Planning, and Geography. He has published over fifty academic articles and several books. Recent publications include **In the Nature of Cities: Urban Political Ecology and the Politics of Urban Metabolism** (with N. Heynen and M. Kaika, eds, 2005), **Social Power and the Urbanization of Water – Flows of Power** (2004), and **Nature, Modernity and Social Power in Spain, 1898-2010** (forthcoming).

# Credits

**Delft School of Design Series on Architecture and Urbanism**
Series Editor Arie Graafland

Editorial Board
K. Michael Hays (Harvard University, USA)
Ákos Moravánszky (ETH Zürich, Switzerland)
Michael Müller (Bremen University, Germany)
Frank R. Werner (University of Wuppertal, Germany)
Gerd Zimmermann (Bauhaus University, Germany)

Also published in this series:
1 **Crossover. Architecture Urbanism Technology**
ISBN 978 90 6450 609 3
2 **The Body in Architecture**
ISBN 978 90 6450 568 3
3 **De-/signing the Urban. Technogenesis and the urban image**
ISBN 978 90 6450 611 6
4 **The Model and its Architecture**
ISBN 978 90 6450 684 0
6 **Cognitive Architecture. From biopolitics to noopolitics**
ISBN 978 90 6450 725 0

5 **Urban Asymmetries. Studies and projects on neoliberal urbanization**
Editors Tahl Kaminer, Miguel Robles-Durán and Heidi Sohn
Text editing John Kirkpatrick
Book design by Piet Gerards Ontwerpers
(Piet Gerards and Maud van Rossum), Amsterdam
Printed by DeckersSnoeck, Antwerp

On the cover: Uneven urban development in Mexico City. Photograph
courtesy of Jose Castillo / arquitecture 911sc.
Special thanks to R. Thijs and P. Lühl for additional work on some of
the maps appearing in this book.

ISBN 978 90 6450 724 3